Yon Lad Out There

Eileen Ward

Acknowledgements

I would like to thank my friend and neighbour Dr. Kenneth Cully for all his help in proof reading and his encouragement in the writing of this book.

Also thanks to all my friends at the Driffield writing group for their support and enthusiasm.

CHAPTER 1

Stanley clicked the gate shut and felt the weight of the two threepenny bits in his pocket. He stamped his feet to rid his boots of their film of coal dust and brushed his trousers with his blackened hands.

He had just spent the last hour moving a ton of coal for Mr Earnshaw who lived further down the road. The old man, although retired, still received his free allocation of coal thanks to his lifetime of working at the coal face. Also thanks to the long years spent underground, he now suffered so badly from pneumoconiosis that he could barely breathe enough to walk, let alone move his coal which was tipped in a heap at his gate.

Stanley had seen him standing looking at the coal with a shovel in his hand and volunteered to move it for him.

"Aye, ah'd be right glad if tha would son. It'll never get shifted if it's left to me, but ah'll pay thee. Ah'll gi thee fourpence when tha's finished t'job. Barrow's down t'yard, wheel's a bit wonky but it'll do."

Within an hour Stanley had moved all the coal and tipped it down into the cellar, and swept up so thoroughly that there was only the slightest shadow of black dust remaining on the road where the coal had been.

As he began to walk down the short path, he thought of all the coal that was delivered every week to the miners and wondered how many of them would be willing to pay to have it moved into their cellars, and he began to form a plan.

He pictured himself knocking on doors and offering to move the coal for a small payment. It could turn out to be a good little business and quickly his mind moved on to where he could keep the money that he would earn. There would be nowhere in the overcrowded bedroom that he shared with five brothers. In the ground in a box, yes, that would be the place. He smiled at the thought.

His two younger brothers, Harold and Cyril, played marbles near the house. As he passed, Cyril's best marble disappeared down the cellar grid into the coal below; his lip trembled but he got little sympathy from his brother.

Stanley left them to it and turned the corner. He almost collided with his father and recoiled back as if he had been stung.

At nearly thirteen, he was almost the same height as his father but a different build, tall and slim and at a gangly stage in his development, all long arms and legs.

His father was short and stocky, strong and hard from years of grafting down the pit. If he had any affection for his son he kept it well hidden.

He glared at him now and grabbed his arm.

"Where's tha been? I told thee to get that garden dug and what's tha doin'wi coal dust on thee?" His eyes narrowed as he stared at Stanley. "Tha's been shifting old man Earnshaw's coal ain't tha? Ow much did he gi thee? Tha won't av done it for nowt. Tip thee money up," and he held out his hand.

Reluctantly Stanley took the two threepenny bits from his pocket and handed them over, and then stepped smartly out of the way, knowing only too well that a blow could be handed out by way of a thank you.

He walked fast down the garden path seething with anger and resentment and knew he would have to miss his dinner if he wanted to stay out of his father's way.

He reached the gate at the bottom of the garden and glanced back over his shoulder.

"Good, he's gone in, the rotten old pig," he muttered under his breath. "Why isn't he in bed? He usually goes straight to bed after a night shift."

He let himself into the allotment which led directly off their garden.

It was a good-sized piece of land and used for growing vegetables. His father had used his older brothers as garden labourers in the past with little success.

But now it was Stan's responsibility, and he had discovered he had a natural talent for growing things and found it soothed and calmed him.

There was an old shed on the allotment converted into a crude pigeon loft. Stanley headed for it now and, locking the door after him, sat on the box that served as a seat. Tears filled his eyes and he fought the desire to break down completely.

The door rattled and his younger brother's voice came whispering through the cracks. "Open t'door Stan, I've got something for thee."

"Go away, don't want to talk to anybody, Ah'm fed up to teeth wi all this bloody family."

"Aw come on Stan, I'm yer best mate, I'll 'elp thee wi t'digging, an av brought thee some snap."

Stanley opened the door a crack and Harold shot in and handed over a greasy paper bag containing a hunk of bread and dripping.

"What's he so nasty to thee for our Stan, he's bad enough wi us lot, but tha always seems to cop it worse."

"I don't know, I sweated me guts out shifting that coal an he's taken me pay, an ah know for a fact he'll be straight down to t'bookies and purrit on an hoss wi three legs, the rotten old pig. But ah'll show him, you wait and see, I'll show em all."

"Yeah, but not me eh Stan? Cos am your best mate aren't ah Stan? Anyway, ah've got some news an all. Ah've just heard me mam say that Aunt Lizzie and our Doll are comin' tomorrow and they're stopping for two days at me Aunt Rose's."

That brightened Stanley up, he liked his cousin Doll a lot, they always got on well and his Aunt Lizzie always made a fuss of him. He stuffed the last of the bread and dripping into his mouth and picked up the old spade from behind the door. He put his arm round Harold's shoulders, ruffled his short, pudding-basin style hair and said, "Well come on then my best mate, let's get digging."

The next day was Sunday, and Stanley knew the routine well. His father would be sleeping off what he called 'a skin full of ale' and often didn't rise before 10 o'clock, and then after breakfast would be off down to the club for the dinnertime session.

But Stanley was up bright and early, glad to leave that tiny bedroom, opening the window wide before he did.

'Let some of the stink out,' he thought as he quietly closed the door behind him carrying his clothes in a bundle under his arm. Downstairs, he strip washed in the kitchen sink in lukewarm water, savouring the luxury of having the kitchen to himself. He dressed quickly, wishing as he did so that he had long trousers.

Grabbing a hunk of bread, he headed out into the garden and checked the digging. It looked good, and he marked out where the potatoes would go, then walked to the fence and stood gazing for a few minutes over the other allotments and beyond, down the fields to the pit at the bottom of the Dearne Valley.

The winding wheel was still today, no cages of men descending down to spend a long shift shovelling coal, and no giant buckets being emptied onto the ever growing black slag mountain behind the pit.

But steam and smoke still rose from the coke ovens, and even at this distance the stench reached him. Stanley looked, and swore yet again, that he would never work there. Spend his life underground? Never! And with that thought fresh in his mind he set off for the local farm to see if he could get work there.

He walked fast, rehearsing what he would say, and almost lost his nerve as he reached the farm. He arrived just as the farmer, Mr Downing, was finishing milking the herd of cows and he looked hot, tired, and irritated.

"Nah then, what's thee after?" he fairly barked at him.

"I'm looking for a job, I'm nearly fourteen," said Stanley all in a rush. "Ah'm used to working, ah can work before and after school."

"Can tha nah? Well tha looks like a good strong lad, let's see how tha performs with a muck fork, and then ah'll let thee know." He nodded towards the tools in the corner and walked off, leaving Stanley to it.

Stanley grabbed the fork and set to work with a will, trying not to stand in the pools of muck and urine with his leaky boots. He finished off with the sweeping brush and was trying to clean his hands on an old sack when Mr Downing reappeared in the doorway. He gave a slight nod of approval, looked Stanley in the eye and said, "Right, be here at six in t'morning, tha can help me wi t'milkin, ah'll gi thee a shillin' a week."

"Thanks Mr Downing. Ah'll be here," and Stanley raced back towards home, eager to tell his mother the good news. He ran all the way, his long legs quickly covering the distance and he was home in ten minutes.

'Almost as fast as being on a bike,' he thought with satisfaction, but he was panting heavily and had to stop for a breather before he entered the house.

His mother was sat at the table with a cup of tea in front of her, she looked pale and strained. Stanley looked at her worriedly and wondered if she was pregnant yet again, but she gave him a smile as he came in and indicated for him to sit down with her at the table. Stanley knew she was trying not to make a noise and didn't want to wake the rest of the family who were still sleeping. She liked to enjoy a few minutes to herself on Sunday mornings before they all got up and the chaos of a large family erupted.

So although he was so keen to tell her his news he spoke quietly, barely above a whisper.

His mother touched his arm and said, "Well done lad, no pit for thee then? I'll be glad of the money; tha can av three pence a week out of it."

Stanley nodded and took a big gulp of the tea that his mother had just poured out for him.

The door at the bottom of the stairs creaked and opened a couple of inches, and his youngest sister Laura peeped around, her long blond curls tangled and her big blue eyes still sleepy. At three years old she was the baby of the family.

Stanley thought about how this was the longest his mother had ever gone without being pregnant again, and hoped that the breeding years were over for her.

Loud noises from the bedroom above indicated that his father was rising and he had no intention of being there when he came downstairs. He hurriedly finished his tea and splashed his hands and face with water at the kitchen sink.

As his father reached the bottom of the stairs Stanley was already halfway to the gate, his face still damp. He combed his hair with the piece of comb that he kept in his back pocket and looked down at his legs, wishing again that he had long trousers.

He headed down into the little mining town and was soon knocking on the door of the terraced house where his Aunt Rose lived.

Straight away the door opened and there was Doll, a big smile lighting up her pretty face. Stanley held her arm and leaning close whispered, "Ah'm off down to Uncle John's at Bolton, see if tha can come wi me."

She nodded and led the way into the kitchen at the back of the house, where her mother and aunt were stood at the sink preparing vegetables for the Sunday dinner.

They both turned as Doll and Stanley came in, and both exclaimed at how much Stanley had grown in the weeks since they had last seen him.

Doll's mother agreed to their trip to Bolton but reminded her that they had to catch the four o'clock Doncaster bus that was the first leg of their journey back to Carlton, and then she pressed a sixpence into Stanley's hand and shushed his thanks, putting a finger to her lips as a sign to say nothing to anyone.

Affectionate as ever, Doll wrapped her arms around her mother and aunt and kissed them both, then went to join Stanley who was waiting at the door picking up two newly baked scones on the way, and looked at her aunt with raised eyebrows.

Her aunt smiled and flapped the tea towel at her. "Go on you two, you'll eat me out of house and home." Doll laughed and handed a scone to Stanley.

Closing the front door behind her, Doll linked arms with him. He didn't quite know how to handle that and said, "Ah can walk on me own tha knows, ah don't need owdin' up."

Doll gave him a punch on the arm and he pretended to hold it in pain. They ran down the street larking about for a while, acting more like ten-year-olds instead of nearly grown-up teenagers.

After a while they settled down to a steady walk and Stanley told her all about his new job.

"That's great Stan, you'll be good at that but it's a bit rough you having to tip nearly all of it up. How's things at home now?"

"Don't ask Doll, it's a nightmare, I'd do anything to be able to get out of it."

They talked then of the time when Stanley had been four years old, and had been sent to live at Carlton with his Aunt Lizzie and her husband after his grandad (who used to look after him) had died. Doll had been just five then but remembered it well. Stanley had been very homesick and eventually had been sent back home to his mother.

"You should have stayed with us Stan; it would have been brilliant having you there all the time. Carlton's ok. There's plenty of open fields and no pits. Lots of farms and animals. You'd have loved it."

"Don't rub it in Doll, I can't tell you how many times I've wished I'd stayed."

They'd reached the bus stop now but decided to save the fare and walk the four miles to Bolton.

The walk took them along the side of the canal, its water black and murky, over the railway crossing and past the pit, almost through the pit yard itself. Past the coke ovens, belching steam that gave off the most terrible stench, like thousands of rotting eggs. The coal dust coated everything and seemed to hover in the air waiting to be breathed in with each breath. Then they went under the railway arch and followed the road to Mexborough and finally reached the outskirts of Bolton.

At last they arrived and went round to the back door of the tiny stone built terraced house. It was wide open in spite of the sharp November wind. As they entered, the heat from the fire place met them. The fire was banked high and glowing red hot. One of the few perks of being a miner was the free coal received every month, and

Uncle John was making full use of it. As always they were made very welcome.

"Na then, look who's ere. Put t'kettle on mother, ar Stan n Doll's turned up. Sit thee sens down and get warm, tha'll av ad a long walk."

Mugs of tea sweetened with creamy condensed milk were soon on the table and while they drank, Stanley told his uncle all about the new job.

"Well done lad, tha could do wi sum long trousers though if tha's guna be farmin'. Thee mother should get thee some."

"Ah know Uncle John, but she's got no money to spare."

"Well tha knows. Ah'd help thee if ah could, but money's tight ere an all, we're on short time."

Stanley's uncle went quiet and seemed in deep thought for a while, then he lifted his head, looked him in the eye and said, "Ah'll tell thee what ah can elp thee with. There's an auld bike in t'chicken run. Ah Jack'll show thee it; tha might be be able to gerrit goin, it'll do to get to work on."

Doll jumped as he gave a great bellow of a shout for Jack. It worked. He came clattering down the stairs and was instructed to show Stanley the bike.

Doll got up to go with them but Uncle John indicated for her to stay in the house. She sat back down and looked at him and waited.

He looked back at her, took a deep breath, and said, "Tha's gerrin' to be a right bonny lass ar Doll. Nah there's sumat am gunna tell thee. Am not supposed to, but tha's got a right to know."

He went quiet again. Doll could hear his breathing, heavy in his chest from years of working in the coal dust.

He looked down at his hands, then at Doll, and then in that blunt direct Yorkshire way of his said, "Tha needs to know this. Yon lad out there, is thee brother!"

CHAPTER 2

Doll was so shocked she couldn't think what to say, the only word she managed was, "But."

John could see how confused and uncomfortable she was, and leaned across to her putting his hand on her shoulder.

"Don't get upset Doll, I know it's a shock but things'll work out, they always do. Av a talk to thee Mam when tha gets home. But it's true what ah've told thee, our Stan's thee bruther. Aunt Ada and Uncle Harold are thee real mother and father. Our Ada had thee before her and Harold were married. Well, he were still married to t'other woman at time, so our Lizzie sort of adopted thee. But then Ada went and had our Stan, and she kept him. Me Dad looked after him most a time, till it got too much for him. Then they tried palming him off onto our Lizzie an' all, but he was that homesick they had to fetch 'im back.

"Ah'm not sayin' owt else. Ah'll be in trouble with our Ada for telling yer, and ah dare say Harold will be down ere, throwin' is weight about, but ah can stand me ground with him. This lot is all his fault anyroad, and ah'll tell him so. No, it's our Ada ah'm worried about, she's a right little spitfire when she gets going."

Doll had to smile at that. It was true about Aunt Ada, she'd seen her in action more than once.

'Oh dear,' she thought, 'will I have to start calling her Mam now? It'll be funny having two mothers!'

Jack and Stanley came back, laughing and jostling each other and pretending to box.

"Hey, we're gonna take up boxin' Dad, look at this."

Both lads adopted boxing poses.

"What do ya think?"

"I think all t'boxers in Yorkshire'll be quaking in their boots. My God, what bodies! Ah've seen more muscle on a sparrow's kneecap."

The lads collapsed laughing on the old horsehair couch. It sagged a bit more under their weight and John's wife Mary called out for them to, "Steady down and behave."

"Aye, come on now, let's get down to it. What does tha think on t'bike Stan. Is it any good to thee?"

Stanley sat up. "Yea ah'll be right glad on it. It just needs a couple a new pedals and a chain and a front wheel."

Jack interrupted, "Give me a couple a weeks ah'll get thee a wheel. No questions asked."

He was well known for his shady deals and his father gave him a warning look.

The church clock struck two and Stanley turned to Doll and said they ought to be setting off back. Doll said she would need to use the privy across the yard and ran off outside, barely saying goodbye.

John stood up, he held his back and gave a groan, put his arm on Stanley's shoulders, sighed and said, "Look after Doll, she's had a bit of a shock, she'll tell thee all about it."

Stanley looked at him but his uncle obviously didn't want to say any more, so he arranged a time to come back and collect the bike and left, waiting for Doll at the end of the yard.

As soon as they reached the road they stepped out, knowing they had a long walk in front of them.

"What's the matter Doll?"

Doll hesitated, then stopped. "You'll never guess what Uncle John's just told me."

Stanley urged her to keep walking. "Come on, tell me on t'way, we'll never get there if we don't walk."

But Doll stood still.

"He said you and me are brother and sister."

He turned around and walked back a few paces till he was close up to Doll, facing her. "What!"

"We're brother and sister!" Doll repeated it all, every word, just as her uncle had told her.

They looked deep into each other's eyes and without another word, put their arms around each other and hugged, then stepped apart a little self consciously.

As they set off again Doll said, "Just think, if Uncle John hadn't told me, we might never in all our lives known that we were brother and sister; I can't believe they would keep something like that a secret."

Stanley was more cynical. "Ah can, ah've never had a proper explanation of why I have a different surname to the rest of t'family; I've had a thump or two for asking about it and been told to mind me own business. If it's not my business, whose is it I'd like to know? This family is full of secrets. I've guessed of course why my name's different but I'd never have guessed you were me sister."

"But how do you feel about that Stan? Are you glad?"

"Course I am, I've always felt closer to you than anyone else."

"Tha's right about the secrets though, I've never understood why Herbert's got a different surname too, and he's the eldest isn't he?"

Stanley nodded,

"Aye, he belonged to me Dad's first wife. He'll be off soon, he's courting now, and they're goin' to get married next year."

"Be a bit more room in the bed then?"

"Aye, and God knows we need more room, we're like sardines in a tin."

By the time they reached Wath, they had arranged that Doll would ask her mother about it all, athough she felt apprehensive. Lizzie had a fiery temper at times.

Stanley was determined to let his parents know the secret was out. No doubt he'd get the backlash, but it had to be said.

He parted from Doll when they got to the roundabout, with just a brief touch of hands and a promise to exchange letters and information. He turned left, straight up Sandygate and past Downing's farm, where he would be starting work early next morning.

His feet were sore now, his heels rubbed raw from the ill fitting boots. He stopped briefly and examined the sole of the right one. He could see his foot through the large hole that had developed. But next week he might be able to afford a cheap offcut of leather and some studs to repair them.

All sorts of things were possible now that he was a working man.

CHAPTER 3

The house was unusually quiet when Stanley arrived home and walked into the kitchen. Everything was clean and tidy, the dishes washed and stacked on the wooden draining board with the dishcloth draped over the taps to dry. The floor was swept and the handmade pegged rugs all straight in their correct position.

His mother's cat sat on the windowsill, enjoying the warmth of the sun through the glass. Petals from the geranium plant had floated down and settled on its shiny black fur. They shone like rubies in velvet. The cat raised its head and glared at him warily. Stanley and the cat were old enemies.

He walked quietly over to the living room door and opened it just far enough to look into the room. The fire was glowing red and reflecting on the brass fender. His father sat slumped in the only comfy chair in the house with Laura sat on his knee, her blonde curly hair spread out over his shoulder. They were both fast asleep, their cheeks flushed from the heat of the fire. The racing pages of the newspaper were on the floor where he had dropped them. Cyril lay on the pegged hearth rug also asleep, Harold sat propped up against his mother's chair, reading as usual. 'Always reading is Harold', thought Stanley.

His mother sat at the table, her work basket in front of her, mending clothes; she looked up at Stanley and stopped Harold calling out to him just in time, pointing at her husband and putting her finger to her lips in a "shush" sign. Then she pointed at the kitchen and mouthed, "Dinner on the table."

Stanley gave a thumbs-up sign and withdrew silently back into the kitchen, just in time to see the cat sniffing at the plate covering his dinner. It jumped down as soon as it saw him and stood near the door, its tail lashing angrily, waiting to be let out. Stanley opened the door and helped it through with his foot, murmuring, "Bloody cat," as he did so.

Dinner was a pile of potatoes, turnip and cabbage, a large slab of squashed looking Yorkshire pudding and a tiny piece of beef. He ate it cold, just as it was.

He took the plate to the sink and turned on the tap, letting the water run, staring at it without really seeing it, his mind on the day's events.

"I think it's clean now, is tha tryin' to wash pattern off?"

His mother's voice came from right behind him; Stanley jumped and turned round to look at her. Now was his chance, he had to say something.

"Mam, Uncle John told Doll something today." He hesitated. "He says she's my sister, is it true?"

Ada returned his gaze, colour flooding into her normally pale cheeks, then she looked down and quietly said, "Yes."

"Why didn't you and Dad tell us?" His voice was strong and firm now, like the man he would become in a few short years.

She looked at him again, her eyes full of tears. "I couldn't luv, I just couldn't."

Stanley put his arms around her then, his anger melted away by the sight of his mother's tears.

"It doesn't matter mam, I just wish we'd known."

He kissed her forehead and realised how small and frail she felt now, and wondered how on earth she had managed to carry and give birth to so many children, and he cursed his father for putting her through it.

He pulled his cap on his head and walked out of the door without saying anything else, automatically heading down the garden path.

Betty, Jessie and Iris, three of his younger sisters, were playing on the sad, well worn piece of grass at the back. They called out to him, teasing, hoping he would pretend to chase them as he usually did, but he was in no mood for games today, and carried on down into the allotment and the privacy of the pigeon loft.

Ada watched him through the kitchen window, her heart full of love and tenderness for this eldest son of hers. She sat down at the little table in the corner, suddenly so tired and weary, thankful the house was still quiet; just the sounds of her daughters chattering as they played outside, and the soft drone of her husband's voice talking to the other three young children. They loved to hear his stories of when he was a boy, and sometimes tales of mysterious happenings down the pit.

This was the nicest time of the week, when Harold was rested and mellow from his lunchtime session down at the 'club' with his workmates. She didn't begrudge him his drink really; he worked so hard all week slaving away at the coal face. Some days he came home so exhausted he fell asleep on the floor before he had even had chance to bathe and wash off the grime and coal dust. But soon the new baths would be opening at the pit top. He'd be able to come home all clean and fresh then.

She murmured to herself, "Yes, he'll like that." He'd always been particular about being clean, and dreaded having the typical miner's complexion, all dark and pockmarked by coal. He spent ages at the kitchen sink scrubbing himself till his skin and hair were spotless, with not a trace of coal dust. That was one of the things she loved about him. She closed her eyes then, and smiled a little and her thoughts went back to the time when they had first met.

CHAPTER 4

Ada and Harold

Ada sat outside on the bedroom window sill, facing the glass with her feet still on the bedroom floor. She slid the window down until it touched her thighs and wondered nervously if she would be able to slide it up again.

'What a position to have to get into just to clean the windows on the outside,' she thought, and proceeded to wash away the grime as best she could, while clinging on to the window frame with her left hand.

She mopped up the water and gave the glass a good rub with a scrunched up piece of newspaper and with relief began to slide the window back up, wincing as it creaked ominously.

'One day,' she thought, 'the rope is going to snap on this sash window and I shall be stuck out here waiting for the fire brigade to come and rescue me.'

As she ducked back inside the room she glanced down the communal yard that was shared by five other houses. Rows of washing hung from each house to the blocks of brick built lavatories at the other side of the yard. Each house had their washing hung in the same order, as if there was an unwritten ruling. All the whites and what few best clothes they had were hung near the house, then the bedding and towels, and finally the work clothes near to the lavatories.

Long props held up the centre of each line, just managing to keep the sheets from trailing on the floor. A group of children too young for school ran about the yard playing hide and seek and dodging underneath the flapping blankets.

"Aye up lass, tha's mekin' a grand job o them windows, tha'll soon a polished a hole in t'middle."

Ada jumped and looked directly below to see their newest neighbour staring up at her. Their eyes met, and Ada felt the blush begin in her cheeks.

He was carrying his snap tin and helmet, his face still black with coal dust, but his smile and blue eyes lit up his face. Ada stared back at him, unable to look away, and felt as if she couldn't breathe as she gazed at his blonde hair and strong jaw. He was medium height and a muscular build. There was a presence about him, a quiet masculine strength that demanded attention. She had seen him before and given him a shy smile in acknowledgment of his nod of greeting.

He had moved into the house next door but one a week ago with his wife and family. This was the first time he had actually spoken to her and Ada, feeling incredibly shy, tried to think of a witty reply, but could only come up with, "Hello, just back from early shift?"

"Aye, I am that, see thee later."

He nodded his head slightly to one side and gave her a wink. Ada waved in reply as she stepped back and dropped the net curtain into place. Her normally pale cheeks were flaming and she stood there for a moment or two, her thoughts in turmoil, then she pressed close up to the thick cream coloured net and peeped through the small hole that had developed near the top. The aroma of the freshly washed curtains and windows filled her senses. The mixed scent of soap, starch and vinegar would forever remind her of this moment.

The wind was stronger now, blowing the washing back and forth wildly. The children had developed a new game which involved running from one end of the yard to the other, letting the blankets brush across their heads.

As Ada watched, two of the dirtiest children she had ever seen ran towards her washing. They had filthy faces and runny noses, with green candles of snot from nose to mouth. They grabbed the blankets as they ran under them dragging them across their faces.

Incensed and furious, Ada lifted the curtain, banged on the window and shouted, "Clear off you dirty little buggers, go and wipe your snotty noses on your mother's washing."

They ran off, laughing, and Ada was mortified to see her new neighbour observing the whole scene. He grinned, clicked his heels together and saluted her, calling, "Certainly madam, this minute madam."

Ada flew down the stairs in a temper, dragged the pegs from the clothes and flung them all together into the basket. She left the prop where it had fallen, and carried the washing basket towards the house.

"Ere luv, tha's forgotten these."

Ada turned to see him standing close behind her. The blush flooded her cheeks again as she saw him holding her best pink bloomers in his hand.

He placed them delicately on top of the washing.

"I'm Harold," he said. "Seeing as we're on bloomer touching terms tha'd better know me name."

"Thanks," she murmured, and balancing the basket on her hip, tucked them deep down the side of the basket out of sight. "I'm Ada."

"Aye, ah know, I heard thee Dad shoutin' thee. Ta-ra for now, ah'll look out for thee tomorrow and see if tha wants any more washing pickin' up."

Returning his smile she went back into the house thinking how glad she was that it was her best bloomers he had picked up and not the shabby old ones that she had to wear most days.

She dropped the loaded basket onto the scullery table and set about putting the soiled edges of the blankets into the copper of still warm water, and left them to soak, wrinkling her nose in distaste at the thought of them. She carried the rest of the washing through into the living room and started folding the clothes mechanically, her mind reliving the moments of eye contact with Harold.

She looked into the mirror above the mantelpiece and patted her hair into place, examining her face, turning this way and that, wishing she was prettier. What she didn't see was the shy appealing look she had. Her warm brown eyes, delicately pointed chin, and dark brown hair made her very attractive to men, but mostly it was her way of looking up from downcast eyes that seemed to promise hidden depths.

But she had no steady boyfriend. No one until now had made her feel like this. 'Trouble is,' thought Ada, 'he's married, very much married, with children. Still, there's no harm in dreaming.'

Harold went into his house with a gleam in his eye and a smile hovering round his lips as he thought of the silky feel of Ada's bloomers.

The scullery was warm and damp from the morning's washing. He kicked the door shut and breathed in the smell of soda and bleach. The fire still glowed faintly under the copper and the bricks around it were still hot. He lifted the round wooden lid and tested the water. His wife Winn had topped it up with clean water after the clothes had boiled in it. It was a milky greyish colour and felt soft and soapy from the remains of the Sunlight soap.

Harold always washed in the copper on Mondays after the clothes washing was done. It saved getting the tin bath down out of the backyard. He stripped off his shirt and plunged his arms into copper, relishing the feel of the soapy water on his skin and dipped his head in as deep as he could. Grabbing the big bar of rough Lifebuoy soap he began to scrub himself, bit by bit.

Winn popped her head round the kitchen door, then came in and picked up the piece of old towelling they used as a flannel.

"Ah'll wash thee back shall ah?"

"Aye, but don't just tickle it, give it a good scrub, ah want that bloody coal dust off."

His top half clean, Harold stepped out of his trousers and sat on the brickwork that surrounded the copper. "Bloody hell Winn, it's red hot. It's burning me arse, pass that cloth for me to sit on, tha should of let copper fire go out earlier."

"Shurrup an' ger on wi it, tha should think thee sen lucky tha's got hot water. Me father had to wash under t'pump when he come back from pit, water were ice cold."

"Aye, and that's why he had skin t'colour of t'fire back. Ah'm not letting mine get like that."

Harold gingerly lowered his feet into the water and scrubbed his lower half, taking care not to let his private bits touch the hot sides.

Satisfied at last that he had got rid of all trace of coal dust, he climbed out, dropped his dirty pit clothes into the water and pushed them to the bottom. Black scum rose to the top and he turned them around a few times then left them for Winn to sort out.

Dried and dressed in clean clothes he felt refreshed, and he noted with satisfaction his pink cheeks and shiny skin in the tiny shaving mirror over the sink.

After his early start and long shift he was starving hungry and went into the living room looking forward to his meal. His dinner was waiting on the oven top, keeping warm, and gently drying round the edges. A fine crusty skin had already formed on the rim of the plate, but Harold was too hungry to complain.

He'd eaten half of it before his hunger diminished and he began to notice the lumps and burnt bits in the potatoes and the gristle in the meat.

'Not much of a cook is Winn, and not much of a house keeper either,' he thought as he looked around at the dirty hearth and the thick dust on the furniture.

He pushed the plate away and decided to leave the rice pudding till later. Rice pudding was one of the things he didn't mind being well done. He loved to run a knife round the edges and eat the dried, milky crust.

Sleep was what he needed now, he'd been up since 4am, walked the three miles to work, done a shift shovelling coal, then walked back again. That had been the pattern of his life since he went to work down the pit at thirteen, so he knew no other way.

He climbed the narrow staircase and found the beds still unmade and the chamber pots still full. He'd have strong words with Winn later, but for now he was too tired to do anything but collapse on the bed and give himself up for sleep, dreaming of Ada's silky bloomers and the delights that must be inside them.

He slept for an hour then went downstairs and ate the rice pudding. As he finished, Winn came back into the room carrying a full basket of washing. She dropped the basket on to the floor and sat in the wooden armchair near the fire and placed her hands around her swollen belly. She felt more tired than usual today and leaned back in the chair, thankful to sit for a while and rest. The baby moved under her hands, reminding her that there would soon be another child to look after. The novelty of child bearing had worn off. With one child born before Harold married her and two more since, she could see a future of bearing a child every year stretching ahead of her. 'Well not if I can help it,' she thought, 'there must be something I can do about it, even if it is an accepted way of life for most women.'

"When's tha goin' to get beds made and pots emptied Winn? It stinks up there, and t'dinner were about fit for t'pigs."

Winn said nothing but grumbled under her breath as she went upstairs to see to the beds.

Next morning Harold was awake early, with half hour to spare before he had to get up at 4am. He had always been an early riser, and never had need to pay for the services of the professional knocker upper who went tapping on the windows of the men on early shift.

He had dreamed all night. Strange dreams of Ada, and long lines of pink undies hung out to dry that constantly blew away, and he kept running after them, and picking them up, but when he turned around to put them in Ada's basket she was nowhere to be seen. She had gone and his arms and pockets were full of pink silky bloomers.

Harold lay awake thinking of the dream and Ada with her warm, brown, come-to-bed eyes and enjoying the early morning warmth of the bed.

As usual at this time he felt aroused and amorous and turned to Winn putting his hand on her waist and nuzzling her neck.

She obligingly moved her body to accommodate him and let out a series of small farts, ending with a large one that blasted the foul aroma throughout the bed, sending it rising up to escape through the top of the blankets just under Harold's nose.

"Bloody hell Winn, tha certainly knows how to put a man off."

"Aw stop grumbling. Ah couldn't help it, tha knows ah alus fart a lot when am expectin."

Harold threw the blankets back, angry to have been deprived of his early morning treat and flounced out of bed, making the saggy, spring wire bed base bounce.

He went downstairs still wearing just his night shirt. First job was to put the kettle on for his essential mug of tea and then he began dressing. First on were his old shorts and singlet that he wore to work in down the pit, they were still hung over the oven door where Winn had put them to dry last night.

They felt cold and clammy, but Harold put them on anyway, muttering to himself that they would have to do and would be wet through with sweat soon enough. They had once been white but were now a dirty shade of grey from the residue of coal dust. Then came his old work trousers, thick and heavy with dust and dirt. They were seldom washed due to the length of time it took to dry them.

Then he pulled on his socks and heavy boots. He was proud of the boots. They were the first brand new ones he had ever owned, and they felt strong and comfortable. He'd had to argue with Winn about the expenditure of the cash for the boots, but won in the end by telling her that a good pair of boots could save his feet from injury.

Lastly came the jacket and the checked muffler. There he was, ready, with still enough time to enjoy that mug of tea. He sat with his hands around the old mug and looked at the untidy, shabby living room. It was littered with children's discarded clothing and dirty pots, the hearth was cold and full of ash, with no warmth left in it.

'No comfort at all in here,' he thought. Harold had never been able to abide dirt and untidiness in his home, and then he noticed with disgust the two soiled nappies beside the other chair, left in a stinking heap. It was almost a relief to be going to work.

He picked up his snap tin and the Dudley that was filled with cold tea, put on his flat cap and joined the rest of the early shift workers walking down the street towards the pit, their footsteps echoing in the silence of the empty streets.

At this time of day there was little conversation, just a curt, "Nah then," as a greeting as more joined the group.

The pit siren wailed, signalling its message that another shift was due to begin. The huge winding wheel would be turning, lifting the

26

cages that carried the men up from the bowels of the earth, weary and glad to breathe fresh air after their night spent underground. Many of them would be tired to the point of exhaustion and black as the coal they had been hewing. Tough men doing a tough job.

While Harold was on his way to work, Ada was lighting the fire and preparing her father's breakfast. At sixty three, William Dale was still a strong vigorous man working every day in the local brick works. 'He looks tired this morning,' Ada thought. He had that sad look in his eyes that he sometimes had since his wife Louise had died.

They had lived at Epworth then, in a farm cottage with a huge garden, where they kept chickens and grew all their own vegetables. They were surrounded by fields and woods, the air was clean and fresh and the family had thrived in spite of having to survive on the low farm wages.

After Louise died William had been overcome with grief, and eventually decided to leave the farming life and the tied cottage and try to make a fresh start at Wath on Dearne.

They had moved into the house in Packmans Row and tried to get used to the cramped rooms and squalid conditions, hoping that with higher wages they would soon all be able to afford to move to a better house. William had found work in the brick yard, while her brothers, John and William, had gone to be miners at the Manvers Main colliery.

Her sisters Rose and Lizzie were both in service now, so Ada had the front bedroom all to herself, apart from when her sisters had one of their rare weekends off.

Her brothers slept in the back bedroom and her father had made the tiny attic into a bedroom for himself. Compared to many of their neighbours in Packmans Row they had lots of space. Most of the houses were full to bursting point with their big families.

Ada put her hand on her Dad's shoulder as she placed his bowl of porridge on the table. He looked up at her and smiled his thanks but his smile rarely lit up his eyes these days.

"You ok Dad?"

"Aye lass, thanks, this looks good, just what I need to keep the cold out," and he scooped up the first hot spoonful, blowing on it before he put it into his mouth.

"Look at thee Dad, tha's got it all over your tache." Ada wiped the stray porridge away from William's moustache

Ada and her father William enjoyed a close loving relationship. Since his lovely Louise had died William lavished all his love on his family and doted on Ada, his youngest, she reminded him so much of his late wife.

"What time you off to work today Ada?"

"Starting at nine this morning Dad, I should be back by one, it'll be a quiet day today."

She had found a part time job cleaning at a local bakery and went in when the morning's baking was finished and after cleaning up she did all the preparation work for the next day. The hours suited her well, the pay was good for an unskilled worker and she usually came home with leftover bread and pies.

Being the only female in the house meant that at aged twenty she was the housekeeper and ran the house like clockwork. Food was always on the table on time. Clothes were washed every Monday and dirt was never allowed to linger. She soon had her two brothers organised into making their own beds and doing their share of the heavy chores.

"I've made a stew for the lads' dinner, all they have to do is warm it up. That gas ring you got is a real god send, it saves having to wait for the fire to get going. I'll get thee a kipper for tea eh? And ah'll bring a couple of cream buns that will have been damaged."

"What you on about Ada, will have been damaged?"

"Well, they could av a bit of an accident when I move em."

"Now then Ada, you be careful, that's a handy little job tha's got, tha don't want to go and be getting t'sack."

"Don't worry Dad, I'm careful not to take advantage, I reckon they owe me a few perks the amount of work I get through."

William left for work shaking his head at her and tutting under his breath.

Ada could hear her brothers moving about upstairs, they were on afternoon shift this week which meant they would be starting as Harold was finishing.

She poured herself a cup of tea and sat thinking of him.

Maybe she would get home from work in time to be cleaning the front step as he passed, and she thought of his blue eyes and the way he had smiled and winked at her.

'Have to be careful though,' she thought, 'he's married, but it's just a bit of flirtation, no harm in that; it's so nice to have an admirer, married or not.'

John was the first downstairs and went into the scullery to wash while Ada bustled about making a fresh pot of tea and slicing thick slabs of bread to toast. The fire was glowing red now and she stabbed a slice with the long toasting fork and held it close to the bars in front of the fire.

"Can you do this John, while I go and stir some life into Will, I can't hang about here all day. I've got to get cleaned up before I go to work."

She went to the bottom of the stairs, just in time to see Will making his way blearily out of the bedroom.

"Well done, tha's getting up, don't forget to bring t'jerry with thee. I'm not emptying it tha knows."

"Ah, you do it this morning Ada, ah feel rotten," replied Will.

John shouted loud enough for all the houses in the row to hear, "Empty thee own piss pot, tha can't expect thee sister to do it for thee. Tha filled it wi suppin' all that ale last neet. Do as she says and bring it down and empty it."

Will knew better than to argue with John when he was in a mood, and sulkily obeyed, then sat on the sofa looking at his socks.

"Look there's a big hole in me sock Ada."

"Aye I can see it, but don't expect me to mend it, ah'm not thee servant tha knows. Get thee girlfriend to mend it. She should do it, she's keen enough to get married. Tha's only been going out wi her for a couple of months and t'wedding's booked already."

Will heaved a big sigh, "Aye ah know, and it looks like we're gonna av to bring it forward to two weeks on Sunday."

John looked at him for a moment then raised his eyes to the ceiling.

"You bloody idiot, she's in t'family way in't she?"

"Well, what if she is?"

"Will, ah warned thee about her and her family, tha's just fallen for t'oldest trick in t'book."

"That's my future wife tha's talking about," shouted Will as he snatched a piece of toast from the pile on the hearth, cursing as he burnt his fingers. He slammed it down on the table and roughly scraped dripping on it, followed by a liberal coating of salt.

He sat down at the table to eat it, the expression on his face saying that the conversation was over. John shrugged his shoulders and held another slice of bread to the glowing embers. The room was warm and filled with the delicious aroma of toasting bread but the atmosphere was icy.

Ada went about her chores and left the house on time, instructing John about the dinner left in the pantry.

By one o'clock she had completed her morning's work and was ready to leave the bakery, and was preoccupied with calculating in her head how long it would take for her to call at the fishmonger's to get the kippers, and be home in time to be casually cleaning the steps as Harold walked past.

There was a queue at the fishmonger's, which seemed to be at a standstill as the fishmonger skilfully skinned a couple of mackerel for a customer who was imparting some piece of juicy gossip to anyone willing to listen.

The fishmonger stood absorbing the gossip as if he had all day while Ada fidgeted and fumed, willing him to hurry. At last it was her turn and she asked for three large kippers, one for her dad and one each for her brothers, she couldn't stand them herself and planned to have some of the left over stew and one of the damaged cream cakes that were packed carefully away in her bag.

"Anything else love? Come on wake up lass, what you doing, dreaming of your nice young man?"

Ada realised he was talking to her and turned a deep crimson with embarrassment. Her thoughts had been on getting home and making herself look as good as possible to impress Harold. She paid for the fish and practically ran all the way home, the steel tips on the heels of her shoes rattling fast and loud on the pavement.

It was almost 2pm by the time she opened the front door and she hastily hung her coat and hat on the peg in the passage. Placing the kippers in the pantry with a cloth over them, she went to the kitchen sink and swore under her breath at the dirty dinner pots left there. Pushing them to one side, she washed her hands and face under the cold running water, then dashed upstairs and combed out her hair. She swept it back from her forehead and pinned in into a deep wave. Leaving it loose would make it look as if she was showing it off, so she knotted it at the nape of her neck into a bun and pinned it securely.

Quickly she filled a bucket with water, dropped a floor cloth and scrubbing brush into it and went to the front door.

It must be time for the men to be arriving home any time now thought Ada and she set about the window sill and doorstep. Normally spotlessly clean and scoured with yellow donkey stone, today they received even more attention than usual.

Just as she was about to give up hope of seeing him, she heard the sound of his heavy boots walking towards her and began to feel flustered and shy. As he approached, Ada looked around as if she was surprised to see him.

Harold began to say something to her in a teasing voice but her eyes met his and neither of them could think of the right thing to say. In the end, oblivious of the chance that neighbours could be watching, Harold touched her hand and simply said, "Hello Ada."

"Hello Harold," she replied quietly.

For a moment she thought he would kiss her right there in the street, but the moment was broken when Harold's eldest son caught sight of him and shouted to his dad, and they moved quickly apart. Harold gave her a smile and a wink and said in his low throaty voice, "See thee later," before following his son into his house.

Ada put the bucket away and stood perfectly still, gazing through the scullery window. Her heart was beating faster than she had ever known it beat before and she relived the moment that their eyes had met, over and over again.

The next day, she managed to be walking home from work at the same time as Harold was returning from his morning shift. He saw her in the distance, tall and slim in her navy blue coat, her hair coiled neatly in the nape of her neck and walked fast to catch up with her. As he drew alongside her he gave a low wolf whistle and said, "Tha's lookin' very smart Ada to say tha's on thee way home from work, and pretty as a picture."

The colour rose in her cheeks again and before she could reply he said,

"Look at thee blushing, tha looks even prettier now."

"Give over Harold, tha shouldn't be saying things like that to me, when tha's a married man."

"How can I help it, when tha's so bonny. It don't matter if am married or not. Can't resist telling the truth," and he gave her one of his brilliant smiles.

Today was Friday and Harold was in good spirits. His week's wages were in his pocket and he had the happy feeling that it was the weekend with a day off on Sunday.

"Give us a kiss when we get to the alley Ada."

"What, with your face black as the fire back. Not likely."

"Well how about it when am washed and changed then?"

Ada was beginning to enjoy the flirtation and smiled coyly saying, "Wait and see," and with that turned into the alleyway ahead of him and walked quickly across the communal ground and into their tiny backyard.

As she inserted her key into the door she realised he had followed her.

"What you doing? Go away, one of the neighbours will see you," whispered Ada, horrified at the thought of being the subject of the local gossips.

"I'm waiting to see if tha's gonna promise me that kiss."

"Okay, at Christmas," said Ada, and slipped inside, shutting the door after her quickly but giving him a little smile as she did so.

Saturday was the busiest day of the week at the bakery so it was work as usual for Ada, but by 2pm she had completed all her work and was on her way home with her wages and a shopping bag full of slightly stale bread and a large meat pie with a damaged crust.

Harold was sitting on the step of his back door trying to repair the family's shoes with a tough piece of leather; he looked up as he heard her footsteps.

"Can you make use of some bread? I've got more here than I can use."

Winn appeared behind Harold in the doorway, she looked hot and tired, her long dark hair straggly and unwashed. She took the bread without a word of thanks and turned her back on Ada.

Harold looked around and seeing his wife had gone, said thanks and showed her the shoe he was struggling to repair. Ada offered to loan him her father's cobblers last.

"I'm sure he won't mind as long as tha brings it back when tha's finished with it."

"Thanks, that'll be grand, ah'll pop round in a bit."

Ada felt uncomfortable and embarrassed about the way Winn had taken the bread and wished she hadn't offered it. She found the house empty when she let herself in, and then remembered her father was out driving the pony and trap for the local doctor and knew that John would be working down at his allotment. There was no telling where Will would be, she thought, probably with his girlfriend.

She made herself a cup of tea, took off her shoes and sat in the wooden armchair with her feet on her father's footstool, enjoying a few moments alone. The room felt quiet and peaceful, the clock in the corner ticking the hours away. The fire glowed, filling the room with warmth and brightness. Ada relaxed and was on the point of falling asleep when she heard the soft knock on the door. She got up, annoyed to have her rest disturbed and opened the door to find Harold standing there.

"Hello Ada, I've come to see if ah can borrow the last and to say thanks for the bread and also sorry about Winn's bad manners. She's not very sociable at the best of times but just now she's not too well and right miserable with everybody, especially me."

As he was saying this Harold stepped into the living room and stopped abruptly, gazing in admiration at the cosy room.

"By heck Ada, tha's got this room lookin' grand. Ours is nought like this, it's a right tip, and a bloody mucky tip at that."

"Well, I like the house nice," said Ada, "me mother were the same, she always said cleanliness cost nothing but a bit of elbow grease."

"Tha wants to come round to our house an av a word with our lass, she could do with some lessons on housekeeping."

Harold turned to go, brushing against Ada as he did so. His arms went round her without a moment's hesitation.

As their lips met, Ada felt as if she was on fire. The kiss was deep and long, bonding them together and Ada knew in that moment she would give everything to this man. Anything he asked she would give.

They drew apart and Harold gently held her face between his rough hands and kissed her eyes, her forehead, her nose and finally her mouth again, his tongue caressing hers. He held her away from him, looking into her eyes and said,

"Th'a gonna be mine one day Ada Dale. Ah'v never felt like this before. Ah'v never felt like this about Winn. One day Ada, tha's gonna be mine. I swear it. Ah'm not messing thee about lass. I love thee and ah'll av thee, one day."

He went then, slipping out of the house in the dim light of the dusk, leaving Ada in turmoil, and instinctively she knew it would be a long time till she had peace again.

CHAPTER 5

And so the love affair that was to last a lifetime began, with a few snatched meetings now and then, always afraid of being seen together. Stolen moments that only served to inflame their passion.

On one special day they managed to arrange to be together for a whole day. Hexthorpe Flats was their chosen meeting place, a well known beauty spot near the River Don and far enough away for them not to bump into anyone who knew them.

They met at the gateway to the park and walked hand in hand until they reached the riverbank. At first both of them were silent and self conscious. They sat on a bench overlooking the river and ate the sandwiches Ada had packed. Gradually they relaxed and talked as they had never been able to talk before.

Harold opened his life and his heart to Ada, telling her about his harsh childhood in the back street slums of Mexborough, and about the terror he felt when he first began to work in the pit at the age of thirteen, and how he had suffered nightmares for weeks before going down in the cage to the bottom of the shaft for the first time. He explained how he could never have disclosed these fears to anyone, least of all to his father for the certain prospect of being ridiculed. And he told Ada how eventually he had managed to overcome the fears and become one of the band of comrades who risked their lives every day to blast and dig what they called black gold out of the ground.

Then he told her how he had come to marry Winn. How he had met her when he was seventeen and she was twenty one with a son from a previous relationship.

He had found her attractive and she had let him have his way with her.

"I thought I was the big man," said Harold, "and strutted about with a head as big as a bucket, but I was in for a downfall, and fast."

Apparently Winn had come to him and told him that she was pregnant. Harold had been horrified and wanted to take to his heels and run.

"But there was no chance of that," said Harold.

Winn's father and mother were only too delighted to have their daughter and her child off their hands and her brothers made sure that he walked her up the aisle in record time.

"So there I was, eighteen years old with a pregnant wife and someone else's son to bring up. Mind you he's a grand lad is Herbert, I've come to love him as me own, and he seems to worship me, always coming to meet me from work and wants to sit and talk to me while I have me dinner."

And so Harold had bared his soul and his past to Ada. In comparison to Harold she felt she had had a privileged life. She told him all about the cottage they had lived in, the big garden where they had grown all their own fruit and vegetables, and about the chickens they kept and the pig which they all petted and fed, and then cried over when it had to go to the butchers. To Harold it all sounded idyllic. Then Ada told him about when her mother had died and the decision to make a fresh start and the subsequent move to Packmans Row.

He put his arm around her and pulled her close, removing her hat with his other hand. Her hair, pinned up so carefully this morning, was falling loose and Ada tried to pin it back but Harold pulled all the pins out and stroked her hair as it tumbled about her shoulders.

"Leave it Ada, it makes you look beautiful. I can just see thee in thee nightie brushin' thee hair and getting ready for bed and me waitin' and watchin'."

Ada looked up at him in her shy way and smiled, her cheeks flushed.

Harold returned her look and stroked the back of her neck.

"When tha looks at me like that I just want to pick thee up and carry thee away. Come on, we'd better go for a walk before I lay thee down, right here, on the path."

They walked along the riverbank, his arm around her shoulders, lost in their own world, neither knowing nor caring what the time was.

Ada sighed, "I wish this day could go on forever, just you and me."

They were far away from the park now, no one in sight and Harold guided her into a secluded spot between the rhododendron bushes. He took off his jacket and laid it, lining side down, on the grass.

Ada removed her coat, folded it carefully and placed it on the ground with her hat on top. She sat on Harold's jacket and looked around at the leafy enclosure the bushes made, and could think of nothing else but being here in this lovely place with the man she loved and wanted.

Harold sat down beside her and gently they lay down together. They neither would nor could stop now.

Afterwards as they walked back Harold stopped, held her tenderly and said simply in his plain Yorkshire way, "Tha's mine now Ada Dale, for life."

It was a great relief to Ada to find the house empty when she returned home. In spite of her efforts to tidy her hair and pin it back into place, one look at her would have brought forth questions from her father and brothers.

Harold went straight to the pub and stayed there until he knew that Winn would be in bed, and hopefully asleep. He let himself into the house as quietly as the five pints of strong ale inside him would allow. He closed the door after himself with exaggerated movements and tip-toed carefully across the room, then cursed loudly as he stubbed his toe on the coal bucket and fell headlong on to the still warm hearthrug in front of the fireplace.

As he lay there gazing at the dying embers of the fire, he smiled to himself, simply because he felt so happy, and then he began to laugh. Once he started he just couldn't stop, and he laughed loud and long till tears rolled down his face.

Winn came ponderously down the stairs in her too tight nightdress, clumsy and ungainly in her seventh month of pregnancy. She looked at Harold in the dim light, shook her head in disgust and said, "Bloody idiot, tha'll be laughin' on t'other side o thee face in t'mornin' when tha as ta get up for work wi a thick head. Tha can sleep there on t'rug. And for God's sake keep bloody quiet, tha'll av kids awake and all t'neighbours an all."

Winn shut the door on him and climbed back up the narrow staircase, dragging her bulky body back to bed.

Harold promptly fell into a deep sleep but woke in time for work the next morning, and just as Winn had said he had a thick head and also a very stiff back and neck. But Harold had his thoughts and memories of his day with Ada and inside he was smiling.

Living as they did in densely populated surroundings it was difficult for them to find opportunities to meet. But they found ways. Sometimes they had to be happy with a passing touch or a stolen kiss which only made them long for more.

Ada took to visiting friends that her family had never heard of, or so she said. In reality of course she was meeting Harold, while he just told Winn he was going to the pub.

Then they had a stroke of luck when one of Harold's drinking buddies offered him the use of his barge, which was moored on the canal between the trips it made carrying coal up to Sheffield. He had to be kept well supplied with drink in exchange and to ensure his discretion, but Harold reckoned it was worth it in order to have somewhere private to be with Ada.

Their lovemaking was like a drug, the more they had the more they needed. As one assignation was over, they were scheming to find the chance to meet again.

Ada went around as if she was in a happy trance. She glowed with love and had never looked more beautiful. She knew the risks she was taking but somehow she couldn't help herself. All that mattered was finding the next opportunity to be alone with Harold.

Of course the inevitable was bound to happen, and happen it did!

One morning Ada woke feeling nauseous and it just happened to be a weekend when Lizzie was at home. Ada tried to fight back the urge to vomit but it was no good, she jumped out of bed and pulling the half full chamber pot from underneath, knelt down and retched violently.

Lizzie was appalled and leapt out of her own bed to hold Ada's head and keep her long plaited hair out of the vomit and urine. By the time Ada had stopped retching she was on the point of collapse and Lizzie managed to get her back into bed, wiped her face and laid a cold wet flannel on her forehead.

Lizzie was no fool; she'd seen it all before and could read Ada like a book.

"Now then Ada, I think tha's got something to tell me hasn't tha?"

"I think I've eaten summat that's upset me," whispered Ada, afraid to move or raise her voice in case it all began again.

"Now don't give me that Ada, don't tell me lies, I can tell tha's expectin', ah can see it in thee face. Ah knew there was summat wrong as soon as ah saw thee yesterday. Who is it? Who's the father? Ah didn't even know tha was courting."

She stopped as she saw the tears start. They welled up in Ada's eyes and overflowed, rolling down the sides of her face, soaking the pillow.

Lizzie took hold of her hand and wiped her face again.

"Don't cry love, it's not the end of the world, tell me who thee boyfriend is. Am sure he'll marry thee and be glad to get such a lass as thee."

But Ada cried all the more and between her sobs in a juddering voice said, "He won't marry me Liz, he can't."

"What does tha mean he can't? Oh no, don't tell me he's married already! That's it isn't it? Oh bloody hell Ada. Tha's a little fool. Tha's got thee sen in a right fix now."

"What am ah going to do Liz? Dad'll be that upset wi me. A'll just av to leave home, go away somewhere."

"Best keep it quiet for t'time being Ada, and see what happens. But ah want to know who the bloke is."

But Ada wouldn't tell her no matter how she pleaded or threatened.

The weekend passed and Lizzie went back to her position as housemaid at Carlton, promising to write to Ada, and advising her to keep quiet as long as possible. In their hearts they both hoped that

Ada would miscarry; at this stage no one would be aware of the pregnancy.

She did write to Ada and also to her sister Rose telling her the whole sorry story about their youngest sister, apart from the fact that the father was already married.

At home, Ada carried on as best she could, although she felt ill so much of the time.

Her father William was not so ignorant of women's problems as his daughters presumed. After all, he had seen his Louise go through several pregnancies and he knew the signs only too well.

He watched his youngest daughter carefully, noticing how pale she looked, and how preoccupied and secretive she had become. Not like his Ada at all.

One day after tea they were sat either side of the fire reading.

William could stand it no longer and folded his newspaper carefully, and placed it on the table. 'Now here goes,' he thought.

"Ada love, ah want to ask thee summat, and ah don't want thee flying off the handle. Am real worried about thee an am gonna ask thee straight out. Is thee in t'family way?"

Ada looked at him, shocked, then bent her head in shame and nodded.

William hadn't realised that he was holding his breath till it all came out in a great whoosh, leaving him feeling weak and lost for words. He put his hand over his mouth and stared at her. Emotions ran through him. Anger, disappointment, pity, love, understanding, but most of all a need to protect her, comfort her and tell her not to fret, he would look after her.

She went across to him and sat on the hearthrug, resting her head on his knee as she used to do when she was a little girl and said between her tears, "I'm sorry Dad, so sorry."

"Well it takes two to get thee in this state Ada. Who is it? Ah didn't know tha had a boyfriend."

But Ada was determined not to name Harold and made up a story about a young man she had been seeing who had joined the army and gone off to fight in France, and added that she wouldn't marry him even if he asked her.

All Ada wanted was the chance to speak to Harold. She waited day after day for the opportunity. It came one day the week after the talk with her father.

She saw Harold walk past the front window on his way to work and pulled on her coat and went after him, walking as fast as she could. She caught up with him just under the railway bridge. He turned around when he heard her call him and looked shocked to see her.

"Harold, I have to talk to thee," she said, gasping for breath and holding her side where a stitch had developed.

"Tha'll av to be quick love, ah'm late for work."

"Harold, I'm in trouble, I'm expectin'!"

For a moment he was speechless, then groaned and said, "Aw, bloody hell Ada, tha's picked a fine time to tell me. Our lass as gone into labour today, that's why ah'm late, ah've ad to fetch t'doctor, she's real bad."

Ada forgot her own troubles for a minute. "What, and tha's going to work?"

"Got to Ada, we need the money. She's got Mrs Shaw there and her mother. God bless the bloody old bat. Doctor's on his way. That's why ah've got to work, doctor'll want paying. Ah'd only be in't road, and her mother'd spend all her time playin' hell wi me."

"What we gonna do Harold?"

"Don't know lass, but ah'v got to go now. If a miss start of t'shift ah'll av more problems," and he turned and began to run, shouting as he went, "see thee," and the sound of his heavy boots echoed under the bridge.

Ada stared after him wondering what on earth she was going to do. A train passed overhead, the sound deafening as wagon after wagon loaded with coal rumbled over the bridge.

Normally she would have rushed to get through the bridge, as she so hated being underneath it when the trains were passing over, but today she just stood still as if paralyzed. The noise went on and on until it seemed to fill her whole body with the vibration and she realised that her hand was pressed to her stomach as if to protect the little life growing in there.

She walked home slowly then, deep in thought, and by the time she reached the alleyway leading to Packmans Row a change had begun in her. A steely determination came over her, and an awareness that she would cope no matter what happened. This would be her baby to love and care for no matter what the gossips might say. She wasn't the only girl that had found herself pregnant with no husband.

But she still dreaded telling her brothers. John in particular would be so angry and out to find the man responsible for her condition. She would put off telling them as long as possible.

While this was going on, Winn was struggling to give birth. After a long and difficult labour, her second daughter was born. A tiny, delicate baby, with a sweet little face and rosebud lips. The doctor doubted that she would survive and advised Winn to have her christened as soon as possible. They decided to call her Sarah after Harold's mother.

Her older sister Edith took one look at her and was instantly and totally devoted to her. She barely left her side and spent hours talking to her, rocking her, and constantly worrying about her. She drove her mother mad with questions, was Sarah too hot? Too cold? Was she having enough milk? Sarah surprised everyone, not only did she survive, she thrived, but remained dainty and petite and soon became the pet of all the family and especially to her father.

Two months went by and Ada's situation was becoming desperate, her pregnancy was beginning to show and she knew she couldn't put off telling her brothers any longer.

Before she managed to find the courage to tell them, matters were taken out of her hands. When she arrived home from work one day she found both of her brothers and her sister Rose sitting around the table in the living room.

Ada smiled a welcome at them, but there were no smiles in return. Rose indicated the chair at the opposite side of the table from her and told her to sit down as they had something to discuss with her.

As she took off her hat and coat and pulled the chair out her heart was racing and she broke out in a clammy sweat.

John was the first to speak. Hesitantly he said, "Ada love, we have to talk, our Rose says tha's expectin'. Is it true?"

She looked at them, from one to the other, her face pale and her eyes brimming with tears which she struggled to hold back, and simply said, "Yes."

Then the recriminations began. How could she behave like this, she'd brought disgrace on the family. What was she going to do? Who was the father? When was she getting married? She should be ashamed of herself.

Suddenly Ada grew very angry and shouted, "What's it got to do with you three? It's my life. Mind your own business." And she walked out of the room up the stairs and closed the door behind her and wedged the chair under the handle.

The arguing and indignant statements continued downstairs, she could hear every word through the thin ceiling, but she just didn't care anymore. She lay down on her bed, pulled the eiderdown up to her chin and stared at the flowers on the faded wallpaper until she fell asleep.

The next day she went to work and told her employers, half expecting them to sack her, but they were understanding and said she could carry on working as long as she was able to do the job.

Overnight it seemed her pregnancy had become common knowledge. A few people shunned her, walking past as if she was invisible but most were kind and sympathetic. Especially her friend Martha who lived at the far end of Packmans Row.

Martha started knitting straight away. Churning out tiny bootees and jackets every week in beautiful soft white wool, bought out of the meagre amount of money she had left after paying for her lodgings.

Ada stuck to her story of the soldier, who had gone to France, and no one seemed to doubt her except Lizzie, and she kept quiet, but Ada caught her giving out strange looks now and then.

Even her brothers eventually became reconciled to the idea. Accepting at last that there was nothing that could be done about it, and they both had their own lives to see to. Will was due to marry his pregnant girlfriend. He had put it off as long as possible, but her family were becoming insistent, and they were not a family to cross. Will was beginning to regret ever having got involved, but it was too late now.

John also was about to make his announcement that he would be getting married very soon, but for a much pleasanter reason. He had been walking out with Mary for a long time now and her widowed mother had offered them two furnished rooms rent free to get them started. It was too good an offer to turn down.

Since the day that Winn had given birth, Ada had barely seen Harold and she longed to speak to him. Then one day as she went across the yard he passed her as he setting off for work. He slipped a note into her hand, winked at her and went off with a quick wave of his hand.

Ada went into the lavatory, locked the door, sat on the seat and opened the note with shaking hands. It was short and to the point with no loving endearments and simply said, 'Can you meet me at the barge tomorrow night usual time?'

When she arrived at the barge, Harold was already there. The kettle was just starting to boil on the little stove, filling the cabin with steam. He locked the cabin door after her and took her in his arms. For long minutes they just stood there holding each other, soaking in the relief at being together again, oblivious to the steam swirling around them, until Ada pulled away and lifted the kettle off the stove.

"We'd better make tea then if that's what we've come here for."

"Come ere love, let me show thee what we've come ere for, and it's not tea!"

Ada giggled as he pulled her towards the bunk bed, and Harold had to put his hand over her mouth as he heard voices on the tow path.

"Sh, there's someone outside. Bloody hell Ada, they're comin' on board. Quick, on the floor."

They both lay on the floor right up to the door, praying that the lock would hold as they heard the handle being tried. They held their breath as a face could just be made out, trying to peep through the narrow cracks in the flimsy wooden door, Harold realised that he hadn't locked the bottom half of the stable type door and leaned against it with all his strength to prevent it being pushed open. At last, whoever it was gave up, and they heard footsteps fading away along the path.

As they lay there on the floor with their arms entwined Harold kissed her gently, then with increasing passion. They never did make it to the bunk.

Afterwards they spent their last few moments together talking about the events since they had last seen each other.

"Ah can't tell thee how much I've been longing for this Ada. How is tha managing love?"

"Oh Harold, it's been awful, but things have got better now that everyone knows, and the sickness has stopped thank God."

They went round and round their situation trying to think of a solution.

Harold said he would leave Winn tomorrow but couldn't desert the children and then he had to tell her his news. He had put it off as long as he could but he had to tell her now.

"We're leaving Packmans Row, Ada."

She looked at him disbelieving.

"Winn gave up the tenancy without telling me and has got a house to rent at Denaby, says she wants to be nearer her family. I've played hell about it, and been to see the landlord but he's already let our house to someone else at more rent than we can afford, so he won't take the notice back. Ah'm gonna av to try an get work at Denaby Main. Honestly Ada, sometimes ah could swing for that bloody woman!"

"Oh Harold, what can we do? I can't stop seeing you." Then she hesitated as a thought hit her. "Are you fed up of me? Are you trying to finish with me?"

"Look at me Ada, look at me. Ah swear ah love thee. Ah'll never stop trying and praying for us to be together."

There were tears from both of them as they parted that night, promising they would meet every week somehow.

It was the following Saturday that Harold and his family moved house, so Ada wasn't there to see it and she was thankful for that. Packmans Row seemed even more depressing now with no likelihood of seeing Harold about the place.

Every Saturday from then on Harold walked from Denaby to Mexborough and Ada took the trolley bus there. They spent most of their time walking, talking, and seeking out places where they were least likely to be seen by anyone who knew them both. On a few rare occasions they were able to use the barge when it was moored nearby.

After the fifth month, Ada had no more morning sickness and carried her pregnancy well. Her body remained slim, just the increasing bump showed her condition.

Then suddenly in the seventh month, as she returned from work, the pains began, faint at first then increasing till she bent over the chair gasping, waiting for it to ease. She climbed the stairs and crawled into bed, laying on her side with her knees drawn up hoping to gain some relief.

Between the pains, Ada dozed a little and kept listening for her father to come home. He was working late today on his Saturday job, driving the local doctor around in the pony and trap to see his patients.

Ada thought how she could do with the doctor herself. If only it had been a weekend when Lizzie or Rose had been here. If only she could get to the window and shout for help. If only Harold was with her. She could find no ease at all now, the pain was almost continuous and she was losing blood. Fastidious as ever, even in her pain she worried about making a mess of the bed.

It was almost dark by the time William finished work. The rounds had taken longer today and he had brushed and fed the pony, talking to him as he worked. Satisfied at last that the pony was comfortably settled, he set off home, expecting to find a warm fire and his tea cooking in the oven. But the house was quiet and the fire almost out when he arrived.

"Not like Ada," he said softly to himself as he piled coal on the fire and lit the lamp. And then he heard the faint moan. Picking up the lamp he went upstairs calling to her as he went, "Ada, are tha in bed? What's the matter? Is tha badly?"

He found Ada in a tangle of blankets thrashing about with the pain. He took one look at her, and ran downstairs faster than he would have thought himself capable of and called the next door neighbour to fetch Mrs Shaw who acted as the local midwife.

William was beside himself with worry, looking through the window one minute, dashing downstairs to see to the water boiling on the hob the next, and all the time trying to reassure Ada that help was on its way. The neighbour returned to say Mrs Shaw would be there soon and sure enough she almost followed her, climbing slowly up the stairs, grumbling that she had just been about to sit down for her tea. Harold was so relieved he almost hugged her but had second thoughts when he looked at her bulky body and whiskery chin.

She wasted no time in pushing William out of the room and instructed him to keep the kettle on the boil and get the copper stoked up to make sure there was a good supply of hot water. Harold obeyed in spite of muttering to himself about all midwives always wanting hot water.

"What the bloody hell's she gonna do, boil the poor little babby," he said aloud, but not quite loud enough for her to hear.

Nevertheless he was glad to go and glad to have something to do. He felt useless and unbelievably angry with the man who was responsible for his Ada being in this position, and speaking aloud again cursed him and wished he could make sure he'd never be able to do it again. He stormed in and out of the tiny rooms ranting about castration by the most extreme methods.

The sounds from the bedroom above were driving him mad. It was when he sat down exhausted that he heard the first faint feeble cry. Not the lusty almost angry cry usually made by a healthy newborn, and William stood up again, his head on one side, waiting to hear a louder sound, but none came.

Upstairs, Mrs Shaw held the tiny baby girl gently in her capable hands, and laid her on her mother's breast and thought that even allowing for the fact that she had given birth in her seventh month, the baby was much smaller than she would have expected. The reason soon became clear when Ada began to push again and a second baby girl was born. This time there was no cry, no movement at all. She laid her on the towel on the dressing table and attended to Ada. No point in calling the doctor now, knowing from her long experience the tiny babies had no chance of life.

Privately, knowing Ada's circumstances, she thought that perhaps it was a blessing in disguise, but doubted that Ada would think so, and how right she was.

The first born baby lived for an hour and Ada lay with both her babies cuddled to her breast, sad beyond the point of tears. She felt as if a large black cloud had descended upon her, and all she could think of was if only they had lived. She could see them both in her mind's eye, dressed in matching clothes, running about the park getting into mischief, or sitting on the hearth rug in front of the fire while she told them stories. Dozens of scenes were going through her mind, but all of them began with 'if only'!

Then she thought of what a waste it had all been, all the long months of worrying, the disgrace and the pain her family had had to endure. Maybe it was God's punishment she thought, for falling in love and being with a married man.

She knew she had to let the babies go, all the warmth had gone from them. They were cold and stiff now like two tiny dolls wrapped in pieces of blanket. Ada unwrapped the blankets and looked at them both. They were perfectly formed but just too small to live. Gently she wrapped them both together in the beautiful shawl she had crocheted and silently handed them over to Mrs Shaw.

It was left to her father to arrange for them to be buried in Wath cemetery, both in the same little coffin. He was so worried about Ada's state of mind that he wrote to Lizzie and Rose telling them how badly their sister had taken the loss of her babies.

Lizzie managed to get a whole week's leave from work on the grounds of a family bereavement, although her employer, who was a woman with little compassion, had made it clear that she would, of course, be deducting the time off from her pay.

When she arrived at Packmans Row she found Ada in a sorry state, unwashed and refusing all food. As she walked into the room the stale smell hit her. She went straight into big sister mode and first of all opened the window as far as it would go. She bent and kissed her sister but wrinkled her nose at the unwashed smell.

"Bloody hell Ada, tha stinks. We'd better get thee sorted out. This won't do. Tha's got to pull thee sen together."

Ada didn't answer, just slid further down the bed and pulled the blankets up, almost over her head.

Lizzie wasted no time. Telling Ada she would be back shortly she went downstairs, filled the copper with water and lit the fire underneath it, then dragged the tin bath up the narrow staircase, cringing as it scraped the paintwork and faded paper. Rose arrived as the water began to boil and just in time to ladle it out and carry it a bucket full at a time, upstairs to fill the bath. A generous handful of Epsom salts went into the water and a couple of cloth bags filled with lavender, which filled the room with fragrance.

Ada offered no resistance when her sisters pulled the bedclothes back, but was so weak it needed both of them to get her into the bath.

Kneeling one each side of her, they washed her from head to foot, both of them shocked at how thin and frail she had become in the two weeks since giving birth. Ada began to cry silently, the tears rolling down her face and dripping into the water.

"That's right, get thee crying done while tha's in t'bath, it'll save a lot of hankie washing," said Lizzie.

A glimmer of a smile started in spite of the tears, especially when Rose and Lizzie were exchanging stories of things that had happened at work.

Lizzie told about the new girl who had started as a kitchen maid, and who was so afraid of boys that she thought just a touch from one of them would put her in the family way.

"Tha knows different to that don't tha Ada," laughed Rose. "Depends where she was touched don't it?"

Lizzie produced a shampoo she had acquired from among her mistress's expensive toiletries and proceeded to wash Ada's hair. Ada relaxed for the first time in weeks as Lizzie massaged her scalp, and finally Rose poured a jug of cool water mixed with rosemary over her head as a rinse.

They got her out of the bath, and wrapped her in a towel, then sat her in the pink basket chair that had once belonged to their mother. As Ada dried her hair and brushed it free of tangles she felt so much better.

"Don't know how to thank you both, I feel so much better, and ah'm starving, can ah av a cup of tea and some toast?"

Lizzie kissed the top of her head, while Rose said, "Don't thee get used to this sort of treatment our Ada, it's bloody donkey work carrying buckets of water up these stairs."

As Ada enjoyed her tea, her thoughts turned to Harold, and how she longed to see him. She wondered if he would have assumed she had finished with him when she hadn't turned up at their usual meeting place in Mexborough. There was a street tucked away behind the market where they usually met every Saturday teatime, and she closed her eyes and imagined him walking up and down looking for her.

The first Saturday that Ada missed their date Harold was torn between disappointment and worry, but convinced himself there would be a good reason for her not being there. On the second Saturday he arrived half an hour early, and waited in the freezing wind for two hours before walking back to Denaby, worrying every step of the way that she could have met with an accident, and then tormenting himself with the thought that she had decided to end their affair.

He spent the whole of the next week in a state of frenzy, wondering what to do, and how to get in touch with her without her family knowing. If only they still lived in Packmans Row he would have been able to see her every day, and he was more irritated by Winn than ever, blaming her for his present dilemma.

In the end he put all his faith in Ada being there at the usual time the following week. He had never known a week to pass so slowly, every day he counted the hours and became so quiet and short tempered that his workmates noticed and said little to him.

When at last Saturday arrived he was out of the house early and off to Mexborough long before the meeting time. Winn's parting comment was,

"Tha's in a big hurry this morning, where's the fire? It's about time tha took these kids out and gi me a bit o time to meself." Harold totally ignored her, not wanting to be dragged into an argument.

He arrived in Mexborough far too early and wandered up and down the aisles of the market looking at the stalls but not really seeing them. He stopped every time a trolley bus from Wath came into the market square, his heart sinking as it emptied and there was no Ada among the passengers.

He crossed to the street where they usually met and waited and waited, till he could stand it no longer and he set off to walk to Wath, not sure in his mind how he was going to contact her, but he just had to see her, had to know if she was alright, and had to know if she still wanted him. As he walked he thought of the events since they had moved to Denaby.

Their house was no better than the one they had had in Packmans Row. There were the same number of rooms, the same lack of amenities and just as many cockroaches that came out from behind the fireplace after dark and scurried back into their hiding places as soon as a light came on.

Harold was well known as a skilled collier and a hard worker and he had been welcomed at Denaby Main by bosses and workmates alike.

The gang he was working with were more than happy to have him with them. He would work all day on his knees in the narrowest of tunnels, instinctively knowing when and where the roof needed to be propped. But Denaby Main was known as a dangerous pit, with more than its fair share of accidents and Harold much preferred his previous job at Manvers Main.

Life at home had not improved. His marriage to Winn was a misery. Harold felt trapped and longed to be free to marry Ada, but could see no way that it was ever going to happen. While Winn had found that being married to Harold held no joy, especially when he was in a constant bad temper over their move to Denaby and resentful of her. The only consolation was that she could pop down to her sister's house to have a good moan.

It was dark by the time he reached Packmans Row and Harold had decided he had no alternative but to go straight to Ada's home and knock on the door. After that he would play it by ear.

The curtains were closed, but he could see lights flickering and hear voices inside as he knocked. The door was opened almost immediately by John who peered into the darkness at him. He was obviously not in a good mood and as he recognised Harold he said bluntly, "Oh, it's thee Harold Corker, what does tha want?"

Harold cleared his throat and quietly said, "Ah've come to see Ada."

"And what does tha want wi our Ada then?" John stopped. "It's thee in't it? It's thee that's got our Ada in this state, an tha's got the bloody nerve to come round to our house ya bastard. Come ere," and he made a lunge for Harold, grabbing him by the neck and pushing him up against the wall.

Harold put his hands up and said, "Do what tha likes John, ah won't fight thee, but ah won't go till ah know how Ada is."

John's father came to the door just in time to witness it all, and grasping straight away what it was all about said, "That's enough John, get inside the pair of you, tha's just providing a sideshow for that lot," and he waved his arms at the crowd of onlookers who had appeared as if by magic. "Piss off the lot of ya, bloody sensation seekers that's all you buggers are."

It was rare for William to swear or even raise his voice, but when he did, the family obeyed without question.

Ada had been sitting upstairs enjoying the tea that Lizzie had brought her and listening to one of Rose's stories about life in the big house where she worked when they heard the raised voices. Lizzie peered through the window; if she stood on tip-toe and looked through the top right hand corner she could just see into the yard.

"It's Harold Corker," she declared, "Him an our John's avin' a right set to." She broke off as she realised that Ada had got up and was intending to go downstairs.

"Wait Ada, tha's not strong enough yet, tha'll fall."

The words were hardly out of her mouth when she heard the bump as Ada fell and slid to the bottom of the steep narrow staircase, calling out for Harold even as she slid down the steps.

The men were just inside the door when they heard her. John was glaring at Harold, while his brother looked on, waiting for the next move. At the sound of the fall they rushed as one to the stairs, but Harold was there first, on his knees with his arm under Ada's head, straightening her clothes and smoothing her damp hair away from her face.

She looked up at him and smiled. Oblivious to anyone else he returned her smile tenderly.

"Tha's fallen for me again Ada." He kissed her forehead gently, and jokingly said, "Is tha alright love, there were no need to fall down t'stairs for me tha knows, Ah'd av waited till tha walked down."

Harold slipped his other arm under her knees, lifted her from the floor and laid her on the couch. He remained on his knees by her side holding her hand, while all the family looked on speechless.

Even John could not deny the love in Harold's eyes, and felt at a loss as to what to do. Looking at his father he said, "Ah'll be off then, ah can see ah'm not needed ere, it's in your hands Dad. Ah'v got me own family to see to. Just look what tha's doing Ada, no good can come o this; and take care of thee sen. If tha wants me, tha knows where I am," and ramming his cap firmly on his head, he left, telling himself it would be a long time till he returned. He'd see his dad later when he went for a pint and let him know his feelings on the matter.

His brother followed him, glad for once to be going home to his wife.

Lizzie and Rose declared they needed to go shopping and left the house quickly, both dressed smartly in their long navy coats and neat narrow brimmed straw hats, and both of them giving disapproving looks at Harold, who was now seated by Ada holding her hand.

There was as uncomfortable silence for a few moments as William gathered his thoughts together. He felt so depressed by it all and in a turmoil, wishing with all his heart that his Louise was still here to guide him. He cleared his throat and turned his chair to face them both, his expression stern and unsmiling.

"Well, let's hear it all then, what's tha messin' about wi my daughter for when tha's got a wife and family?" He looked from one to the other.

They both began to speak at once but Ada fell silent and let Harold do the explaining.

For a man of few words he gave an eloquent and detailed explanation of his young life and of his early enforced marriage to Winn. Looking William in the eye, he declared his powerful feelings of love for his daughter.

William thought deeply of Harold's words before he replied. He knew well enough of many such loveless marriages and the misery endured between the partners. He had seen young wives turned into old women before their time, bearing child after child and the husbands become bitter, turning to alcohol and gambling as their only relief from the daily grind of backbreaking work.

He knew only too well how Harold felt, but that didn't mean he could abandon his wife and turn to his daughter for comfort and love, and he said so in his firm quiet voice.

Harold nodded in agreement and replied, "Mr Dale, right or wrong, ah'd leave Winn tomorrow without a second glance, but ah'd never leave the bairns, they need me, they're my responsibility. Ah av to stop wi em till they're old enough to fend for themselves."

"Well that's gonna be a long time, seein as t'youngest ain't walkin' yet. It's not fair on our Ada to expect her to waste her life waitin' around for years."

Harold looked down, silent, knowing he spoke the truth, and then Ada said, her voice shaky with emotion, "Dad, it's Harold ah want. I'll never want anyone else. Ah don't care what busy bodies say, ah'll av this man anyway ah can. There'll be nobody else for me. Ah luv im Dad and ah won't finish wi im."

William knew his daughter well enough to recognise the depth of her feelings, and knew how determined she could be. Just like her mother he thought, and remembered the fierce arguments with Louise's parents all those years ago when they hadn't approved of him and Louise marrying. But they had gone ahead and proved them wrong, and he recognised that he was going to have to give way or risk losing his daughter.

"Well, all ah can do is hope and pray things work out eventually, but ah'll tell thee both now, there's troubled times ahead and of plenty of heartache. This is not what ah wanted for me daughter tha knows. Tha'd better treat her well. Oh, ah think tha's a good enough bloke but no good to her when tha's already married." Shaking his head William stood up, pulled on his working jacket and left the house.

He walked down the street pondering on the events and went to check on the doctor's pony. As always, he had a warm welcome from Beauty, especially when he produced a mint from his pocket. She took it gently, her velvety soft mouth nuzzling his hand then nudging his pocket for more, and William began to brush her mane, taking comfort from the simple routine of grooming her.

Left alone for the first time in weeks Harold and Ada sat holding hands. Both had so much to say to each other, but were overcome with emotion.

Harold put his arm around her, pulled her close and said, "Come on then love, tell me all about it," and Ada talked of all that had happened since they had last met and about the loss of their two babies.

Harold held her quietly, his blue eyes full of tears, not just for the loss, but for what she had had to endure without his support.

Exhausted, Ada leaned on Harold, relaxing in his warmth and strength. When she stopped speaking in mid sentence Harold looked down at her and realised she had fallen asleep. He kissed her forehead and lowered her on to the cushions, gently easing his arm out from beneath her.

Knowing he could stay no longer, he covered her with the knitted blanket which Ada kept on the back of her father's chair, then wrote a note telling her that he would be back next Saturday. He banked the fire down with damp slack and carefully put the guard in place. Giving Ada one last look, he closed the door and set off on his long walk back to Denaby.

CHAPTER 6

Harold walked fast, swinging his arms in rhythm with his legs, taking in deep breaths of the cold air and exhaling till his lungs felt empty, trying to rid them of the residue of coal dust that always seemed to reside there. And as he walked, the events of the last few hours went over and over in his mind.

He could think of no solution, but now that Ada's family knew, at least they would be able to see each other without hiding, and that thought brought him a feeling of happiness, and before he knew it he began to sing softly to himself. It was a long time since he had felt like singing.

The mood lasted until he reached the outskirts of Denaby, then gradually seeped away the closer he got to home.

As he opened the door to the little house in Victoria Terrace he strode over the grimy step and the noise hit him. Then the stench reached him in spite of his poor sense of smell.

Sarah was screaming as Edith struggled to change her nappy while Herbert and Bill chased each other up and down the uncarpeted stairs firing imaginary guns. The smell of unwashed nappies and their contents filled the room. Flies hovered above the remains of breakfast, walking over spilt sugar and breadcrumbs. A string of stained washing hung low over the fireplace where a few pieces of coal struggled to stay alight in an overflowing grate.

Winn lay on the sofa fast asleep. 'How the hell can she sleep in this lot?' he thought. Even relaxed and sleeping she looked pale and weary, older than her years. The guilt and pity he felt was soon replaced by anger when he noticed the empty beer bottles underneath the dirty, sagging sofa.

Taking one look at their father's face the boys stopped their noisy game and exchanging glances headed to the door, but turned around and crept upstairs quietly as Harold simply pointed at them.

Edith looked up as she struggled to pin the nappy. "Come here lass, let's have a look at thee, let's get this babby sorted out shall we?"

Edith began to cry. "I couldn't do it Dad."

"Ah know lass, tha's done thee best," and he patted her shoulder.

Lifting his youngest daughter, he laid her against his chest and gently rocked her. She nuzzled against him and Edith silently handed him a half filled bottle of milk. Harold looked at the grubby discoloured teat with distaste and held it under the tap but it made little difference.

Feeling in his pocket he produced a sixpence and handed it to Edith.

"Run to t'shop Edi, and get a new teat, and bring three sherberts wi t'change."

Edith's face lit up at the thought of the sherberts, but as she took the money she said sadly, "Me Mam's poorly Dad."

"Aye, ah can see that, now get off quick, and run all t'way. This babby's hungry."

As soon as Edith was out of the door he nudged Winn off the sofa, not caring if she fell on the floor or not, and laid Sarah carefully in her cot.

"Come on Winn, get thee sen up, idle bugger, these bairns need looking after."

Winn slid to the floor and sat there looking around sleepily, "What's tha dun that for, ah war just avin' a bit of rest."

"Rest!" Harold shouted. "Tha's nought to do all day except see to house and t'kids, an tha can't be bloody bothered to even do that, an tha's been drinkin'. Has tha had that awd ma Jenkins in ere again?"

Winn pulled herself to her feet and faced Harold. "What if ah ad? Tha's never ere."

"Well ah'm ere nah, and tha can get this place cleaned up, it stinks. Ah'm going for a pint, and tha'd better av it done when ah get back."

Harold turned away from her, his face red with anger. He had never been a man to use his fists on his wife the way that many of his workmates did, 'but my God,' he thought, 'she pushes me close

57

sometimes'. He went out of the house, seething with anger, just as Edith returned.

Winn sat on the sofa holding her head in her hands. Edith handed her the teat and looked sadly at her mother as sobs shook her body and tears coursed down her cheeks.

"Don't cry Mam, are ya still poorly? Come on, ah can help ya," and she handed the bottle to her mother. "Put teat on t'bottle mam, and ah can feed Sarah, she likes me to feed her."

Silently, Winn fitted the new teat and left Edith to feed her sister. She put her head back on the old cushion and gave a deep shuddering sigh.

Back in Wath, Ada woke to find herself alone in the house. For a while she lay perfectly still, soaking in the comforting atmosphere of her home. She looked slowly around from her unfamiliar position on the old sofa, taking in the chenille curtains and the matching table cloth, and remembered how she had saved to buy them and haggled to get the price down at David Haig's, the local second hand shop, where almost anything you needed could be found.

She found and opened the note that Harold had left and smiled as she read, 'Got to go. I love you. See you next week.' He had signed it simply Harold, but had drawn two hearts with an arrow going through them.

Ada hugged the note to her face, kissed the paper and dreamed as the fire glowed and filled the room with its warm light, while twilight fell outside. And then she noticed the hearth was filled with ash and the furniture had a fine film of dust. Automatically she began to get up. 'I must clean the hearth,' she thought, but the room span as she sat upright, giving her that nauseous feeling again.

She took deep breaths and waited for it to pass, then carefully stood and made her way gingerly back upstairs to bed.

As she sank thankfully into the feather mattress and pulled the blankets up to her chin, her thoughts turned again to Harold and the note tucked into her nightdress pocket, and smiled as she thought that tough miner he may be, but deep inside she knew he was just a romantic young man.

Within days, Ada was almost back to normal and set to work cleaning the house with a vengeance. Not an inch of floor was left unswept, no curtain escaped without being washed, and as she worked she thought of Harold and counted the days till she would see him again.

At the end of the week she ventured out to the shops and was pleasantly surprised at how many people stopped to ask how she was and seemed genuinely concerned. At the bakery she bought pies, bread and teacakes, and was astonished when the baker came out from his kitchen to put his arm around her shoulders, refused payment for the goods, and asked her if she was interested in having her old job back.

In a whisper he confided that the girl who had taken her place was a useless lazy lump, and would be getting her marching orders the next day. Ada replied that she would love her old job back but didn't want to deprive the girl of a place.

"Don't thee worry lass, she's going anyway, ah'm not paying good money to her any longer, even if I have to do the work meself, I'll be glad to have you back as long as you feel well enough."

So it was arranged that Ada would start on Monday, and she went home with a smile on her face, swinging her basket and feeling better than she had done in months.

Lizzie and Rose had returned to their work, leaving just herself and her father to keep house for.

There was an uneasy peace between them. Being a very private man who found it difficult to express his feelings, he refused to discuss Ada's affair with Harold. He had said his piece and could not face churning his emotions up again, so he said nothing. But Ada could tell by the set of his mouth exactly what he thought every time she said Harold's name.

When Saturday came around William declared that he had to work, and thankfully went to the doctor's stables where he poured out his troubles to the patient horse while he groomed him.

Alone in the house, Ada locked the kitchen door and washed herself from head to foot. She brushed her hair and plaited it carefully then wound it into a circle and pinned it at the nape of her neck.

She ran upstairs to peer at her reflection in the dressing table mirror, pinching her cheeks to bring some colour into them.

Her best cream blouse suited her and she tucked it firmly into the waistband of her navy blue skirt, pulled her stockings into place, and secured them with the blue lacy garters she had made the previous night. Finally she slipped her feet into her black shoes with the smart silver buckles.

Satisfied that she looked her best Ada went back downstairs and laid the table with a clean cloth and the best willow pattern crockery that had been her mother's pride and joy.

She sliced the new loaf, buttered it and washed the crisp celery that one of the neighbours had given her, freshly dug from his allotment. She had boiled a piece of bacon that morning and she sliced it thick and arranged it on a plate in the centre of the table.

Harold knocked at the door as Ada put the kettle on to boil and she rushed to open it. She suddenly felt flustered and shy, but melted into his arms as he stepped into the kitchen and embraced her.

For long moments they stood motionless with arms wrapped around each other, just thankful to be together and both close to sentimental tears, till Ada broke away and led him through into the cosy living room.

Harold sat down at the table and stared around the spotless room and the simple tempting meal laid out in front of him.

"By this looks grand Ada, how did tha know celery was me favourite? Tha's gone to a lota trouble."

"Aw, it's nought, just a bit o' tea."

Harold stood up again, went outside and came back holding a shoe box tied up with string. Holes had been cut in the side of the box and Ada stared at it as she saw something move inside.

"Ah'v brought thee a present. Tha don't need to av it if tha don't want it, ah can tek it back. Hold it careful, put it on t'floor and unfasten it."

Ada did as he said and lifted the lid. Inside was a tiny black kitten with white paws and blue eyes that gazed back at Ada. It opened its mouth and gave a pitiful meow, showing sharp white teeth and pink tongue.

Instantly, Ada fell under its spell and Harold knew there was no danger of the kitten going back.

"Aw, it's lovely Harold, is it a he or a she?"

"Well am damned if ah know love. Time'll tell."

"Harold for goodness sake, let me av a look."

And country girl at heart, she tipped up the kitten and checked.

"It's a tom, so Monty is his name, but he'll av to be doctored when he's old enough, can't av him tomming all over the town and spraying all over the house."

Harold stroked the kitten and said, "Poor little bugger, tha don't know what's ahead of thee does tha?"

"Oh he'll be alright, it won't hurt will it Monty?"

Harold sucked in his breath. "Well it's makin' my eyes water just to think on it."

Ada laughed, put the kitten down on a cushion and poured the strong tea into the china cups. Giving him a soft kiss on the lips, Ada sat down and they enjoyed their first meal together.

That Saturday set the pattern for many months to come. It was the one day they both waited and longed for. As Harold toiled below in the dark tunnels he relived their afternoons together, sitting in the firelight enjoying their tea. He could almost taste the crunchy celery that Ada always managed to get for him and remembered every detail of their stolen hours in Ada's bed.

Her family had come to accept their relationship even though they did not approve of it. Her brothers stayed away from the house when they knew Harold would be there. Lizzie and Rose still came home on their weekends off, but less frequently. Both of them were walking out with their own young men and preferred to spend their weekends courting.

Ada and Lizzie were still very close and poured out their secrets to each other whenever they met and exchanged letters every week. Lizzie's letters arrived every Thursday morning regular as clockwork and Ada posted her replies every Friday morning.

And then just as it seemed life was running smoothly, there came the morning when Ada awoke feeling very sick and she needed no other sign to know she was pregnant again.

For the first few days she swung from one emotion to another: panic, joy, fear, but most of all apprehension about what her family would say. She couldn't wait to tell Harold and longed to confide in Lizzie. But as she wouldn't be home until the end of the month, Ada decided to tell her in a letter and spent hours composing in her head exactly what she would write.

Another surprise came on Thursday before Ada had managed to get her news written down. Lizzie's regular letter arrived and it announced that she and her young man, Reggie, were to be married in four weeks' time.

"And it's not because I'm in the family way that we are getting married at short notice," she wrote. "It's because Reggie has been offered a cottage to go with his new job at Carlton. You should see it Ada, it's lovely and it just reminds me of where we lived at Epworth. It's got two bedrooms, a big living room and a great massive garden, you and Dad will be able to come and stay for a holiday."

The rest of the letter went on to describe the cottage in greater detail, then almost as an afterthought added that she would be getting married from home and telling Ada that she would buy her the material for a new dress and pay for it making, as she expected her to be her bridesmaid. Then she added a postscript that she could choose the colour and style of dress herself.

How generous and typical of Lizzie she thought, and how she longed for it to be herself and Harold that were getting married. Useless to wish it she knew, but nothing could stop her daydreaming.

She decided not to burden Lizzie with her news until after her wedding and simply wrote back saying how pleased she was for her and Reggie and how happy she was to be her bridesmaid.

When Harold arrived at the weekend she told him almost before he was in the kitchen, so eager was she to share her problem.

He looked at her, raised his eyes to the ceiling, closed them and in his quiet throaty voice said, "Bloody hell Ada," and pulled her into his arms, his mind racing round in circles. "I thought I'd been so careful, we could do without this."

It was not the reaction Ada had hoped for but understandable knowing his circumstances.

Plans for Lizzie's wedding began, and desperate to conceal all signs of her pregnancy Ada took peppermint to try and ease the sickness and avoided all foods that made her feel nauseous just by their smell.

The banns were called at the local church, and Ada took the money that Lizzie had sent and bought five yards of a pale blue silky material from Barnsley market. The stall holder gave her a small packet of pearl beading just for luck, to sew on the neckline of the dress.

On her way home she called at the dressmaker that Lizzie had mentioned. Ada knew her by sight from working in the bakery but had never been to her home before. She lived in a large terrace house on Barnsley Road.

The steps were scrubbed clean and the edges scoured with dark yellow donkey stone. As Ada admired the red geraniums flourishing on the window sills, the door opened, and there stood a tall middle aged woman who looked at Ada with her eyebrows raised slightly. She gave a little toss to her head as she said, "Yes?"

For a moment Ada thought she had made a mistake and gone to the wrong house until the woman smiled and stood on one side to allow her to pass into the hall. Without another word she took the brown carrier bag from Ada and looked inside.

"Mmmm, I see you've been to Edward Thompson for your material, not bad. How much did he charge you?" And then peering at her as if she was short sighted, she said, "You're Ada Dale aren't you?" Without giving Ada chance to reply, she said, "Right, what have you got in mind?"

Ada mentioned the price she had paid which was greeted with a tut and a shake of her head, which left Ada wondering if she had been overcharged.

Between them they settled on a dress with a long straight skirt that would suit her slim figure, and the pearl beading would be sewn around the neckline. A small bolero jacket would complete the outfit. As the dressmaker took her measurements she hovered a while near Ada's stomach then glanced upwards at her quizzically. Ada said nothing, but blushed, and prayed again that her pregnancy wouldn't start to show until after the wedding.

She left feeling thoroughly confused and uncomfortable and it was not until she was on her way home that she realised she had not asked how much it would cost. The only thing she had established was when she had to go for the fitting. 'Wait till I tell Lizzie,' she thought. 'Why on earth did she send me to her?'

The bakery where Ada worked made the wedding cake and she carried it home carefully, covered with a white pillowcase, but had to keep removing it to show neighbours who declared it to be a wonderful creation and what a shame it would be to cut into it.

Ada promised so many of them a piece that she wondered how on earth it would go round, and set about baking another one at home to supplement it.

As the cake cooked, she wondered how many of those neighbours would be indulging in malicious gossip when her condition became obvious, but tried to put the thoughts aside and concentrate on the wedding.

The next three weeks passed quickly. Ada's dress was finished with just four days to go before the wedding. and Lizzie arrived home the following morning carrying her dress carefully folded in a large suitcase, along with all her other clothes and belongings.

Her mistress had terminated her employment as soon as Lizzie had announced her forthcoming marriage, explaining to her that she never employed married women. Lizzie had more than a few choice words to say about her but insisted to her family that Reggie had a good job and they would manage very well. Privately she told Ada that she would find some part time work to keep her in pin money.

It was quite like old times to be sharing a bedroom with her sister again. They snuggled down together in the old feather mattress giggling and chatting. Lizzie entertained Ada with stories of the goings on between the gentry, as she called her old employers, and their visitors.

"They pretend they're so much better than us, but some of their ladyships have slept with more men than they've had hot dinners. I'm sure that's why they put us staff up on the top floor out of the way so we don't hear what's going on. Little do they know we don't miss a thing. Huh, talk about scandalous behaviour."

Then she whispered to Ada something that made her gasp and declare,

"What, three of them with one woman, and they didn't force her?"

"Not a bit of it, and the next day there she was walking about the garden with her parasol, all dainty and prim. I tell you what Ada, it's a wonder she wasn't walking bowlegged."

Ada burst out laughing so loud that Lizzie pulled the blankets over her head.

And then she began telling her about Reggie and their new home.

"He wouldn't have been so keen to get married if I'd let him have his way," went on Lizzie.

"Then you haven't, erm, you know, done it?" asked Ada.

"Not likely, I only let him go so far, just enough to get him excited but not all the way. I've made him wait for the wedding night."

Ada went silent, thinking of her own situation.

"What's the matter Ada? You seem upset. Is it Harold?"

"No, it's nothing. Blow the candle out and let's get to sleep."

But sleep was a long time coming for both of them. Lizzie lay awake thinking of the wedding and going over all the arrangements yet again. And at the back of her mind was concern for her sister. There was something worrying her and Lizzie had a good idea what it was.

Ada was used to sleepless nights, all too used to laying awake thinking of Harold and wondering what they could do. But tonight, instead, she thought of wearing the blue dress and walking down the aisle following her sister as her bridesmaid. If only Harold could have been there too. If only.

At exactly the same moment in Victoria Terrace, Harold lay in bed at the side of Winn, thinking of Ada, remembering her slim body, always so sweet and fresh, and he drew away from Winn, her bulk and loud snoring. But in spite of his irritation, when Winn turned to him and ran her hands over him it was hard to resist.

Ada woke at 5.30 the next morning and lay listening to the faint noises coming from downstairs. She recognised the sound of the fire grate being scraped and the rattle of the coal bucket, and knew her father was up extra early this morning. Her sister was still sound asleep and looked like a school girl, with her dark hair plaited loosely into two pigtails. Slipping quietly out of bed, Ada tiptoed down the stairs into the living room, opening the door at the bottom of the stairs carefully, cringing as the hinges squeaked.

She smiled at her father sitting in his wooden armchair, watching the sticks burn and ignite the shiny black coal. Going across to him she bent and kissed his forehead.

"Mornin' Dad, tha's up early."

"Aye, av gorra surprise for ar Lizzie. Doctor said ah could borrow t'pony and t'trap. So am off down there early to get Beauty all dolled up. Don't tell Lizzie, ah want it to be a surprise, she's expectin' to av to walk to church. Am gonna tek you and her on a ride round Wath in all yer weddin' finery. Then ah'll tek Lizzie and Reggie to t'reception after they're wed."

"Eh, that'll be grand, what about ar Rose though, won't she feel left out?"

"No, ah've ad a word wi her, and am goin' back to pick her an her young man up an drive em up Sandygate and then down New Road. And ah'll be doin' t'same for er when she gets wed."

"Poor old Beauty, she'll be tired out."

William laughed and shook his head. "Nay, she luvs showin' off."

Ada put her arms around him. "Ee, tha's a good dad, ah just wish me mam were still ere."

"Aye lass, so do ah. Come on nah, that's enough sloppiness. Let me go an get this ere hoss sorted out."

Ada waved him off, made two cups of strong tea and carried them upstairs on the little tin tray.

Lizzie was awake and they sat side by side propped against the brass bed rails, drinking the tea and enjoying the sight of their dresses hanging on the big oak wardrobe.

The wedding dress was ivory satin. It had started out as an evening gown for the mistress but had been passed on to Lizzie when it was considered to be outdated. She had unpicked the full skirt and reshaped it into a slimmer style and made a short jacket out of the spare fabric.

Ada admired the dress. "It looks lovely Liz, that satin is beautiful."

"I know, ah would never av been able to afford summat like that meself. It's one thing that ah av to be grateful to that auld bugger for. Mind you, ah ad ta wash it due to t'smell of er sweat and stale scent. And it were a devil to get creases out after it ad been washed."

As they were alone in the house, they ate their breakfast still dressed in their long flannelette nighties, sitting each side of the glowing fire, taking turns to toast their bread with the long toasting fork.

Ada's cat lay stretched out on the hearthrug, as close to the fire as he could get without actually burning himself. Lizzie tickled his belly with her bare toes and he instantly responded by curling himself around her foot, sticking his claws in and biting her.

"Gerroff tha little bugger."

Ada laughed, "Tha should know by now that he doesn't like being disturbed."

William returned just as Lizzie and Ada were coming down the narrow stairs, all dressed ready for the wedding.

Ada came first in her pale blue outfit and small neat hat decorated with delicate forget-me-nots. She had dyed her shoes just a shade darker than her dress and carried a white handbag borrowed from her sister Rose. Close behind came Lizzie in her ivory satin dress and matching hat with an organza veil pinned in place around the brim and decorated with white rosebuds.

They stood together in the living room and waited for William's verdict.

But William found it hard to speak for the love and emotion he felt for his daughters. Taking his handkerchief out of his pocket he blew his nose loudly, and coughed a couple of times before he could speak and declare,

"Well, what a pair of bobby dazzlers."

Taking Lizzie's hand he led her to the door and smiled as he saw how delighted she was to see her transport.

Beauty stood as proud as the finest bred racehorse with her mane and tail braided and her coat brushed till it shone in the sunlight, but spoilt her manners by lifting her tail and depositing a large steaming pile on the road, just as Lizzie and Ada climbed into the decorated carriage.

Cheers and laughter came from the crowd of friends and neighbours, gathered to see Lizzie on her way.

"That's lucky Liz, nought like hoss muck for good luck, especially when it's fresh," shouted one.

Lizzie smiled and nodded, holding on to her wide brimmed hat, and waving as William touched the horse's back with the whip and clicked to her.

Beauty gave a blow of breath through her lips and shook her head before setting off sedately, carrying her passengers proudly in her finery and confident the whip was only there for show. William would never have dreamed of using it on his faithful old friend.

A crowd of the local children ran alongside shouting and singing until William urged Beauty into a trot and left them behind, causing Lizzie to hang on even tighter to her hat.

They slowed to a walk as they reached the centre of Wath. Saturday morning shoppers stopped to see them pass, waving to them and calling out good luck, and they were rewarded by radiant smiles from Lizzie who declared she felt just like royalty.

Beauty walked sedately into Sandygate, snorting and tossing her head at the sight of the steep incline. William murmured soft words of encouragement to her, thinking to himself that he would get out and walk a little further on to ease the load.

At the entrance to the Red Lion they passed a group of miners heading into the pub, there were cheers and calls. "Ee lass, come an marry me, ah'll look after thee."

"Who's the lucky bloke then?"

"Tha looks good enough to eat, ah could av thee both wi a slice o bread n butter."

The girls smiled, but a stern look from William froze the men's calls and they lifted their hats in salute and turned into the Red Lion for their Saturday quota of ale.

It was fifty yards further on that Ada saw the familiar figure walking slowly up the hill. He stopped and turned, waiting for them to overtake him. As they approached, Ada's heart did its usual somersault as he smiled and winked at her. Instinctively she put out her hand to him and he took it for a few moments as he walked alongside. Softly he said,

"Tha looks lovely, ah'll see thee next week," and he pursed his lips in a kissing motion.

William concentrated on his driving and the road ahead, but their actions had not escaped his notice.

Their actions had also not gone unnoticed by one of the men who worked on the same shift as Harold at Denaby Main. A man by the name of Horace Moor, who just happened to be in Wath to see his mother. Walking behind them he observed it all, and gloated as he thought of the juicy bit of gossip that he could pass around at work. 'Just wait till our lass knows,' he thought, 'she's right pally with Harold Corker's missus'.

William turned left into New Road with its high stone walls on either side, topped with shards of broken glass to deter unwelcome visitors from climbing over into the gardens of the large private houses beyond.

Lilac and cherry trees hung over the walls, almost touching above the narrow road, making it feel like a flower tunnel. This was their favourite place in all of Wath. Even Beauty seemed to love it and gave a little whinny as they passed through.

Harold followed them down the road and thought that the picture of the decorated pony and trap carrying his beloved Ada would stay with him forever. He turned right at the bottom of the road to begin his long walk back to Denaby, dreading the thought of returning, but brightened up considerably as he reached the Manver's Arms near the pit, and found several of his old workmates there.

William and his girls had turned left at the bottom of the road, back towards the centre of Wath again. Beauty picked up her feet and broke into a smart trot as they passed through the shopping area and headed towards the church.

William held out his right arm to signal he was turning into the church yard, and the oncoming traffic, mostly horses and trade carts, halted to allow them through, the horses whinnying to each other in greeting.

"Last chance to change thee mind Lizzie."

Turning to see who had spoken, Lizzie smiled broadly at her sister Rose. She wiped the imaginary sweat from her brow and continued, "Just finished, everything's ready, kettles boiled, sandwiches made, cakes on t'stand. Oh, and ah remembered to lock t'door. Don't want them little Bs gerrin' in an eatin' it all."

Rose was referring to the crowd of ragged urchins that always hung about the hall where they were holding the reception. Given a chance they were up to all sorts of mischief. Raiding the food was the most likely. Couldn't really blame them thought Ada, poor little devils were half starved, and she resolved to see that there would be plenty of leftover cakes for them.

Just as William brought them to a halt right in front of the church door, a tall young lad appeared from the corner of the church and stood by Beauty's head. William pressed a few coppers in the lad's hand and told him to look after the horse, and said he would give him another three pence when the service was over. The lad looked at William.

"Don't worry mister, ah'll look after er, ah like hosses."

"Aye, ah can see that, she's a very special horse in't tha Beauty?"

He stroked the horse's face gently. "She belongs to t'doctor tha knows."

Meanwhile Rose helped her sisters, tidying their hair, straightening hats and clothes, until, finally satisfied that they looked their best, she left them and went to take her place in the church. As she went, Lizzie whispered to her that she looked lovely. And so she did.

70

Rose was wearing her best navy blue suit that had a long three quarter length jacket and underneath it a pink high necked blouse. She had pinned a large pink rose to her lapel and trimmed her navy blue straw hat with pink rose buds. She looked the picture of elegance as she walked into church carrying her neat little beaded bag.

The organist began playing the familiar wedding march and Lizzie took her father's arm, and gave him a kiss on the cheek as they set off to walk up the aisle, where Reggie stood waiting for her.

Ada followed after in her role as bridesmaid, proud to know she was dressed well and enjoying the admiring glances from friends and family. The service began, William looked at Reggie and couldn't help wondering yet again what on earth Lizzie saw in him, and why he found him such a disappointment as a future son-in-law.

As they took their vows several of Lizzie's family hid smiles as she promised to love, honour and obey. It was the obey part that would be the stumbling block as they all knew only too well. Lizzie had a big generous heart but also a fiery temper and hated being told what to do. Reggie would have to handle her very tactfully.

William's attention wandered as he stood and listened to the parson's words. His mind went back to the time when he and Louise had married and the years afterwards when the babies came. He remembered how they had struggled to feed and clothe their growing family, and wondered why, just as life was becoming easier with the eldest ones working, that Louise had had to die. Sometimes, William decided, he didn't think much to this God that the parson was always ranting about.

Before he knew it the service was over and there was Lizzie, walking back down the aisle as Mrs Heaton, holding on to the arm of her new husband, exchanging smiles and greetings from family and friends.

William walked behind them alongside Ada feeling very proud that he was the father of the bride.

Outside, he went straight to Beauty and gave the lad threepence for looking after her.

"Ee thanks mister, ah'll do it again if tha needs me."

"Ok son, tha's done a good job," replied William, "ah'll remember that."

Lizzie and Reggie climbed into the trap amid a cloud of blossom petals that were showered on them by the congregation as they came out of church. The brim of Lizzie's hat was full of pink and white cherry blossom and she tipped her head forward over the side, leaving a trail of petals as they made their way to the hall where the reception was being held.

Rose and her two helpers were there before them and had the door open awaiting their arrival. The tables were laden with homemade cakes and sandwiches, in spite of the shortages and the rationing due to the war which was now in its second year.

An audience of hungry children hung about the doorway, peering inside and fairly drooling at the sight of all the food. Rose came out holding a large brown paper bag and gave each one a sandwich and a bun and told them to clear off. Then she gave them a smile and whispered, "Come back later, and don't be telling all yer mates or we'll not be able to shift for kids."

Lizzie and her new husband were seated at the top table with close relatives either side of them. Reggie looked uncomfortable and ill at ease in his tight fitting collar, gradually getting redder and redder in the face. Ada could see he was longing to undo the collar stud and guessed that he was dreading the moment he would have to make his speech.

How right Ada was. Poor Reggie was no speaker, and expected to make a fool of himself. Lizzie grasped his hand under the table and gave it a squeeze, but it didn't help and he stuttered and stammered his way through and sat down again with great relief. After the stress of the speech was over, Reggie began to relax, and helped by several glasses of best Barnsley bitter, launched into a tale of how he had first met his new wife.

"Well," he said, "it were like this, there ah was out for a walk in me best Sunday suit. To tell the truth ah were hopin' to bump into Lizzie, ah'd seen er a few times out walkin', and fair fancied er, an ah were tryin' to pluck up courage to speak to er.

"Anyway, there ah was all done up like a dog's dinner, when ah heard t'cows bawlin', and ah knew straight away there were summat up. One of t'heifers (that's a young lady cow to you colliers that don't know about such things) were calvin'. Ah couldn't leave er like that, so ah takes me best jacket off and hangs it on t'fence and ad a look at poor lass. Nose and one foot were out, but t'other were bent back wrong way. So by the time Lizzie come on t'scene there ah were wi one arm in t'cow and covered in cow shit. Sorry, ah mean muck. Then all t'other cows in t'field decided to ger'in on t'act and were crowded round mekin' a right racket. A herd of thirty odd cows can gerra bit rough tha knows; even if tha's used to em.

"But Lizzie went into action. She grabbed a stick and waded in, and kept em away till ah'd got calf out; a lovely little heifer it were an all, a right beauty. Ah picked it up and headed for t'gate wi it's mother following close behind. Lizzie shouted she'd get me jacket, but cows ad beaten er to it and trampled it into t'muck. Ah can see Lizzie nah, shoutin' and waving t'stick. She's gorrra a right voice on er ah can tell thee. Anyroad she rescued me jacket and were just runnin' to t'gate wi t'cows behind er when she slipped in t'shit, I mean muck, and sat right in it. She didn't know whether to laugh or cry. In t'end she did neither. She got up," Reggie hesitated, "ah didn't think ladies knew such words, but she let fly at them cows, slappin' em and swearin' like a trooper.

"A right sorry pair we looked by the time we got back to t'farm. When t'boss stopped laughing, he said he would pay for a new frock for Lizzie and a new jacket for me. He were that pleased. It were a pedigree calf tha sees. Ever since then he's bin right taken wi Lizzie. Good job he's already married or ah wouldn't av stood a chance."

That was the most William had ever heard Reggie say and he began to warm to him, but made a mental note to make sure to give him a couple of beers if he ever felt like having a decent conversation with him.

The next couple of hours passed very pleasantly, friends and family happily swapping news and yarns. Everyone remarked how good it was to meet up and what a shame it was that they only managed to do it at weddings and funerals.

By 4pm the beers and sherry were gone, and the guests prepared to leave. The bridal couple were wished luck many times over. Reggie lost count of the number of hugs and kisses he'd received, mostly from aunts he had never seen before, and also slaps on the back and whispered risqué comments in his ear from newly met uncles and cousins.

Ada took a plate of sandwiches and cakes outside while Rose and her friends cleared the tables. As she stepped out of the door Ada was surrounded by children all hoping for leftover treats. The plate was cleared almost as soon as she held it out. With shouts of, "ta missis," they were off again, back to their street games. She smiled and shook the few remaining crumbs out for the birds and went back inside.

William took the newlyweds to the station where they caught the train to Cleethorpes for their two day honeymoon.

Ada walked slowly home and changed into her everyday clothes, hanging her blue outfit carefully on the satin covered hanger she had made. She brewed herself a cup of tea, coaxed the fire back into life and sat quiet and alone, feeling relieved that the wedding had gone so well, but sad it was all over, for now there was nothing to stop her dwelling on her problems, and worse still, reflecting that it would be a whole week till she saw Harold again.

But the week passed and at last it was Saturday again. 'Harold will be here this afternoon,' thought Ada the moment she woke. The previous day a postcard and a letter had arrived from Lizzie. The postcard had a picture of Cleethorpes on the front with its endless beach. Lizzie's letter said they had enjoyed their honeymoon in spite of the landlady at the guest house where they had stayed; she said she was as ugly as sin and a bad tempered old cow.

Ada smiled at that, how like Lizzie not to mince her words. She went on to describe the beach, which was much bigger than she had expected and said the sea was so far away they had ponies and traps to take the holiday makers down to the water to paddle. They had enjoyed the salty air but were both glad to be back in Carlton in their cosy little cottage. She added that she hoped her sister would come to visit them soon as she had so much to tell her. Ada thought regretfully that she had something to tell Lizzie too, and expected a strong telling off from her.

This week the sickness had returned. It was almost as if it had been held at bay while she was busy with the wedding preparations but was now back with a vengeance. She had felt wretched all week, but somehow had managed to conceal it from her father and go to work every day. This morning she actually felt much better and lay in bed an extra ten minutes planning the day.

Harold's week had been his worst for a long time. On Monday and Tuesday he had endured hints and jibes about having a bit on the side. By Wednesday he had had enough and challenged the man who said "how good it must be to have a bit of young stuff". After Harold had pinned him up against a wall and threatened him, he had pointed out who was responsible for starting the rumours and Harold recognised Horace Moore, who he knew had relatives living in Wath.

He waited for him when the shift finished just outside the Denaby Arms pub. As he approached, Harold stepped up close to him. "Nah then, Horace Moore, ah want a word wi thee."

Horace stepped back, startled. "Well ah dunt want a word wi thee," and he tried to go around Harold and into the pub. But Harold was having none of that and grabbed him by the checked scarf that was knotted around his neck and dragged him round the corner out of sight.

Both men were of similar height but Harold was by far the stronger and Horace knew it; he also knew that Harold was not a man to hold back when angry, and he now regretted passing on the gossip of seeing him holding hands with that bonny young piece dressed in wedding finery. The information had made him popular with his workmates at snaptime but it wasn't worth it if it meant getting on the wrong side of Harold Corker.

"What the hell's up? Ah've not done owt wrong to thee av ah?"

"Yes, that bloody has, an tha knows it. Flappin' thee gob about my business. Ah've a good mind at smash that long beak o'thine into thee face. Then tha'll not be so keen on poking it into things that don't concern thee."

The long beak that Harold was talking about was running now, leaving two trails of moisture down his thin grimy face. Somehow that seemed to make Harold angrier, and he drew back his fist ready to carry out his threat.

A hand on his shoulder stopped him and he turned to see the local bobby towering above him in his helmet and cape. His first thought was, 'bloody hell, it's the copper, he's just like a rash, everywhere tha dunt want it.'

"Nah then lads, what's all this about, it's not like thee Harold Corker to be fightin' in t'street."

Harold lowered his arm and turned away from Horace.

"It's nowt, just a difference of opinion."

"Well clear off home, pair of you, an dun't let me catch either of you again or ah'll av ya both down at t'station."

Harold nodded and walked away, giving a warning look to Horace who shot off like a rabbit, straight into the pub.

There was no more talk at work. At least, not in front of Harold, and they worked together at the coal face as a team, but there was an uneasy atmosphere, and Harold knew it was only a matter of time till someone passed the gossip on to Winn.

He woke early on Saturday morning and rose and dressed quietly, leaving Winn curled up under the blankets breathing heavily through her mouth. Her hair looked tangled and greasy on the grubby pillow. Harold wrinkled his nose in disgust, and muttered, "Dirty bitch," under his breath as he left the room, hoping that Winn would stay where she was for an hour or so. He didn't relish her company at breakfast.

Herbert was already up, munching on a piece of bread and reading his comic. He smiled tentatively at Harold, trying to judge his humour.

"Ah've boiled kettle Dad, shall ah mek sum tea?"

Harold ruffled his hair as he passed him, glad that Herbert had always called him Dad from the moment that he and Winn had got married. The room was freezing cold. Harold raked out the ashes as quietly as he could, knowing how the sound carried up into the bedroom above.

Thankfully, he had brought in coal and sticks the night before and soon had the fire going, adding the shiny lumps of coal one by one until they were piled high, wondering as he did so if this was some of the coal he himself had shovelled. What a difference the fire made, the flickering light making the shabby room look almost cosy. He sat back in his chair, with the mug of tea in his right hand. Herbert sidled up to him and perched on his knee.

"Tell us about t'pit Dad."

"What about it son, what shall ah tell thee?"

"Tell me about Champion, the best pit pony."

"Oh aye, Champion, he really is a champion, he's t'strongest pony in t'pit, he can pull more tubs than any other hoss, but he hates mice tha knows. If he so much as smells a mouse, he's up on his hind legs dancing about like a ballerina."

Herbert started giggling at that and snuggled up against Harold, sighing with contentment at being close to his Dad.

"When ah grow up Dad, Ah'm gunna come to work wi thee in t' pit, will ah be able to av a dudley an a snaptin?"

"Well aye, tha'll av to av them."

"How fast does t'cage go when it's goin' down into t'pit Dad?"

"It goes that fast tha as to owd on to thee hat in case it gets left behind."

Herbert slapped his knee, "Tha's jokin' me nah int tha Dad?"

"Aye, but ah'll tell thee what am not jokin' about, that muck in thee ears, an t'tide mark round thee neck. Ah've teld thee before about gerrin' washed. Ee tha's gor a right tide mark ere, look thee, when did tha get bathed?"

"Em, er a week last Sunday."

"Ye gods, what's thee mother playing at? Right, tomorrow's goin' to be big bath day. We'll av t'copper on and t'tin bath outta yard. But for nah, ah want thee ta put rest of t'warm water outta kettle inta a bowl, then get thee shirt off and give thee sen a good scrub. Top half first then t'bottom half, and use that carbolic soap, Later on if tha's clean ah'll take all on ya down to t'shop an get sum spice an a comic."

"Ooh can ah av a gobstopper Dad."

"Aye, ah'll get thee one each an ah'll get thee mother a box full. We might gerra bit o peace then."

Billy came downstairs next, face grubby and hair stood on end and his ears in the same state as Herbert's.

Harold shook his head in annoyance, poured more water into the bowl and without a word handed Billy the soap and towel, pointing as he did so at the sink. Billy began washing, slowly wiping the flannel delicately in the region of his neck, until he saw the look that his father was giving him and quickly decided it would be a good idea to wash with some energy.

He had learned from past experience that Harold was likely to wash him from head to foot if he judged he was unclean, and would do it none too gently.

Harold started on the breakfast, thick slices of bread toasted on the now glowing fire, then spread with dripping and sprinkled liberally with salt.

Herbert and Billy munched slowly, savouring every mouthful of the crisp, slightly singed bread.

As the last piece disappeared, Edith came into the room carrying baby Sarah on her hip the way she had seen her mother carry her. She laid her gently on the floor well away from the fire, and went to wash her hands and face. Her hair was already neatly plaited and tied with checked ribbons. Harold stared in wonderment at his eldest daughter who behaved more like a miniture adult.

"Come on Edi, there's some toast on top o t'oven for thee, then we're going to t'shop for comics."

Edith sat at the table and tucked into the toast but not until she had pulled off a big piece of crust for Sarah to chew on later.

Sarah lay on the floor kicking her bare legs in the air, giving little hungry cries that would turn into a full blown angry wailing any minute. She stopped for a while, screwing up her face and clenching her hands into fists.

"Hey up Dad, Sarah's filling her nappy," called Herbert.

"Aye, ah can see that; Edi, is thee mother still asleep?"

"No Dad, she's sat up in bed looking at Herbert's comic, she asked me to get her a cup o tea."

"Tea, tea.Cheeky bugger."

Harold went to the bottom of the stairs and called, "Winn, get thee sen up. Now! This babby needs seeing to. Ah'm takin' kids to t'shops."

He could hear her grumbling and the bed springs creaking as she reluctantly did as he said.

As he walked down the hill to the main street Harold watched his children in front of him, chasing each other and dodging round the lamp posts, their hands already grubby from the coal dust that seemed to settle everywhere.

His spirits lifted and he smiled as he thought of the coming afternoon when he would be with Ada again.

Ada opened the door almost before he knocked, she took his hand and led him into the living room. Harold sat on the couch and pulled her on to his knee, wrapped his arms tightly around her slim body, gently kissed her forehead and said quietly, "Ah've missed thee so much Ada."

The tea set out on the table looked delicious and tempting, and the kettle was boiling on the bars at the front of the fire, but they gave it not a thought as they made their way up the stairs to Ada's bed.

By the time they came down again the fire had burned low and the kettle was almost boiled dry. The cat lay stretched out on the hearth rug, luxuriating in the heat, and looked at Harold reproachfully as he moved him to one side to put more coal on the fire. He lashed his tail in annoyance and jumped on to the wooden armchair.

"Sorry pal, tha can't stay there either," said Harold, as he tipped the cat unceremoniously off the chair, smiling as it went under the table with its tail swishing and giving just the faintest growl.

"Tha spoils that cat Ada, he's gerrin' fat and lazy, it's time tha turned him out to catch some mice."

But Ada just laughed at him and poured his tea, then told him of her idea.

She had decided to tell Lizzie about the baby as soon as possible, ask if she could stay with her and Reggie for the last few months of the pregnancy and have the baby in Carlton.

Harold met her idea with dismay, declaring that he didn't know how he could manage without seeing her. Then, after a moment's thought said,

"But what's tha goin' to do when tha's ad t'babby Ada? Tha can't just turn up wi a new born babby an say tha's found it, can tha? Folks are gunna know anyroad aren't they?"

Ada admitted he was right, and that she hadn't yet decided what she would do after the baby was born. At the moment all she could think about was what people were going to say. Having one baby with no husband was bad enough, but having a second would cause such a scandal and she could just imagine what her family were going to say. Her father would be so upset.

By the time Harold left they had agreed that she would tell Lizzie the following week and if she was willing, Ada would move to Carlton after Christmas when she was four and a half months pregnant, and would decide what to do later, after the baby was born.

The very next day Ada made herself sit down and write a letter to Lizzie. It was such a difficult letter to write. She sat on the couch chewing the end of her pencil and staring into space for an age before she finally wrote.

Dear Lizzie,

You will be surprised to receive a letter from me today, so soon after my Friday letter but there is something I need to tell you, something I should have said weeks ago. I delayed telling you because of the wedding but I can't put it off any longer.

Lizzie, I'm in such a fix, I'm expecting again. Please don't be angry with me. There is nothing you can say that I haven't said to myself.

I want to ask you a really big favour. Can I come and stay with you and have the baby at your house? It's due in four and a half months. I'm praying you will say yes, I don't know what else to do. I've got a little money saved, I can pay for my food, I don't expect you and Reggie to keep me for nothing. No one else knows yet, not even Dad. I'm dreading having to tell him. I would like to come to you just after Christmas if you will have me. Please let me know as soon as you can.

Your loving sister Ada xxxxx

As she dropped the letter in the box she crossed her fingers, and sighed as she sent up a little prayer for help. It was only four weeks till Christmas and a bleak time for most people with a war going on in France.

It was a bitterly cold afternoon, and Wath looked more dreary than usual. 'The only good thing about living here,' thought Ada, 'is the fact that coal is freely available.' The miners all got an allocation of coal as part of their wages and often sold some of the surplus to neighbours who didn't work down the mine, although, of course, it was forbidden by the mining bosses.

Ada was feeling very low as she began the walk back home. The morning sickness had stopped, but in its place was a terrible tiredness that she couldn't seem to overcome. But it was not in Ada's nature to be unhappy, and as she walked her spirits began to lift as she thought of the warm cosy home waiting for her, and she decided to buy herself some sweets and a 'Woman's Weekly' magazine as a treat. There was the scarf she was knitting for her Dad's Christmas present. That needed finishing. Then she thought of all the clothes that would need making for the little life growing inside her, and she began to plan them.

In spite of her difficult circumstances, there was a big part of her heart that was delighted at the thought of the baby.

There was a group of men outside the pub at the top of the road. She knew most of them by sight. They all had the benefit of several pints of best Barnsley bitter inside them, and were louder and coarser than they would have been without it. As she approached, one of them called out,

"By, tha gets bonnier every day Ada."

Two of them started singing, "Ada, Ada, give me your answer do, I'm half crazy all for the love of you.

It won't be a stylish marriage,

I can't afford a carriage,
But you'll look sweet, sat on the seat
Of a bicycle made for two."

Ada blushed, but gave them a smile as another went on his knees as she passed, and said, "Oh marry me Ada, marry me, the missis won't mind," and she couldn't help laughing, but her smile froze as Horace Moor stepped from the back of the group and said, "Aye, but Harold Corker's wife will mind won't she Ada? By, that's wiped the smile off thee face ant it."

Ada's blushing cheeks had turned chalky white, but before she could do or say anything, her brother John appeared. He had walked out of the pub just in time to hear what Horace had said. He made no comment, he simply gave a punch to Horace's chin that sent him staggering back, and as he made contact with the wall he slid down it until he was sat on the pavement, with his legs outstretched and a dazed expression on his face.

"Aye, and that's wiped the smile off thee face, yer loud mouthed weasel. In future keep a bloody civil tongue in thee head when tha's talkin' to my sister. Nah then, is there anybody else wants the same?" and he turned to look at the other men, but they were already scattering in different directions.

John took Ada's arm. "Is tha alright lass?"

Ada nodded but felt shook up by the incident. As they walked back into the house Ada thanked John, but he brushed her thanks aside, saying roughly, "Aye well, tha knows, that's the sort o thing that's gonna keep happening if tha's playing about wi a married man," and he jammed his hat down firmly on his head and left, slamming the door behind him.

If it hadn't been almost dark outside, Ada would have sat in the chair and given way to tears, but the coal buckets needed filling, and as she knew only too well, visits to the coal house across the yard were best avoided in the dark.

So she picked up the two large buckets, emptied the few remaining lumps of coal onto the fire, collected the key, and hurried to get them filled. The padlock on the door was a recent safeguard after their pile of coal went down faster than usual and Ada suspected that they were helping to keep a neighbour's home warm as well as their own.

She'd bought the lock from Mexborough market and got it cheap as there was only one key attached to it, but Ada had fastened it to a large empty cotton bobbin and thought there was little chance of losing the lone key. It was hung on a nail near the back door, but even so William invariably went without it, and came back grumbling and muttering about the necessity of having to lock the coal up.

"Thieving buggers around ere ad av yer teeth if yer didn't keep yer mouth shut," he'd say.

Ada staggered in with the buckets piled high, and the last of the sticks balanced precariously on top. She put the sticks in the hearth under the oven to get dry, so they would be ready to light the fire in the morning, then washed her hands and laid the table for tea. She'd bought a piece of tripe for William.

He liked it just as it was with lots of salt and vinegar, and a couple of slices of brown bread, buttered generously. Ada couldn't stand it herself but there was a small piece of Cheshire cheese left in the pantry and she made it into a sandwich with a spoonful of homemade chutney. There were two Eccles cakes to finish off with, courtesy of the bakery, a little battered round the edges but Ada knew her father would enjoy his just the same.

Tea prepared, Ada sat down on the couch to get on with her knitting. Monty made a half-hearted attempt to chase the wool, but soon gave up and snuggled down beside her to sleep. Ada stroked his shiny fur and said, "Harold's right, tha is gerrin' fat and lazy Monty."

The cat opened one eye briefly, gave her a disdainful look and turned on his back with his legs in the air. Ada looked at him and laughed, "Aye, ah can see tha's right upset at being called fat and lazy in't tha?"

William arrived home before she had even finished one row of her knitting, and she hastily bundled the partly completed Christmas scarf under a cushion.

William looked troubled. Ada took his coat from him, handed him his slippers and waited for him to say what the problem was.

"Ah've just seen ar John, he were telling me about the bit of trouble tha had. It's a good job he were there to sort it out."

"Yea Dad, he came out of t'pub just at the right time. They'd all had too much ale as usual, but they were ok till that there Horace Moor started mouthin'."

Ada brought the plate of tripe and placed it in front of William.

"Tha knows Ada, tha'll av at expect that sort of thing. Gossip soon gets round."

"Ah know Dad, that's what John said, ah shall just av to put up wi it. Trouble is, it'll probably get worse in a few months." She hesitated and William looked at her quizzically, and Ada saw his face change as he realised what she meant.

"Is tha saying thas expectin' again?"

Ada nodded.

Her father sighed and said, "Well am not surprised, ah've been waitin' for it to happen. What's tha gonna do lass?"

She told him then about her decision to go to Carlton to have the baby if Lizzie and Reggie were agreeable.

"And then what's tha gonna do? Tha'll not be able to keep folks from finding out. Tha can't stay hidden away in Carlton forever."

Ada thought to herself, 'Yes I could stay in Carlton, and get a job there. No one would know me, I could say I was a widow. Lizzie would help me to look after the baby. What about Harold though? I couldn't live without seeing him again,' but she kept her thoughts to herself and just said, "Ah don't know Dad. We'll av to decide later."

One of the things that worried Ada was leaving William on his own, with no one to cook and clean for him. He insisted he could manage without any help, but that didn't stop Ada from feeling as if she was deserting him.

However, that particular problem was solved the following day when a letter arrived from Rose, telling them that she and her young man were getting married on new year's day, and that they had got the tenancy of a house in the next street. Ada was relieved, knowing that Rose would be happy to look after William while she was away.

Rose explained that the wedding was to be a very quiet affair with only the closest of family invited. There was simply no money to spare for fancy clothes and a reception when they had a home to get together.

In the same post there was a reply from Lizzie. Ada opened it with nervous hands wondering what her sister had to say. Relief spread through her as she read Lizzie's letter.

Dear Ada,

What a silly girl you are, do you really think you have to ask if you can come to stay? My home is yours for as long as you want and Reggie says the same, (or he would have done if I had asked him), he is working such long hours at the moment that I hardly see him. But I know he won't mind you being here.

I have to say it came as no surprise to me to hear you are expecting. I felt sure you were the last time I saw you but I hoped I was wrong.

I know it's a waste of time scolding you. I think you and Harold are made for each other; if only he wasn't married already!

I won't be able to see you and Dad over Christmas as Reggie has to work. As he says, the animals still need feeding at Christmas, but I look forward to seeing you very soon. Let me know what date you want to come here and I will meet you at the station. Get the train to Doncaster then change to the Selby one and get off at Snaith. We can walk from there, or maybe we'll be able to get a lift with the carter. It's only a couple of miles.

That's all for now, will write again later, give my love to Dad.

Love from Lizzie xxxxxx

PS. Have you told Dad yet? Worse still, have you told John? Rather you than me xxxxx

'Yes,' thought Ada, 'telling John is one ordeal I could do without, better to get it over as soon as possible,'

She also needed to tell Rose, so she sat down right there and then and wrote her a letter. First of all telling her how happy she was to hear about her forthcoming marriage on new year's day, and what good news it was, that she would be living just around the corner. And then she went on to tell her that she was pregnant and about her plans to go and stay with Lizzie.

Ada sealed the letter and pushed it through the letterbox with great trepidation. She could just imagine the tongue-lashing she would be in for from Rose.

The next day was Friday, so Ada planned to go and see John and Mary straight after work. She knew that John was on 'days' that week, which meant he should home by three pm, and hopefully he would have had his bath and eaten his dinner by the time she arrived. Like most miners he was likely to be in his best humour on a Friday due to it being payday and the start of the weekend.

Ada went into work early and managed to complete everything by four o'clock. She was feeling tired and drained of energy by the time she set out for John and Mary's house, and to make matters worse it began to rain heavily before she was even half way there. It was tempting to turn around and go home, but she pressed on wearily.

Her wide brimmed felt hat kept the rain off for a while until it became sodden and the brim drooped down, channelling the water straight down her back. By the time she arrived at John's home she was soaked through and beginning to shiver. It was Mary who opened the door. She stared for a moment then grabbed Ada's hand and pulled her inside.

"Ada luv, tha's wet through, come an get thee coat off. Eeh tha's freezing luv, go an sit by t'fire an ah'll mek thee a cup of tea."

Ada caught sight of herself in the hall mirror and had to laugh in spite of her discomfort.

"Bloody hell, ah look a sight don't ah Mary?"

"Well, ah av to say av seen thee look better," replied her sister-in-law with a wry smile.

Thankfully Ada sat beside the blazing fire. As she pulled the pins from her hair and shook it loose, she looked around the comfortable room with its deep bay window.

Living with Mary's mother had worked well for the couple. They had the front parlour for their living room and the large room above for their bedroom. They shared the kitchen and scullery. John looked after the long back garden, producing most of their vegetables. Mary's mother respected their privacy and never entered their rooms without knocking. John got on well with his mother-in-law and she treated him like a son.

Ada leaned back in the chair soaking up the warmth of the fire, and when Mary returned with the tea she found her fast asleep. Placing the cup quietly in the hearth with the saucer on top, Mary went back to her knitting. It was a good half hour later when John came downstairs washed and changed and smelling of Lifebuoy soap that Ada woke. She stared blearily up at him for a moment until reality came back to her and she said, "Eeh am sorry, ah must av dropped off for a minute or two."

"Aye, for half an hour actually. Tha must av be tired out luv, thee tea's there in the hearth," said Mary.

John pulled the wooden dining chair up to the fire close to Ada.

"Well Ada, ah can guess why tha's here. Ah saw me dad on t'way home from work and he told me the news." He hesitated. "Tha's chosen a hard path luv. Tha must think a lot about im. Ah can't pretend ah'm pleased, but if ah can help in any way tha only as to say. And that goes for Mary an all, dun't it lass?"

Mary nodded, and Ada took John's hand, too close to tears of gratitude to be able to speak.

Mary, sensitive as usual to other people's feelings, quickly changed the subject. "It's Christmas in just over two weeks Ada, and me an John wondered if you and Dad would like to av Christmas dinner wi us. We've gorra a special treat this year," and she looked to John to explain.

"Aye well it's like this, ah've ad a cockrell runnin'wi me hens, and he's gerrin' too big for is boots, he's teken to flyin' at me when ah go to collect t'eggs. Look at this," and John rolled up his sleeve to show Ada the long scratch marks. "He'll not be so bloody clever when he finds hisen in t'oven on Christmas morning wi an onion shoved up his arse."

Ada laughed till tears rolled down her face. "By heck Mary, he dunt get any better."

Mary shook her head in mock exasperation.

John volunteered to walk his sister home and Mary brought out her own hat and coat for Ada to wear despite her protests, and carefully folded the still-wet coat into a shopping bag and placed the hat on top of the basket that Ada carried.

As they set off Ada linked arms with her brother, matching her steps to his so that they walked in rhythm. The rain had stopped but had been replaced by a strong wind, and Ada was glad of John's strength and bulk to hold on to. They talked little, but it was an easy silence, and Ada felt comfortable and more relaxed than she had been for weeks. Something or someone had changed John's attitude towards her and Ada was thankful for it.

They arrived at Packmans Row to find the house empty. William had eaten the meal Ada had left him, washed his plate and banked down the fire with slack. A short note propped behind the clock on the mantelpiece said he had gone to see to Beauty, and would be calling for a pint at the Red Lion on his way home. William was a keen domino player and Friday night was match night, so Ada guessed he wouldn't be home till ten o'clock. She wrapped up Mary's coat and hat for John to take back and said goodbye.

At the last moment she remembered the shortbread that she had brought home from the bakery the day before and pushed a large slice of it down the side of the bag. John smiled his thanks, pulled his collar up against the cold wind and set off home.

As she had the house to herself Ada took the chance to have a good wash. She poked the fire into life sending plumes of sparks up the chimney as the slack dropped down into the glowing embers below. The water in the boiler at the side of the fire was hot and Ada ladled it out carefully and scooped out the odd flakes of soot that always seemed to settle there. Then having refilled the boiler with cold water, she set about washing herself, using the tiny slither of scented soap that Lizzie had left behind.

After she had washed herself from head to foot, she set about washing her hair, rinsing it thoroughly with a large jug of cold water that made her gasp. She combed out her long hair and placing a towel on her shoulders, she spread her hair out on it to dry, then sat on the couch with her feet on the stool, reading her 'Woman's Weekly'. Monty jumped up on to her knee and turned round and round till he made himself comfortable, purring loudly and pushing aside the magazine so that Ada would stroke him.

Ada relived the day in her mind and smiled as she thought how it had turned out so much better than she had expected. She went to bed happy that night and thankful that she had John's support. It meant more to her than she had realised and as she slipped into a deep sleep, her last thought as always, was of Harold.

Winn was also thinking of Harold, and trying to remember the last time that he had turned to her in the night to satisfy his needs. She looked at him sitting at the table reading the racing page, and noticed the light shining on his blonde hair, and suddenly felt a strong urge of attraction. Going up behind him she put her arms around him, kissed his neck and ran her tongue at the back of his neck, breathing hot breath down the back of his collar.

"Let's go to bed Harold," she said softly.

"Gi up Winn, ah'm trying to study these hosses, and ow long is it since tha ad a bath, tha smells sweaty."

Winn giggled girlishly, "Tha didn't used to bother if ah ad been bathed or not."

"Aye, well ah bloody well do nah. There's no excuse for it, an thee breath stinks an all."

The next time Harold looked up from his racing page he could see Winn washing herself in the scullery. She had taken off her blouse and dropped her vest down to her waist, she had stopped wearing a brassier a long time ago and her breasts drooped low. Harold wondered what it was he ever saw in her. Winn saw him looking and said coyly, "Tha can wash me back if tha likes."

Harold rustled his paper pretending not to hear, then hastily folded it and went to bed. He was sound asleep by the time Winn joined him.

By mid morning the next day, Harold was well on his way to Wath. He had been up early, given the children their breakfast and taken them to the shop for their weekly treat while Winn was still in bed. As she had come downstairs Harold had been just leaving the house, muttering that he was going to help his mate with the pigeons.

He felt as excited as a teenager on his first date as he thought of spending the afternoon with Ada, and stopped at the pawnbrokers to buy her a gift for Christmas.

The shop window was covered with a strong wire grill and filled with a wide variety of goods that had been pawned and not redeemed. There was everything from bedding and clothing to furniture and jewellery. In the centre of the window an attempt had been made to make a Christmas gift display. Seeing nothing that he liked Harold was about to turn away and look elsewhere when he spotted the brooch almost hidden by a large leather-bound Bible. It was made in the shape of a half-moon with a black cat sitting on it and surrounded by a circle of tiny blue stones.

Harold knew the pawnbroker well. He was a little man with bow legs and had the unfortunate name of Samuel Bowly. For years he had been known as Sammy Bowlegs! But never to his face. Too many found themselves having to use his pawnbroker services in hard times. He was reputed to be one of the richest men in Wath, although, thought Harold, you would never think it from the way he dressed. Summer and winter, he wore the same navy blue suit that looked at least two sizes too big for him. His only concession to the cold weather was the pixie hood and fingerless mittens that he usually put on in November and took off in April.

He peered up at Harold from below the brim of his pixie hood, and gave a nod of his head as an indication that he should state what it was he wanted.

"Morning Mr Bowly," said Harold, struggling to keep the smile off his face at the pawnbroker's comical appearance, "how much does tha want for that little brooch in t'middle of t'window?"

"Three bob, it's a very unusual design, and worth double, young man."

"No, ah'll gi thee two bob."

In the end they settled on half a crown with Samuel Bowly declaring he would soon be bankrupt if he had many more customers like Harold. As he was about to leave Harold stepped aside to allow a man to enter the shop. There was something familiar about him, although the dirty checked cloth cap pulled low over his eyes made it difficult to see his face.

He was a good head and shoulders taller than Harold but thin as a whippet, and Harold watched as he approached the counter and slid a bundle of papers across to the pawnbroker. Then it dawned on Harold that the broker was also one of the many illegal bookmakers, and the tall thin man was his runner. He'd seen him hanging about in the alleyways taking bets.

The slightest hint of the police and he was off, dodging in and out of yards and down back alleys till he lost them. And could he run, thought Harold, who had seen him several times with the local bobby in pursuit on his bike. The bobby never had a chance of catching him; the man's long legs and lean build made him a natural runner.

Harold was partial to a bet now and then, and checking how much money he had left, he asked if he could have a look at the list of horses running that afternoon. Silently, he was handed a grubby piece of paper with twenty names on it and the odds printed at the sides.

Running his eyes down the list he spotted one called Blue Moon at twenty to one. That had to be an omen he decided, thinking of the brooch he had just bought, and he chanced a whole shilling on it. If it won he would be richer by one pound. He could certainly do with an extra pound to help him over Christmas.

Nodding his thanks he tightened his scarf, told them he would see them later, and went out of the shop. As he closed the door after him, the old man cackled and said, "Tha'll be lucky, Blue Moon's got no chance. Another mug!" and he dropped the shilling into his money belt.

Feeling pleased with himself Harold walked over the canal bridge and turned left along the tow path. Six barges were tied up and Harold's day was complete when he spotted the one that he and Ada had borrowed several times. He stepped aboard and rapped on the roof. There was no answer but Harold knew where to find the owner, and headed straight for the Red Lion in the centre of town. He entered by the jug and bottle entrance and sure enough, there was

Wally, the owner of the barge, stood at the bar with a pint in his hand and a grin on his face that said it wasn't his first.

"Well look who's here. It's the Monarch, king of the shovellers."

Harold flinched at the use of his nickname. Monarch was an ironic name bestowed on him by his workmates, due to him usually moving more coal than anyone else, and one of them had said he was the king at shovelling. To Harold's embarrassment the name had stuck with him for years.

"Harold me auld mate, come an av a pint."

Harold took his arm, and led him to a seat.

"Tha'd better sit down lad, afore tha falls down. Come on, ah've got summat to ask thee."

"Aye, an ah bet ah know were it is an all. Tha wants to borra me boat dunt tha? Tha's gor an assassination ant tha?"

"Assignation tha means, silly bugger. Am not planning on assassinating anybody tha fool, tha's more pissed than ah thought. And keep thee voice down. Ah dunt want all bloody Wath to know."

Wally's grin grew wider and his eyes more glassy as Harold continued,

"Is tha gunna be usin' t'barge over Christmas?"

"Not likely, ah've got lodgins wi a nice plump little widow woman, down on Doncaster road, an ah've got me feet under t'table if tha knows wor ah mean." Wally gave a broad wink and nearly fell off the stool.

Harold knew exactly who he meant, and plump was a very complimentary term for her. Fat or obese would have been more accurate. She was almost as broad as she was tall. But Harold thought it better not to say as much. He just nodded, then asked, "Well, can ah av use of thee barge on Boxing Day, usual arrangement?"

"Aye, course tha can Harold. Nah then, what about that pint?"

"Nay Wally, no time today, but ah'll leave sum cash wi t'landlord for some drinks over Christmas for thee. And remember what ah telled thee. Keep thee gob shut about this little arrangement."

"Oh aye, Harold, tha can depend on it," and Wally stood up to walk to the door with Harold, but his legs seemed to have turned to rubber and he sat back down again abruptly and called for another pint.

Harold looked ruefully at the handful of loose change left in his pocket after he had paid for Wally's Christmas drinks. He could just about afford a hot meat pie from the bakery for his dinner and a couple of pints on his way home.

Ada was pinning her hair up when Harold arrived. He took the brush from her and said, "Ee, ah shud leave that love, it'll be a waste of time, ah'm starved for thee, let's go upstairs."

Ada looked at him solemnly. "Sorry, we can't Harold, me Dad's at home."

His face fell. He looked devastated and Ada laughed, "Only kidding. Dad's out. Got thee going then, didn't ah?"

Harold reached for her. "Why yer little bugger yer, wait till ah ger owd of thee."

Ada skipped out of the way and ran for the stairs, she could hardly climb them for laughing, and Harold scrambled after her, his hand up her skirts tugging at her bloomers. He had them off by the time they reached the top and pushed them into his pocket.

"There Ada Dale, ah've gor em, tha'll not be able to wear any on a Saturday nah. Ah know these are thee weekend pair."

Ada giggled as she tried to wrestle the bloomers out of his pocket, then looked at Harold as they both realised that there would be no more Saturday meetings after next week. Harold pulled her to him.

"Ada love, how the hell am ah gonna manage wi out seeing thee for months?"

Ada took his face between her hands and kissed him slowly.

"Let's not think about that, let's just enjoy today while we can."

Harold gave no answer, he picked her up and laid her tenderly on the bed.

Before he left that day he gave Ada the roughly packed parcel containing the brooch, explaining, "Ah want to gi thee this Ada. Ah won't be able to see thee on Christmas day tha sees. Ah'll av to be at home wi t'kids."

Then he went on to tell her about his plans for Boxing Day, and how they had the use of the barge for the whole day.

"Go on open it," insisted Harold as Ada stood with the gift in her hand, unsure if she was meant to save it or open it immediately.

As the paper fell away to reveal the brooch she looked at it in delight.

"Oh it's lovely Harold, ah shall wear it always. Look Monty, it's you sat on the moon."

"Aye, an that's where he will be sitting if he sticks his claws into me anymore."

"Get away Harold, ah know tha loves that cat as much as ah do," laughed Ada.

"Ah wouldn't be too sure of that," he replied, as he kissed her goodbye.

Harold had almost passed the pawn brokers when he remembered about his bet.

As he opened the door Samuel Bowly appeared from behind an oak sideboard, piled high with old blankets and pillows that gave off a rank, musty smell. Rattling the money in his pocket he peered at Harold.

"Sorry mate, tha weren't lucky. Blue Moon fell at the first fence. Better luck next time," he said, barely hiding his amusement.

Harold felt like wiping the smirk from his face but said nothing, and left the shop. He headed for the Manvers Arms to console himself, muttering as he went, "So much for the bloody cat being lucky!"

It was fine but cold and windy on Boxing Day morning as Ada headed down the path towards the barge, thankful that there were few people about at that time of the day. Her thoughts and feelings were a mixture of excitement at spending a whole day on the barge with Harold and sadness that soon they would be parted for months.

She was determined to make this a day they would remember and had brought a basket filled with some of Harold's favourite food and a pack of cards and dominos.

The key was hidden under the painted flower pot as usual. Ada let herself into the tiny cabin tutting at the untidy state of the place. But within the hour the stove was lit and everywhere had received a good dusting and a wipe over.

Finally she shook the pegged rug over the side of the barge and replaced it in front of the stove. "There," she said to herself, "that's all it takes. Just a bit of effort, but it's no good expecting a man to bother with it."

Then she sat back on the bunk bed to wait and daydreamed that the barge belonged to her and Harold. In her imagination she could see them travelling the canals through Sheffield and out into Derbyshire. They would travel by day and stop wherever they pleased in the evenings.

As she got to the part of the daydream where she was repainting the barge, Harold arrived, looking cold and tired after his long walk from Denaby.

He held his hands to the stove thankfully, rubbing them in the warmth. Ada untied his boots and he slid his feet from them. Placing a mug of tea beside him, she took his feet one by one and rubbed them. Harold leaned back and closed his eyes blissfully for a few moments before pulling her into his arms. Soon they were lying side by side on the narrow bed under the quilt. Harold ran his hands over her body, pausing over the tiny swelling that showed her pregnancy, and kissed her tender breasts.

The day passed all too quickly and Ada prepared to light the oil lamp as dusk fell, but Harold put his head on one side and raised his finger, half pointing, as he signalled to her to listen. Clearly then, they could hear raucous voices coming towards the barge. Harold peered through the heavy net curtain that covered the tiny window. "It's that bloody Horace Moore," he whispered, "with two of his mates. Pissed as usual."

As they reached the barge they stopped.

"Daily news. Daily news, come and get yer Daily News."

Ada knew that was intended for her. 'Daily News' had been her nickname at school. Then the voices continued, "What a Corker tha's got there Harold, Daily News, come and get yer Corker."

They stood outside jeering for a full five minutes and Harold, seething with anger, began pulling on his boots, saying quietly to Ada as he did so that he would have to go and sort Horace Moore out once and for all. Ada grabbed his arm and begged him not to go outside, but Harold said firmly, "Ah av to see to this Ada. Stay there. Don't come out whatever happens."

As Harold stepped off the barge and on to the tow path, he could see that Horace Moore was at the rear of the threesome, urging on his drunken friends.

"Let's gi im swimming lessons lads. Daily News'll not be so keen on im then when he's cold an wet. Mebbe she'll let us av a go, eh lads?"

Harold stood his ground saying nothing, just waiting for them to make the first move.

"Come on then Corker, let's see what tha's made of."

The tallest of the group moved towards Harold and gave a drunken swing at him, but before the punch reached him, Harold's steel toe capped boot connected with his shin. Screaming with pain, he clutched his leg as Harold's fist hit him hard in his mouth. His mate turned and ran, stumbling and spewing up beer from his overloaded stomach as he went.

"Nah then, Horace, it's just me an thee in't it? Not so bloody brave nah is tha?"

"No offence Harold, it were just a bit o fun," stammered Horace.

"Aye well, this is just a bit o fun an all," came the reply, as he grabbed him by the back of the neck and the seat of his pants and, rushing him to the edge of the canal, threw him bodily into the freezing water.

Harold stood on the deck of the barge and waited till Horace swam to the bank and scrambled out coughing and spitting.

Turning to run away, he fell over the first of Harold's victims who was sat holding his leg with one hand and his mouth with the other. They struggled to their feet and made unsteady progress back towards town. They looked a comical sight but Harold knew he had made another two enemies.

As he sat back down in the cabin Ada noticed his hands were shaking and she knelt back down beside him.

"Oh Harold," she murmured, "tha can't go throwing blokes into t'canal, even if they deserve it."

"Well ah can tha knows, cos ah just did!" and they looked at each other and burst into laughter.

Under cover of darkness Harold walked Ada home, with his arm around her shoulders and hers around his waist. As they neared Packmans Row he drew her into an alley and gave her one last lingering kiss. Then he left her, fighting back his tears. As he walked he thought of the new year soon to begin and sighed deeply, wondering if it would bring a way for him and Ada to be together.

CHAPTER 7

For Ada and her family the new year began with Rose's wedding. It was a very quiet and modest affair and that was exactly how Rose and Wilfred had planned it. They had chosen to spend all their money on the house that they had rented in New Hill Crescent just around the corner from Packmans Row.

When Ada saw their new home she thought it a sensible idea and couldn't help feeling just a little bit envious.

They had managed to furnish the entire house apart from the back bedroom. Wilfred's mother had given them a bed and feather mattress, and the titled lady who Rose had worked for had presented her with a beautiful set of linen sheets, together with several old sheets, some of which Rose had repaired and some she had turned into pillowcases which she had patiently embroidered.

Together, the young couple had visited Samuel Bowly, the pawn broker, and after much bartering had purchased all the bedroom and living room furniture that they needed.

Thanks to Rose's persuasive bargaining, Samuel had agreed to have the furniture delivered free of charge. Tough business man he may have been, but he had a weakness for a pretty face and he fell for Rose's beguiling smile.

When the furniture arrived, Ada had helped Rose to scrub every inch of it, followed by a generous coat of beeswax. They had polished till their arms ached, but the shine and the smell of the furniture had made the effort worthwhile. Ada had made her sister a fine set of cushion covers and William had carved a pipe rack and a box to hold letters, and promised to complete the set with a holder for gas lighters.

Rose was so proud of her little home, and walked round it every day, flicking away any dust that dared to settle, and counting the time down to the day that she and Wilfred could move in. Ada looked round it and dreamed of the day that she and Harold could have similar home, but knew deep down that it was never likely to happen.

Early on the second of January, Ada and Lizzie set off for Carlton. It had been a bitterly cold night and daybreak had revealed a white frost and icy roads. William had borrowed Beauty and the trap to transport them to the station.

His eyes were full of tears as he kissed his daughter goodbye and Ada broke down and sobbed on his shoulder, saying over and over that she was sorry to be leaving him alone.

But train timetables make no allowances for emotions and the porter blew his whistle on time. Lizzie pushed Ada on board, dragging the rest of their luggage behind her. William stood on the platform waving until the train disappeared from sight. He was going to miss Ada so much, but he dug in his pocket for his handkerchief, gave his nose a good blow, squared his shoulders and went outside to Beauty.

By the time the train reached Doncaster, Ada and Lizzie were frozen through and glad of the roaring fire in the ladies waiting room, where they sat and ate their sandwiches until it was time for them to catch the Selby train.

If it hadn't been for Rose's marriage, Ada would have been travelling alone. Lizzie had wanted to be at the wedding, but Reggie was not able to take the time off work and they could ill afford the cost of two train tickets, so it was agreed that Lizzie would go alone and travel back with her sister.

Ada was grateful for her presence. She felt as if she had a huge empty void inside her, and it was hard to act and speak normally. Lizzie was sympathetic to her, but was feeling cold and irritable and not inclined to pamper her younger sister, and briskly told her to pull herself together and get on with it! Then seeing how downcast Ada looked she gave her hand a squeeze and assured her that everything would work out fine.

At last the Selby train was due, and they made their way to the platform just as it came steaming in right on time. Filling the air with smoke and steam, it drew to a halt with a final loud belch and a whistle, and the passengers poured from its carriages. Ada and Lizzie got into the first available empty carriage and settled their luggage in piles near their feet, double checking that they still had the correct number of bags.

"Not long now sis," said Lizzie.

Ada nodded thankfully and moved closer to her sister to make room for the large family who were being herded into the carriage by their mother. She was a large flabby woman who sank into the corner of the seat spreading herself comfortably with her feet planted wide apart, her open legs displaying a pair of bloomers that had once been white.

She grinned in a friendly fashion at Ada and Lizzie, at the same time giving one of the boys a casual flick round the side of his head that sent him sprawling into his brothers and sisters. Then she fixed the rest of the tribe with a look that immediately had them sitting quietly.

"Where's yer Dad?" she shouted.

The eldest boy looked around, under the seats, on the luggage rack and replied, "Not ere Mama, ah think wiv lost im."

"Tha cheeky little bugger. Come ere," and she reached out to give him another blow.

At that precise moment a short man of slight build appeared at the door and peered in, looking bewildered. He was immaculately dressed from his highly polished boots to his smart bowler hat.

He was obviously looking for someone and had come to the wrong carriage, thought Ada, but the mother shouted from her corner, "There yer are Derek, come on luv, ah've saved thee a seat ere by me."

She leaned across to Ada and confided, "He likes to sit near me. Tha knows how it is, ah av to humour im, he's a devil if he don't ger is own way," and she gave a broad wink. "Tha knows what ah mean."

Ada nodded and smiled, at a loss for an answer. She dare not look at Lizzie for fear she burst out laughing.

The little man fastidiously picked his way across to his woman, avoiding the feet and sticky fingers of his offspring. As he sat down in the narrow space saved for him, his wife gave him a smile and fluttered her eyelashes. He smiled back and placed his hand on her vast stomach.

"How is the little one in there Emily my love?"

Emily giggled coyly and kissed his cheek, then gave another swipe at the same lad who received the last one. Expertly, he dodged the blow and retreated out of reach.

Ada and Lizzie both had coughing fits at the same time and sat with handkerchiefs over their mouths, trying to regain control.

"Are you ok me dears? Yer want to be careful wi coughs like that. I hope it's nothing contagious."

With red face and streaming eyes Lizzie shook her head, and bending down, made a great show of searching for something in her bag.

In spite of stopping at every village along the way, they were soon pulling to a halt at Snaith station, and the sisters said goodbye to their entertaining travelling companions and stepped down on to the platform.

Ada rearranged her bags and commented to Lizzie that she felt so much better now, the laugh had done her the world of good.

To which Lizzie replied, "Ah dunt know about it doin' us good, ah think ah've dun mesen a mischief trying not to laugh."

The lamps were lit in the station and as they left its warm light neither of them relished the long walk in the gathering darkness. But they had only gone a few steps when Lizzie stopped and pointed down the road, shouting excitedly, "There's Reggie, just look at im, he thinks he's a bloody Roman driving a chariot."

And sure enough, there coming over the bridge was Reggie, standing with his feet planted wide apart, balanced precariously on a flat farm cart pulled by one of the heavy shire horses. The giant horse was going at a fast trot, mane and tail flowing and heavy feet pounding on the hard road.

As they drew near, Reggie slowed to a halt and jumped down to greet them, but stopping first to pat and talk to the horse.

"By, Blossom, tha were flyin' weren't tha. Tha did well auld lass," and he stroked the horse gently, calming her. She snorted and nudged him for the treat that she knew would be in Reggie's pocket, and sure enough he pulled out a handful of oats mixed with sugar, and held them in his open hand for her to nuzzle. Only then did he turn to Lizzie, put his arms around her and kiss her.

"See that Ada, t'horse comes first."

"Well so she should. Ah told her we were late and asked her to hurry, an ah ad all on to stop her breaking out into a gallop. So say thank you to her."

But Lizzie was already petting the giant horse and talking to her, telling her how wonderful she was, and Blossom pricked up her ears and nodded her head, jangling the harness.

Reggie gave Ada a hug and said, "It's grand to see thee lass, ah hope tha likes Carlton. Ah'm lookin' forward to avin' two women to keep house for me."

Lizzie interrupted, "Cheeky devil, she's not ere to run after thee tha knows."

Reggie slapped her backside playfully and helped her onto the cart, then turned to Ada and said, "Come on then princess, let's get thee on board."

Ada was astounded. This was a completely different Reggie to the tongue-tied young man who had visited Lizzie at home before they were married.

Blossom carried them to Carlton at a sedate pace, but the road was rough and in spite of the sacks filled with straw that they sat on it was an uncomfortable journey. Ada placed her hand on her stomach, thinking to herself that if the journey went on much longer the baby would be shaken from her body.

So it was a great relief when at last they reached the village and pulled up in front of a cottage on the main street. Even in the dusk Ada could see that the garden in front of it was full of interest and added to the charm of the house.

Two large holly trees, grown into conical shapes, stood either side of the gate, and yellow winter flowered jasmine bloomed over the wooden porch. Already there were snowdrops sprouting from the ground, ready to burst into flower in a few short weeks.

Ada thought the cottage was every bit as delightful as Lizzie had described and couldn't wait to see inside.

The front door led straight into the living room, and the first thing Ada noticed as she walked in was the large fireplace and oven which took up almost half of the wall that faced the door. A huge log smouldered in the grate, giving off a fragrant aroma. Around the fireplace were dozens of horse brasses, all bright and shining. Many of them were regularly used to decorate the horses at times of celebrations.

In the centre of the room there was large square table covered with a dark green chenille cloth that had long fringing all around the edges. Ada recognised it as the one Lizzie had bought on Barnsley market the year before. It had been a huge expenditure at the time and Lizzie had agonised for an hour before she had taken the plunge and bought it, but it looked just perfect here in the cottage and had been admired by many of her neighbours.

Two wooden chairs stood at either side of the fireplace similar to the ones back in Packmans Row, but Lizzie had knitted cosy woollen blankets to drape over the backs of them. Ada remarked what a good idea it was, and resolved to make some for her father's chair as soon as she could get hold of some wool. The only other furniture in the room were two small chairs that fitted under the table and a leather sofa which Lizzie said was the hardest and most uncomfortable thing she had ever sat on.

"No wonder Reggie's mother give us it, trust her not to give us owt that was any good. It'll be off on t'bonfire as soon as ah can replace it."

Then Lizzie led her through into the back kitchen and showed her the flat stone sink, and the pump from which flowed delicious, icy cold water. Ada drank a full cup of it and remarked how different it tasted to the water in Wath.

As Lizzie opened the door to show Ada where the logs were kept, two ginger kittens that looked like balls of fur hurtled indoors wrapping themselves around her legs, purring and meowing. She bent to stroke them, then pushed them firmly outside.

"Not allowed to spoil em Ada or they won't learn to catch mice." Then she whispered, "I giv em milk when no one's ere."

They went upstairs then, Lizzie going first carrying two candles. She showed Ada her bedroom, leaving one candle in her room and the other in the main bedroom where she and Reggie slept.

"You'll be able to see it all better in the daylight tomorrow. Ah'll just go an get t'oven shelf to warm yer bed," Lizzie informed her as they felt their way back down the unlit stairs.

Ada protested that she didn't need to warm the bed, but Lizzie insisted, and withdrew the heavy iron shelf from the oven and wrapped it in an old sheet, then slid it into the bed that would be Ada's for the next few months.

As Lizzie prepared their evening meal, Ada stoked up the fire, feeding pine cones and sticks down the sides of the large log in the grate. In no time at all they were blazing and sending sparks flying out in all directions. Quickly wedging the fine mesh spark guard in front of the fire she checked to see that none had landed on the hearth rug.

Just as the kettle boiled Reggie returned, bringing Rob, his black and white collie with him.

Rob stopped and stiffened as he saw Ada, and gave a low growl as a token warning, then sidled across to her, placed a paw on her knee and gazed at her adoringly with his deep brown eyes.

"Bloody fine guard dog you are Rob," commented Reggie.

The dog turned and looked at him apologetically, and laid his chin on Ada's knee, and somehow managed to look insulted as they all laughed.

Reggie shook his head. "Tha knows everything we say, dunt tha Rob?"

And Rob bared his teeth in a doggy grin and wagged his tail.

Ada went to bed early that first night in Carlton. As she sank into the deep feather mattress warmed by the oven shelf she felt protected and loved by her family, but she thought of Harold and wondered how she would be able to cope without seeing him.

104

She soon settled into the country life and loved the clean fresh air and the absence of coal dust gathering on every surface, the way it did back in Wath. Lizzie had a part time job in the dairy and left the house soon after Reggie.

Within the first week Ada got into the routine of cleaning the house and doing the shopping. By the time Lizzie arrived home at noon, dinner was on the table and most of the housework done. Before the end of the second week, Ada had found herself a little job at the local bakery doing the same kind of work that she had done before.

It was only for two hours a day, but the wages were just enough to payfor her keep at Lizzie's and meant she didn't have to use her meagre savings. Ada wore her mother's old wedding ring and her employer assumed her husband was a soldier. She had guilty feelings about it but didn't disillusion him, although she did blushingly tell him that she was expecting and would only be able to work until the end of March.

In January, Harold was always in poor spirits, but this year he had hit an all time low. For weeks on end in winter, like all miners, he barely saw daylight. The lack of sunlight combined with him missing Ada made him more depressed and irritable than usual. The only bright spot was the camaraderie with his workmates.

"Like bloody moles we are, living and working underground," was an often quoted phrase as they made their way to the coal face. Thankfully Harold was on a different shift to Horace Moore and his mates, so their paths seldom crossed.

News of the Boxing Day incident had reached Harold's mates however, and according to rumours he had thrown three men into the canal single handed. He had tried to put the record straight without giving away the fact that he was with Ada at the time and hoped the news wouldn't reach Winn.

As he toiled away on his hands and knees in the narrow tunnels he schemed to try and find a way to visit Ada. Eventually he came up with a plan and wrote to tell her of his idea. Harold was not much of a letter writer; there were no flowery verses from him but Ada cherished every word. She was only able to reply to him thanks to Rose reluctantly agreeing that she could send Harold's letters to her house, for him to collect on alternate weekends.

One Saturday in February, Harold told Winn that he was helping out with the pigeon racing again and he was up extra early the next day and off to catch the first train to Doncaster before Winn was even awake, praying that the weather would hold good.

If snow set in he knew he would have real problems. But happily it turned out to be a rare, dry, sunny winter's day, and he was overjoyed to find Ada waiting at the station for him.

She looked so good he could barely keep his hands from her. They spent the first hour walking down quiet lanes, hardly seeing the sweet smelling violets or the clumps of snowdrops in the hedgerows.

The flat countryside offered little privacy for courting couples. But then they reached a lane where the hedges had been left to grow tall and they were at last hidden from view. In the distance Harold had seen a barn and he firmly steered Ada towards it.

As they came level with the building he slid his hand inside her coat and caressed her breasts and the small distension where his unborn child lay. He kissed her and led her across the grassy bank and into the barn, and then rather spoilt the romance of the moment and made Ada giggle by pretending to growl at her and saying, "Come on Ada, wiv got sum catchin' up to do."

They spent an hour in the barn and a further hour picking out bits of straw from their clothes, and generally making themselves presentable.

Harold tilted Ada's hat to the correct angle, kissed her nose, and said,

"How ah luv thee Ada Dale," then wiped his lips and said, "But tha's gorra cold wet nose!"

The next two months passed quickly for Ada. She packed her days with jobs about the house. Lizzie scolded her, saying she was doing too much, but Ada seemed incapable of slowing down. The busier she was the less time she had to dwell on the future. Only at night when she lay in bed with her hands held over her unborn child did she allow herself to think of Harold.

But by mid April her body had become clumsy, and she was forced to give up her job and sit with her feet raised on the little wooden stool. Rob sneaked into the house at every opportunity to sit with his head on her knee gazing at her and nudging her hand to stroke his head. He seemed to know if the baby moved and would put his head on one side with his ears raised and look directly at her stomach. Reggie would shake his head at him and say, "That dog's in love wi thee Ada, am sure he thinks he's the father," and Rob would look at him in a knowing way.

Lizzie and Ada became closer than ever in the last few waiting weeks and it was as they sat together one evening sewing and chatting that Lizzie made her suggestion.

"Why not leave the babby here Ada? Ah've talked to Reggie, it's ok wi im. Tha cud comean see t'babby any time that tha wanted," and then she added, "ah dun't think me an Reggie are gonna be able to av any kids, we keep tryin' but nowt happens. Think about it please."

And Ada did think about it, and the more she thought the more it seemed like the ideal solution. She wrote to Harold about it and he answered, saying she must do what she thought best and added that he would come to see her the last Saturday in April and bring her some money to pay for the midwife and the doctor if one was needed.

By the time his letter arrived there were only two days to go before his visit. Wanting to look the best she could for him Ada unpicked the waistband of her best skirt and adjusted it to fit her swollen body. Her coat still fitted her if she left the buttons unfastened and the loose tunic she had made covered her bump discreetly. As she set out to meet Harold, her sister kissed her and told her she looked bonny.

Ada walked as far as the edge of the village and sat on the wall near the lake to wait for him. From where she sat she could see the swans moving elegantly across the lake. All around her the air was filled with the fragrance of spring flowers and the trees were covered with new pale green leaves.

Above the tops of the trees she could see the towers of the stately home of the family who owned most of the land and the farms in and around Carlton. How rich they must be, she thought, and day dreamed about having so much money that you never had to work or struggle to survive.

And then she turned as she heard the train whistle in the distance and she walked a little way towards the station until she caught sight of Harold.

He saw her and began to run, shouting and waving to her, but slowed to a walk before he reached her, his breath coming in gasps. Then she saw him stop and lean over the stone wall and knew he was coughing up some of the coal dust that had settled in his chest. She hurried to him anxiously, as fast as she could, and together they sat on the wall until he had regained his breath.

They sat quietly together, talking, thankful that so few people were about, and they discussed Lizzie's suggestion. They both agreed it was the ideal solution, but Harold pointed out that she would be giving up the baby forever.

"Tha wouldn't be able to change thee mind luv, it wouldn't be fair to Lizzie and Reg. They will be the parents once tha's handed it over."

Ada held his hand and said, "Ah know Harold, but at least ah'll be able to come and see t'babby whenever ah want to."

Harold took the money that he had brought for her from his pocket and told her to put it in her bag, stopping her protests by telling her it was from extra work he had done.

By the time Harold caught the return train it was all decided. Ada would have the baby and hand him or her over to Lizzie and Reg as soon as possible.

CHAPTER 8

Ada's baby girl was born early one bright sunny morning in May with the song of sky larks drifting through the open windows. As she looked at her beautiful daughter her heart was full of love for her but she handed her to her sister saying in a whisper, "Go to your mum darling."

Lizzie took her with a big smile, but tears were running down her cheeks and she looked at her sister and knew the sacrifice she was making.

Ada was soon up and about, revelling in the fact that she had her slim figure back. She had named her daughter Doris but when Reggie held her he said she was a perfect little doll, and from then on she was almost always known as Doll.

Registering her baby's birth was something Ada had been dreading. At the end of May, having put it off as long as possible, she went alone to the register office in Selby. The registrar was a bald-headed man with a huge moustache that was twirled into points at each end. Ada could imagine him grooming it at every opportunity. His beady eyes stared her up and down as she entered the office. He neither rose from his chair nor spoke as she approached the desk. She felt her colour and temper rise as he lifted his head and raised his eyebrows as an indication for her to state what she was there for.

As she told him she was there to register a birth he opened a drawer and withdrew a large leather bound book and a wad of forms. He spoke briefly then, simply asking for name and addresses, wrote her answers down without looking up at her. Until that is he asked for the father's name. Ada answered quietly, "Unknown."

He looked at her then, a little smile threatening to break out beneath his pretentious moustache, and demanded loudly, "Pardon?"

That was enough for Ada, she snapped, "Tha heard what ah said. Get the bloody form filled in, tha jumped-up little creep."

His mouth fell open with shock and he stared back at Ada stammering as he completed the form, "Th-th-there are laws to to protect servants of the gov-gov-government madam."

"Tha'll need more than laws to protect thee if tha dunt watch it. Ah'll av me bloke down ere to sort thee out," replied Ada, who was completely past caring by now.

She snatched up the certificate and placed it carefully in her bag. She leaned as close to him as she could across the desk and said very quietly and clearly, "Ah think tha's the ugliest little man ah av ever seen." And she left, slamming the door behind her.

Back in Carlton with Reg and Lizzie she told them the whole story, and said she was beginning to feel ashamed of herself for losing her temper, but Reg roared with laughter and said he knew the man well, and he deserved it. "By heck, he fancies hisen as a bit of a ladies man. It'll tek im weeks to ger his confidence back. Wait till ah tell my mates about it. It'll cheer em up no end."

The next few weeks passed by quickly for Ada, but her emotions were in a constant turmoil. Half of her longed to be back in Wath and able to see Harold regularly, but the other half dreaded leaving Carlton with its clean air and peaceful way of life, and worst of all, leaving her baby behind.

Every time she nursed her, she gazed down at her lovely baby face that was changing almost every day, and wondered how on earth she would be able to cope without her. By the time Doll was three months old she was almost weaned on to cow's milk and a few solids, and she knew the time was coming close for her to leave.

It was September when Lizzie walked to the station with her sister, pushing Doll in her pram, with Ada's luggage balanced on top. As they waited on the platform, she lifted her baby out for one last cuddle before she left, and tears flowed as she breathed in her baby smell. They could hear the train in the distance and Ada knew the time had come. She handed her to Lizzie and kissed them both. Lizzie said tenderly, "Say bye bye to your mam, Doll," and held up her hand in a wave.

"No, Lizzie, you're her mam now, ah'm Aunt Ada. That's the way it's got to be," and she thanked Lizzie again for all that she and Reg had done for her.

But Lizzie shook her head. "No, Ada, it's us that will be forever in your debt, ah can't tell thee what this means to us."

Then she became the brisk sister that Ada knew and loved so well, and putting Doll back in her pram, she organised her sister on to the train and kissed her one last time.

Ada leaned from the window as the train steamed out of the station and waved till they rounded a bend and disappeared from view. Then, grateful that she had the carriage to herself she wiped her face and repeated under her breath what Lizzie was fond of saying, "Pull yourself together girl, and get on with it."

While Ada was travelling towards Doncaster, Harold was sitting with his workmates in the deepest part of Denaby Main, eating the sandwich that Winn had packed in his snap tin. Opening the two pieces of bread he peered inside trying to see in the dim light what it was that he was eating. Unable to decide he gave a sigh, slammed the bread back together again and took a huge bite, and swilled it down with a gulp of cold tea.

"What's up Monarch, in't it very good? What's she gi thee today?" asked one of his mates.

"Am buggered if ah know John, it tastes like shit," came Harold's reply.

They all laughed and John offered him one of his sandwiches.

"Ere av one o mine, ar lass alus gis me too many. See thee, ah've got beef."

"Nay, tha's all right lad, Ah've ad enough."

And Harold tucked his dudley and snap tin away where the mice couldn't reach them and went back to work.

His thoughts turned to Ada again, he could hardly believe that she was arriving back in Wath tonight and they would be together again tomorrow. The last eight months without her had been almost unbearable. They would have to make sure it didn't happen again.

He decided he must tell her to use one of the vinegar soaked sponges that he had heard about from one of his drinking buddies.

Apparently they stopped women becoming pregnant, or so the man had said. But Harold had his doubts, seeing as the man passing on the information had nine children at the last count and another on the way. And, he reasoned, there wouldn't be all the hoards of ragamuffin, half-starved kids running round the streets if all it took was a sponge soaked in vinegar. Still, it was worth a try.

His thoughts then turned to the months without Ada. January and February had been the worst. The only relief in that miserable time had been his visit to Carlton when they had found the barn. The memory of that day had got him through many dismal times.

Then in March he had had a stroke of luck when he got the tenancy of an allotment just outside Denaby. The old man who had gardened it before had left a sturdy shed. Harold fixed up an old stove in the corner and the shed became his refuge. Sometimes he fantasised about living there all alone like a recluse. He spent all his spare time there and became part of the allotment holders' society who met over mugs of tea and put the world to rights. He often took Billy and Herbert with him to help and sometimes Edith joined them with baby Sarah, who was now toddling, and followed her sister like a shadow.

Edith loved playing the little housewife, and would sweep the floor of the shed and scold the boys if they walked in with muddy boots. When it was time to go home, they went back happy and excited if they had a few vegetables to take home for their mother. Harold thought the allotment was the best thing that had happened to the family for a long time.

There was not a happier man than Harold that day as the cage carried them up out of the pit at the end of the shift. It was all he could do to stop himself from singing.

At home, Winn had filled the copper with water and lit the fire underneath so as to heat it ready for Harold. As soon as he came in she sent the children out to play and slipped the bolt on the door. Harold stripped off his filthy pit clothes and thankfully sank his arms into the water. As he washed himself bit by bit, he thought of nothing but seeing Ada again and making love to her, and became so aroused that he almost took Winn right there on the scullery floor.

Flattered at his ardour, which Winn thought was due to her washing his back, she coyly told him she that was going upstairs to tidy the bedrooms. Harold finished washing himself, threw his clothes into the copper and followed her upstairs.

Afterwards he fell asleep, and Winn pulled the sheet over him and went back downstairs smiling, happy in the thought that her husband still desired her.

It was 3pm by the time the train arrived in Wath, and Ada, after a struggle with the door handle, managed to get herself and all her luggage out on to the platform. As she stood there organising her bags among the clouds of steam and smoke from the engine, she heard her name being called, and the next moment, there was her father, pulling her into his arms and hugging her tightly. William had missed his daughter so much. Eight long months she had been away and he could hardly believe she was back home.

She looked as slim and elegant as ever and her face glowed with health, but knowing her so well he thought he could detect a sign of what she had been through. There was a sad look in her eyes despite her huge smile of delight at seeing her beloved father again.

Beauty was waiting patiently outside and greeted her like an old friend, snickering and shaking her harness as Ada stroked her long mane away from her eyes. William discreetly handed her a mint, and pretending to take it from her pocket she offered it to the horse on the palm of her open hand. Beauty's velvet lips caressed Ada's hand as she took the mint gently, and closed her eyes as the minty taste dissolved on her tongue.

They were soon on their way home, with Beauty trotting through the streets of Wath, and her shoes making the clip-clopping sound that Ada loved to hear.

It seemed strange walking back into the house after such a long absence, it almost felt like seeing it for the first time, but for all that it looked homely and familiar. The banked up fire filled the room with warmth and sent its flickering light to reflect on the brass fender.

"Ah polished all t'brasses, Ada, ah did em last night, an ah've put Beauty's martingale up on t'wall. Ere look," and William pointed out the leather strap with four bright shining horse brasses hanging from it.

"Oh, it looks grand, and everywhere is lovely and clean Dad, ah bet ar Rose's been. She's polished all t'furniture wi bees wax, ah can smell it."

And then Ada saw the newly baked loaf wrapped in a tea cloth that her sister had made and the bunch of chrysanthemums from John's garden and thought how good it was to be welcomed home by her family.

Her cat Monty was less welcoming, he gave her a blank stare as she bent to stroke him, and then got up from the warm hearth rug and stalked indignantly across the room and hid under the sofa.

Ada smiled at her Dad and pulled a face and said, "Oh, he's gorra right sulk on im, ant he Dad?"

William nodded and told her to take no notice, the cat would come round soon enough when he wanted feeding.

Ada slept soundly that night, glad to be back in her own bed, and woke early next morning, coming slowly out of the deep sleep and flinching as she moved her neck. Pain ran from her neck and into her shoulder. This would happen today, she thought. There were dozens of jobs she had planned to do this morning.

Easing herself over on to her other side she sought a comfortable place to ease the pain and thought of her baby back in Carlton, and wondered if, at that moment, she was in bed with Lizzie and Reg, drinking her bottle and stopping every now and then to give them a gummy smile.

And then she thought of Harold and mentally added up the hours till he would arrive. That familiar thrill ran through her as she pictured him taking her in his arms.

A knock on her bedroom door brought her daydreams to an end as William called, "Is tha awake Ada? Ah've brought thee a cup of tea."

"Tha's spoilin' me Dad."

114

"Aye ah am that, but don't think ah'm gonna mek a habit of it," smiled William as he set the cup down.

"By, am right glad of this," said Ada gratefully, "me neck's real bad this morning."

"Aye, ah can see that, tha looks as if somebody gi thee a rabbit punch. Does tha want an headache powder luv?" and without waiting for an answer went down the steep staircase to get her one.

He was soon back with a hot cloth and a small packet of headache potion. Ada tipped the powder into her cup and gave it a stir, then thankfully wrapped the hot cloth around her neck.

"Thanks so much for this Dad, ah'll be alright in a bit. Ah won't be long."

"Tek it easy today lass, tha's probably pulled a muscle carrying that luggage yesterday." He turned to go, than asked, "Is Harold coming today?"

As Ada replied yes, William's face tightened and he closed his eyes momentarily before nodding and going downstairs. He sighed as he went into the kitchen wondering where this affair of his daughter's would end.

Harold arrived just as William was leaving, they exchanged curt 'nah thens' but said nothing else. Ada was waiting at the door for him and he pulled her into his arms almost before the lock clicked behind him. Picking her up, he carried her across the crowded living room, narrowly missing treading on the cat's tail who was lying under the table. He put her down on the sofa and kneeling above her said, "It's no good luv, ah can't carry thee upstairs. For a slim lass tha weighs plenty."

"Tha's a fool Harold Corker," giggled Ada.

"Gerrup them stairs woman, an ah'll show thee who's a fool. Ah'm counting to ten then ah'm coming after thee."

Ada jumped up from the sofa, forgetting about her bad neck and ran up the stairs and hid behind the bedroom door. Harold pounded up the stairs after her, doing his lion's roar impersonation till Ada shushed him, pointing to the adjoining wall and whispered that the neighbour would probably have a glass to the wall in an effort to hear what was going on.

Becoming serious, they sank on to the feather mattress and Harold turned on to his side facing towards her.

"Ada Dale," he said, "Don't thee ever ever leave me again. Ah can't survive without thee. Tha's so lovely ah could eat thee up bit by bit. Ah think ah'll start here." And Ada closed her eyes in ecstasy as he gently kissed her neck.

It was afterwards, as Ada lay in his arms with the heat of his shoulder easing the pain in her neck, that they talked of their baby. Harold had only seen her once but he carried the image of her blue eyes and dark hair as clear in his mind as if he was looking at a photograph. Her christening was to be next month and Ada asked tentatively if Harold would be able to accompany her to Carlton.

At first he shook his head, but seeing the disappointment on Ada's face said, "Leave it with me luv, ah'll see wor ah can do."

On the Saturday before the christening Harold informed Winn that he would be helping his mate again with the pigeons on the following day. Winn was not pleased and stamped about the house in a rare old temper banging pots and pans.

Harold left the house quickly, followed by his two sons, and headed for the peace and quiet of the shed on the allotment. They could still hear Winn's voice shouting and swearing as they left the yard. Harold looked at the lads, raised his eyebrows and asked if they had done something to upset their mother. Herbert exchanged glances with Billy, and received a nudge which meant that Herbert had been appointed as spokesman.

Still he hesitated, till his father urged him to speak up.

"Well Dad, it's not us, it's you she's mad at, cos she wanted to go to me granny's tomorra on er own. An you were gonna look after us."

"What does she think ah am, a bloody nursemaid?"

"It dunt matter Dad, ah can look after us lot, then tha can go off an see to t'pigeons."

"No, am nor avin' that, it's thee muther's job to look after you lot, she's got nowt else to do. Ah'll see to it when we get back. When

116

she's cooled down a bit. Tell you what lads, let's av sum pies from t'bakery eh?"

Bringing out a handful of coppers, he sent the lads for the pies while he got the fire going.

Sitting round the fire eating the pies was as good as a feast to Herbert and Billy; they licked every last delicious crumb from the paper they were wrapped in. Harold smiled at them, enjoying seeing them happy. Just as they finished, Edith turned up with Sarah clinging to her hand. Sniffing, she asked if they had been eating. Of course, Billy couldn't resist teasing her about how good the pies had been.

Edith looked so downcast that her father asked what their mother had given them for dinner.

"We had a slice of bread and jam cos Mam hadn't time to get anything ready," replied Edith, laying on the sad hungry look.

"Hadn't time! That's a bloody joke!" snapped Harold as he found more money for pies for the girls. Edith's face lit up and she shot off to the bakery clutching the money tightly. Sarah began to whine after her sister left, but Harold by now was in no mood to pacify her and told her abruptly to sit down and shut up.

He counted what money he had left and realised he hadn't enough for the train fare to Carlton. Sitting down on the old stool he put his head down on his hands and felt so depressed he could have cried.

'What's the point of it all,' he thought, 'I've grafted all week, an ah aven't even gor enough cash for t'train fare to Carlton.'

Feeling that there was someone standing beside him he looked up to find Sarah stroking his hair,

"Don't cry Dad, ah'll mek it better," she said in her quiet little voice and she kissed his hands.

Harold felt as if his heart would burst with love for her and he scooped her up in his arms and sat her on his knee.

"You better now Dad?"

"Yes luv, ah am better. Tha alus meks me better, dunt tha? Tha's just a little treasure."

And he blew kisses on the back of her neck till she scream with laughter.

While Edith and Sarah ate their dinner, Harold dug up the last few potatoes, and not having anything else ready, he begged a cabbage from one of the neighbouring allotment holders and sent them home to Winn, hoping it would put her in a better mood.

"Tell yer Mam, ah'll be late back, ah've got sum business to see to," he told them and set off to walk to Wath, knowing he was going to have to disappoint Ada.

As he walked his spirits rose as he thought about it, and decided that it was probably best that he didn't go to the christening considering all the circumstances. But he did worry about how Ada was going to take it. If he had but known it, Ada was thinking exactly the same thing. She had received a letter from Lizzie that very morning, saying that she thought it better if Harold didn't attend the christening. Since the moment she read the letter Ada had agonised about how she was going to break the news to him, especially when she had practically begged him to go with her.

As he walked in the door she began, "Harold," almost at the same time as he said, "Ada," then he continued, "you go first lass, what's up?"

Before she had finished telling him, he interrupted her and explained his own thoughts and financial situation.

Ada breathed a large sigh of relief and kissed his cheek. "Oh, thank goodness, I thought tha were gonna be so angry, ah didn't know how to tell thee."

"Let's say no more about it luv, and enjoy our bit of time together, ah can't stop late tonight. Just make sure tha tells me all about our little lass when tha gets back," and he sat beside her on the old sofa and pulled her towards him.

Life settled down for a while into an uneasy sort of calm. Christmas came and went uneventfully and then on New Year's Day the family welcomed a new member, when Rose gave birth to a daughter on the first anniversary of her marriage. Rose and Wilfred were beside themselves with happiness and they named their blonde, blue eyed baby, Hiney.

It was at the end of February that Ada noticed a change in Harold. There was a strange quietness about him, as if his thoughts were elsewhere. Repeatedly, she asked him if there was something on his mind, but Harold just shook his head and said there was nothing, he was just tired, but privately he thought back to the scene he had had with Winn a couple of weeks ago.

He had walked in from work to find her crying. His first thought was that she had found out about Ada and initially relief had flooded through him when she said she was expecting.

He soon realised that Winn's tears were more due to anger than sadness, when she picked up a cup and threw it at him, and shouted, "Tha selfish pig, tha's got me bloody pregnant again. Why dunt tha keep thee dick in thee pants? Ah told thee ah didn't want any more kids. Ah can't face it, ah can't."

Harold was on the point of losing his temper but managed to keep calm, and said, "Well ant tha bin usin' that vinegar sponge like ah told thee to?"

Winn went wilder than ever.

"Fat lot of good that's dun, whoever told thee that wants their bloody head looking at."

Words came to the tip of Harold tongue, and horrified, he realised he had almost retorted, 'Well it seems to be working for Ada!'

Wearily he sat down at the table, stared at her, and said, "Just shut up Winn, am too tired for this, as tha got t'water hot for me bath?"

"No ah bloody aven't," she shouted in reply, "tha can stop in thee muck for all ah care."

That was the moment when Harold finally lost his temper, and shouted loud enough for the entire street to hear, "Tha can gerroff thee arse, right now, tha idle cow, and get me bath ready, ah'm buggered, an ah want me bath. Tha knows ah can't go to bed like this."

The children had scuttled off upstairs at the first sign of trouble and stood listening on the tiny square landing between the bedrooms. Sarah was crying silently, sobs shaking her narrow shoulders. Herbert whispered to Edith to take her into bed and he'd come and tell her a story. Needing the comfort of each other, they all piled into bed together and listened as Herbert, in a voice barely audible, told them one of his made-up stories.

Downstairs Harold banged his fist on the table, making the pots dance and clatter. "Get on wi it woman, ah've ad enough nah."

Sullenly Winn got up and set about heating the pans full of water needed for Harold to clean himself, while he laid his head on his arms across the table and fell asleep.

From then on he stayed away from the house as much as possible, spending more and more time in his shed at the allotment, until his mates joked it was his second home. He carried coal there every time he went, and the first thing he did was to light the stove and then sit staring into the flames. The children became unnaturally quiet and often followed their father to the shed, crowding inside with him when the weather was bad.

Winn felt as if she was in a downwards spiral into more misery. She hated being pregnant and dreaded the thought of giving birth again.

Their mean little house offered no comfort, nor had living near her parents made her life any happier.

Her mother constantly interfered and criticised Winn's housekeeping to such an extent that they had fallen out and not spoken for two weeks. Even the children seemed to prefer their father's company and were seldom at home.

Something would have to be done Winn decided, as she lay on the hard sofa trying to ease her uncomfortable body. She would have to find a way out of all this. Once the growing baby inside her had been born, she would show Harold, she'd make him sorry.

CHAPTER 9

It was only to be expected that the neighbours in Packmans Row would have noticed that Harold was such a regular visitor to the Dale household. The speculation about it had provided much entertainment for the local gossips, and it was not long before snide comments were being made to Ada. She met them, and usually silenced them, with a fierce glare or a terse, "Mind your own business."

There were still a few however, who remained loyal friends. Martha, who lived in the last house in the row, would hear no wrong of Ada and Mrs Hudson who had been a family friend for years remained a staunch ally.

Gradually it became accepted that Harold was Ada's lover, and apart from it being a bit of spicy gossip that brightened up their dull lives from time to time, other events soon overtook the scandal of their affair.

In May however, almost a year to the day of baby Doris's birth, Ada discovered, like Winn before her, that a vinegar soaked sponge was unreliable as contraception.

As before, she woke one morning feeling extremely nauseous and knew immediately that her third pregnancy had begun.

Downstairs William had heard her retching, and raising his eyes to the ceiling, declared aloud, "Here we go again. That bloody Harold Corker. For two pins I'd castrate him."

When Ada came into the living room, looking pale and frail, William asked her quietly, "Ah heard thee being sick, is it what ah think it is?"

Ada, feeling too miserable to speak, just sat down and sipped the cup of water her father had placed in front of her.

This had happened on the Tuesday morning so there were a four days to go until she would see Harold.

Four days to think it out, and get used to the idea and make her plans. By the time Saturday came, she had reached her decision. There was to be no running away to hide this time she decided, she would face her critics and have the baby at home.

When Harold arrived on Saturday afternoon she felt determined, positive, and confident that she would have his support.

It was exceptionally warm that day and he looked hot and tired from his long walk; he'd taken off his jacket and carried it over his shoulder. Ada took it from him and poured him a glass of beer that she'd collected in a jug from the pub earlier. Harold took a long drink and set the glass down while he took off his boots. "That tastes grand luv, just wor ah needed."

Ada sat down beside him. She could hold her news no longer, and told him all in a rush that she was expecting.

"Oh bloody hell lass," he said, "not thee an all."

It took Ada a moment to realise the meaning behind his words. Sitting back she stared at him, a cold stillness about her. "What does tha mean, not me an all? Who else is?" She hesitated. "Winn?"

Harold nodded and looked down at his feet, unable to meet her eyes.

"Oh Harold, ah thought tha said tha didn't sleep wi Winn any more?"

"Aye well," he said, "ah know ah said that, but we are married tha knows, an sometimes ah av to."

Ada's temper boiled up and overflowed. "Oh aye, ah bet it were a right hardship for thee," and leaving him she almost ran from the room, up the stairs to lay on the bed and torment herself with mental pictures of Harold in bed with Winn.

In her anger she took her pillow and began to punch it with all her strength, not seeing or hearing Harold as he stood by the bed.

"That's it lass, if it makes thee feel better tek it out of t'pillow. Ah'm sorry luv. Ah ad to sleep wi er or she'd a known summat were up."

And so Ada just had to resign herself to the knowledge that both herself and Winn were carrying Harold's babies.

As Harold walked back to Denaby that night, he contemplated his life. What a mix up it all was. What a situation he was in. The Red Lion inn beckoned as he went through Wath and he felt in desperate need of a drink. Happily a few of his mates were in there and he joined them, all full of beer talk and putting the world to rights.

"Nothing's the same these days," said one, "there's no taste in any of the grub we get nowadays, and does tha know, even t'bloody vinegar's not the same as it used to be!"

Harold agreed, "Well tha can say that again."

When eventually he left to continue his journey home, it was surprising how much better he felt. Things certainly looked more rosy with a few pints inside him. His spirits were so much better that he even began to feel just the tiniest bit proud that he had two women pregnant. After all, nobody could doubt his virility could they? And he pulled his shoulders back as he stepped out towards home.

CHAPTER 10

Winn gave birth to a son at the beginning of November on a wild, windy day, with the rain lashing against the windows. It had been a long, tedious pregnancy for Winn, full of aches and pains and bouts of sickness, and as if it hadn't gone on long enough, the baby had been two weeks overdue.

Over the last few months her relationship with Harold had gradually deteriorated until they were barely speaking. When at last Winn went into labour she cursed her husband with every contraction that she endured. But, at last it was over, and the midwife put her fine healthy son into her arms.

Despite Harold's feelings for his wife, which were now mostly of dislike, he managed to put on a show that was expected of a new father in front of the midwife and the detested mother-in-law, and then disappeared as fast as he could to the local pub.

The women in the tiny bedroom looked at each other, tutted, and said in unison, "Men!" Just one word that conveyed all their feelings.

Proud that he was able to boast to his mates that he had another son, Harold accepted the congratulations and the drinks they bought him until, by the time he walked home, he was in a blurry cloud of something that resembled satisfaction and contentment.

Sadly the feeling was short lived, especially when the baby constantly suffered from colic and cried for hours on end.

Winn's mother was a frequent visitor and considered herself an expert on baby care. She recommended cinder water for the colic and dropped cokes from the hearth into a cup of hot water, allowed it to cool, then fed the water drop by drop into the infant's mouth. It did no good of course, and as Winn felt better she argued with her mother who stormed out of the house vowing never to return.

Harold raised his eyes skywards, whispered, "Thank you God," and put cotton wool in his ears to block out the sound of his son's wailing.

What to call their new son was yet another thing they could not agree on. They bickered about it for the first three weeks of the baby's life, until Harold, thoroughly sick of the arguments, called at the registry office and registered his son as Ernest Corker.

When he returned home and firmly told Winn what he had done, she flew into one of her frequent rages. Harold left early for work that day, thankful that he was on the afternoon shift and would not be back until late evening.

The following day would be Saturday, the day he usually saw Ada, and he thought of little else that afternoon as he laboured underground. His body went into automatic work mode as he shovelled the coal into the tubs, filling one after another, with sweat running down his back and soaking into his shorts.

But in his mind he was sitting in the armchair in front of the fire with Ada by his side, and he imagined the tea they would have. Freshly boiled ham and soft bread spread thickly with dairy butter, and of course his favourite, crisp green celery. And then he thought of their time in Ada's soft feather bed. Oh, he could hardly wait for Saturday afternoon.

When he walked into Ada's orderly home the next day, the tension left him and he relaxed for the first time in days. A bright fire glowed, reflecting on the polished wood and brass, and the table held their tea, all set out on a white cloth just as he had imagined it the day before. Harold settled himself down in the high-backed wooden armchair and closed his eyes with contentment.

Monty sprang onto his knee and stood nose to nose with Harold, staring into his eyes.

"What's up wi thee then?" Harold asked him seriously. "Does tha love me then?" The cat began purring loudly but jumped down when Harold laughed at him. "He's a bloody weird cat is this one Ada."

"Ah, don't laugh at him luv, he dunt like being laughed at."

"He's only a cat, he's not a bloody person tha knows."

"Well ah'm not so sure about that," replied Ada as she sat on his knee and kissed his forehead.

Unlike Winn, Ada had enjoyed a trouble free pregnancy after the first two months of early morning sickness and it was only in the seventh month, when her clothes became tight, that her condition became obvious.

Christmas was only three weeks away and Ada had made her plans. Aware of course that Harold needed to be at home with his children on Christmas Day, she had invited John and Rose with their families to come to tea on Boxing Day, and intended to persuade Harold to be there too.

When she first suggested it, he looked doubtful.

"Ah dunt know Ada, is it a good idea? Ah'll be about as welcome as snow in summer. Tha knows how John is wi me, and Rose in't much better."

"It's time they got to know thee Harold, go on, give it a try, for me."

Harold was dreading Christmas. The thought of being cooped up all day with Winn, trying to remain civil for the sake of the children made him feel as if he would rather be at work. If it had been possible to do an overtime shift he would have been the first in the queue.

And now he had the prospect of facing up to an afternoon of disapproval from Ada's family on Boxing Day, 'I'll have to do it,' he thought, 'for Ada's sake,' but decided that at the first sign of trouble he would leave.

Ada spent Christmas Day quietly at home with her father. Her baby was due in four weeks and she felt clumsy and ungainly, so it was a relief to spend the afternoon sitting with her feet on the little stool, knitting and talking to William.

John and Mary were the first to arrive on Boxing Day with their young son Jack, closely followed by Rose, Wilfred and Hiny. Somehow Ada had managed to find enough stools and chairs to seat everyone around the table.

John looked at the food laid out. "By, tha's been busy Ada, that looks good enough to eat," and he reached across and picked up a mince pie.

"Put that back John," Mary told him, but grinning he put the whole pie in his mouth.

"Ada, what can ah do wi im, can't tek im anywhere. It's a good job the kids are too young to copy im."

"Oh, dunt worry Mary," said Ada, laughing at her brother's bulging cheeks, "ah know what he's like, we dunt call im big gob wi out reason."

Mary counted the plates. "Ah think tha's put one too many places out luv."

Ada took a deep breath. 'Wait for it,' she thought to herself. Clearing her throat she said loud and clear, in a tone that signalled she was standing firm, "There's a place for Harold, and please dunt start any trouble. It's Christmas and ah want im ere, an that's all there is to it."

John looked at his father who shrugged, and then at Rose who remained silent. Taking the lead from William, he did the same as his father and just shrugged and said, "Ok," then put his arm around Ada, gave her a squeeze and a kiss on the forehead. Ada smiled in thanks and relaxed.

It was five minutes later as Rose poured the boiling water into the big brown teapot that Harold knocked on the door. Ada ushered him into the crowded sitting room, holding his hand for a moment. She could sense how nervous he was but John stood up, shook his hand and put him at ease.

Before long the men were deep in conversation discussing the mines. Harold described the conditions down Denaby Main, which was well known as a difficult mine to work and had more than its fair share of accidents.

"Ah've got good mates there but I'd rather be at Manvers," said Harold.

Ada interrupted and called them to the table, overjoyed to see how well Harold had been taken into the family. No mention was made of

Winn or Harold's children over tea. It seemed a truce had been called, for today at least.

As Christmas Day had been on a Friday, it meant a longer holiday than usual and there was one more day before everyone had to return to work.

Harold had promised to take Herbert, Billy, Edith and Sarah to the local pub, where a children's party had been organised.

They were all wildly excited about it, anticipating the food and games, and the gift they would each be receiving. Harold and most of his fellow miners had been paying into a fund every week for a year ready for this party, and it seemed most of Denaby planned to be there. To Harold's relief, Winn had refused to go. The less he saw of her the better, he thought, as he walked down the hill towards the pub with his own children galloping ahead with at least twenty others from their street.

The New Year came and with it several inches of snow, making it difficult for Harold to see Ada. Knowing that her confinement was close he became very anxious about her and he set off to walk to Wath, wearing an old army surplus overcoat he had bought on Mexborough market.

It was heavy and scratchy, and had obviously been intended for someone much taller than himself as it almost reached his ankles, but he was grateful for its protection when it began to snow heavily before he had even gone half way. Pulling his cap down low over his eyes and tightening his scarf, he sank his hands deep into his pockets and strode out, thinking as he walked of the person who had worn the coat before him, and wondered if he had survived the war.

Ada was overjoyed to see him and pulled him into the house exclaiming how cold he was. Holding her close, he told her he would happily have walked twice as far to see her.

It was the nineteenth of January when Ada went into labour, and in the early hours of the twentieth her son was born, just one day before her twenty seventh birthday. Cuddling her baby, she gazed into his deep blue eyes that were so much like his father's, and

128

whispered to him that he was the best birthday present she had ever received, and announced to her father that she was going to name him Stanley.

CHAPTER 11

Due to the bad weather, Stanley was almost two weeks old when Harold saw him for the first time. Ada was up and about and had already registered his birth at the local registry office. Again she had left the column for the father's name empty, but thankfully the registrar was not as judgmental as the one at Selby and admired her baby boy, declaring him to be a handsome little chap.

Harold had mixed feelings as he held his second new son. He was well aware how demanding a young baby could be, and was afraid his arrival would reduce the time he and Ada could spend together. But, he had to admit he was a bonny baby and seldom cried, unlike Ernest, who continued to be restless and was still troubled by colic pains.

Ada was blooming with good health and he desired her more than ever as he watched her move around the room, preparing their meal and tending to Stanley, and he caught her hand and pulled her to him and held her, breathing in her fragrance.

It was in February, just as it looked as if they were settling into a routine and spring was not too far away, that Harold returned home from work to find that Winn had left him. She had just simply walked out, taking all her clothes and the housekeeping money.

Shocked, he sat down at the table and stared into space while he gathered his thoughts. The children sat in a row on the shabby sofa, all subdued and silent. Herbert handed him a piece of paper.

"It's from Mam," he said quietly, putting his hand on Harold's shoulder as if he were the adult and his father the child. Taking in his dirt covered face and the black rims of coal dust outlining his eyes, he added, "Ah've got water hot for thee Dad, tha can av a bath."

"In a minute son, in a minute, let me read this first. Can tha get me a mug o tea Edi, there's a good lass."

As Edith made his tea he read the note which was short and to the point, and more civil than he expected it to be.

Harold,

I'm leaving and won't be back. Can't cope with looking after the kids any longer. You have a go at it. Get your fancy woman to help. Yes, I've known all about that for the last month. I don't need you any more. I've got somebody better to look after me. I'll write to the kids next month.

Winn.

Harold questioned Herbert and Billy about where their mother might have gone to, but they knew nothing. And then as if on cue, Ernest began to cry. 'That's all ah need,' thought Harold, 'what the hell am ah going to do, ah can't look after a four month old baby and go to work to support them all. God help us, we'll end up in t'workhouse.'

With all these thoughts going round and round in his head Harold went into the scullery and set about washing himself in the copper, while Edith gave the baby his bottle. As he washed, he tried to take stock of things. Thankfully it was Friday and pay day, so at least he had some money, and a couple of days to sort out some kind of care for the children.

Maybe his mother or his mother-in-law would take Ernest and look after him. But no, what was he thinking? His own mother was too old to start looking after children again and he wouldn't give his mother-in-law a dog to look after, let alone his own baby son.

All evening Harold expected to see Winn walk back through the door, laughing at him and telling him that she had only done it to teach him a lesson, but when it got to nine thirty he realised that there was little chance of it.

Edith and Sarah went hand in hand across the yard to the privy and came back crying that the old woman who lived next door had stopped them and told them that their Dad would have to send them to the workhouse.

"Wait til ah see that auld bugger, ah expect she's ad er mucky lugs to t'wall all day. Don't thee worry luv, nobody's going to t'workhouse, while ah've breath in me body! Except that auld bugger next door, she'll be goin, and soon."

Herbert awkwardly put his arm around Edith and Billy, following suit, did the same to Sarah. The usual brother and sister hostilities were forgotten and they stood together, bonded by the family crisis.

Herbert, as the eldest, spoke up again, "Well ah'm glad she's gone," he said, his lips tight and his dark eyes huge in his pale face. "All she ever did was shout at us. We'll be ok on us own won't we Dad? Tha'll look after us won't tha Dad?"

Harold seemed to have acquired a large lump in his throat and in spite of his efforts to hold them back, two large tears arrived and ran down his cheeks. "Aye, ah will that son, we'll manage. Come on nah, off to bed wi yer, we'll all feel better in t'mornin."

Half an hour later he followed them, carrying Ernest in one arm and a candle and bottle of milk in the other. He took the baby into bed with him and fed him some more milk, struggling to keep his eyes open. Sleep won, and when he awoke again the candle was still flickering but burned down to a stub. Ernest was fast asleep, his cherub lips sucking now and then on an imaginary teat. Harold eased him over on to Winn's side of the bed and tucked the blanket around him. As the candle finally spluttered and went out, Harold closed his eyes and slept soundly, his worries forgotten for a few hours.

He woke early next morning just as Ernest began to whimper for his feed. It was still dark and Harold climbed out of bed and felt his way to the shelf where matches and a spare candle were kept. In the flickering candlelight he managed to change the baby's nappy, then, carrying him tucked under one arm, groped his way carefully down the stairs. He lit the gas light, cursing as the match caught the mantle, leaving a large hole in one side of it.

The gas irritated him as it hissed and plopped, but at least it gave a good light and he set about preparing Ernest's bottle. The baby lay on the sofa, his legs sticking out of the bulky nappy, the cloth turned

132

grey from dozens of inefficient washings. His whimpers were threatening to turn into a full blown screaming tantrum just as Harold got the bottle ready and thrust it into his mouth.

Sighing with relief at the silence, Harold propped the bottle on a cushion and left Ernest to feed himself. He set about washing his pit clothes and then emptied the dirty water out of the copper, ladling it out a jugfull at a time into the stone sink. Thankful to have that job out of the way, he cleaned the fireplace and lit the fire. The flickering firelight raised his spirits and he began to make his plans for the day

Today was Saturday, the day he always went to see Ada. He would still go he decided, but he would have to take Ernest with him. He could leave Herbert in charge here at home, he was very capable. He hated to leave them alone but he just had to see Ada and discuss the situation with her. Having made his decision he felt stronger and more positive, and set about tidying the room and preparing breakfast.

Harold left the house at ten o'clock with Ernest tucked up in his pram, well wrapped up against the cold damp February morning. At the bottom of the pram, underneath the thin mattress, he placed a brick heated in the oven and rolled in an old blanket. Edith held her hands inside the bedding and declared that Ernest was as snug as a bug in a rug. With a bottle of milk and a change of nappy they were ready for off.

Harold had explained to them all that he had to go out and had put Herbert in charge, and promised he would be back before dark. He was wearing his khaki ex-army coat again and his checked scarf. Edith handed him his cap as he manoeuvred the clumsy pram out of the house, and he stopped long enough to give the girls a kiss. Billy got a warning to behave himself and added that if he didn't, he'd get his backside tanned when he got back.

"Can ah walk as far as t'allotment wi yer Dad?" asked Billy, not in the least perturbed with his warning.

"Aye, but tha comes straight back, does tha hear me?" instructed his father knowing full well that if there was mischief available, Billy would be up to his eyes in it.

The snow had gone and been replaced by a steady, light drizzle that wet everyone through. The streets of Wath looked especially dirty and depressing today and Harold thought longingly of spring, and particularly spring in Carlton, as it had been when Doll was born.

It was half past eleven as Harold approached the centre of Wath. He had practically run past Manvers Main pit and the Manvers Arms pub next to it, dreading the thought that some of his mates might see him pushing the pram.

Glancing to the side of him he saw an old tramp keeping pace with him as he walked, he was dressed in an army overcoat just like his, and by a strange coincidence was pushing a pram. Then he realised with horror that it was his own reflection in the shop window.

"Bloody hell Harold," he muttered to himself, "tha'll av to buck thee ideas up."

Two women passing by gave him strange looks and a wide berth, and he heard one of them say, "What a shame, poor bloke's gone a bit loopy."

He decided to walk up New Road and down Sandygate, mostly because it was the one road on his route that could claim to be attractive, but it turned out to be one of the best decisions he had made in a long time.

As he passed one of the wrought iron gates that opened into the private grounds that lay beyond the high stone walls, something shiny on the ground caught his attention. Bending down and scraping away the grime and rotting leaves he picked up a gold sovereign.

His smile would have lit up a room as he checked that there were no witnesses and after giving it a good rub on his coat, he thrust it deep into his pocket. Raising his eyes skywards he murmured, "Thank you God, I believe in you. Ah really do."

Ada was surprised to see Harold so early, especially as he had Ernest with him. She and William had just been about to sit down to their midday meal. The rabbit stew and dumplings that were steaming on the plates set Harold's mouth watering. Without a word, Ada piled a plate high, deftly taking one of the dumplings from her own plate and sliding it on to Harold's without anyone seeing.

If William was surprised to see him arrive with the baby in his pram, he made no comment. He just finished his dinner and excused himself, leaving his daughter and her man alone. His actions had not gone unappreciated by the young couple and as he pulled on his hat and coat, Ada followed him to the door, put her arms around him and whispered, "Thanks Dad."

"That's ok luv, ah can see summat's up, ah'll leave you two to sort it out." And he left, missing out on his usual mug of tea and afternoon rest.

Ada resumed her dinner and waited for Harold's news. Between mouthfuls of stew, he explained all that had happened.

"So," he added, "God only knows what ah'm goin' to do."

Ada thought for a moment. "Ah've got an idea," she said, "the house you used to live in is empty. Why not see if tha can move back ere, then ah'll be able to look after t'kids while tha's at work. The landlord's comin' for his rent this afternoon. Tha could ask im."

Harold needed no time to think about it. "Ada, ah knew tha'd think of summat, bless thee luv."

"Only thing is, Arthur Bramham'll want sum money up front, tha knows what he's like."

Harold's face lit up, and going to his coat he delved into the deep pocket and brought out the sovereign. As he held it up the light reflected on it. "Does tha think this'll be enough then?" he said with a big grin and he explained how he had found it.

"Oh Harold, ah think sumbody up there loves us," cried Ada, and she threw her arms round him.

Less than ten minutes later the landlord arrived and readily agreed to rent the house to Harold, who, thinking it best not to pay with the sovereign, brought out his wage packet and carefully counted out exactly the right amount of cash.

Arthur Bramham, the landlord, made it clear he would have to take the house as it was, without it being scrubbed out.

"Can ah move in tomorra?" asked Harold.

"Ah don't see why not, tha's paid thee rent. Good luck, and make sure tha pays on time every week, tha knows the score." With that he turned abruptly and left with a wave of his hand, walking quickly out of the yard, an imposing figure in spite of his short stature.

Ada clapped her hands together. "Just think Harold, we'll be able to see each other every day."

Ernest decided it was feed time and demanded his bottle with loud cries that woke Stanley who joined in the chorus. Peace was only restored when Harold produced the bottle from under the blankets and Ada put her baby to her breast.

As they sat in the cosy living room listening to the sound of the two babies suckling and the loud tick of the clock, they looked at each other and Harold thought he had never seen Ada look more beautiful and planted the image deep in his mind, a picture that would stay with him forever.

Practical as ever, Ada's mind was racing through things that would need to be done, and she asked Harold if he knew a carter who would move him on a Sunday.

"Ah were just thinking about that luv, ah'm goin' to call at Sammy Bowlegs on way back an see if his carter'll do it. He won't care what day it is, as long as there's money in it for him. It's goin' to be a right rush to get packed up on time, so ah'll gerroff in a minute. Ah'm on late shift on Monday, so that'll gi me a bit more time."

Harold bit his lip, thinking. "Ah'll tell thee what. Winn's goin' to ger a right shock if she comes back an finds us all gone an t'house empty."

"Well it'd serve her right wouldn't it?" retorted Ada. Then added, "Does tha want to leave Ernest ere wi me overnight? It'd make things a lot easier for thee gerrin' t'packin' done."

And so it was agreed. Harold set off soon after, his step quick and purposeful, his head full of jobs to be done, and his heart lighter than it had been for a long time.

His first call was at the pawn brokers. Samuel Bowley's eyes shone as bright as the sovereign that Harold handed over as part payment for the carter's costs. He fondled the gold coin as tenderly if it were a beautiful woman, already he could see it joining the rest of his secret hoard.

He counted out Harold's change, double checking to assure himself that he had not given him too much, and informed him that the carter would be there at 9.30 on the dot.

"Just make sure tha's all ready and packed up. Time's money tha knows. If it takes longer than t'stated time it'll cost thee more. So think on."

Harold nodded and checked his change before dropping it into his pocket.

As he came out of the shop he saw the Doncaster bus approaching, and sprinted for the stop, making it just in time. He climbed on board and settled down on the hard wooden slatted seat and handed over his fare, reflecting as he did so that it would be worth the cost for the extra time it would save.

The house was quiet when he walked in. The fire was still lit, the pots washed and everywhere looked tidy. Edith and Sarah were playing with their dolls. As usual Edith was in charge with Sarah following her instructions. They looked up as Harold entered the house and asked them where the lads were.

"Herbert's gone to t'allotment and Billy's gone down to watch t'trains. We've cleaned up like you said Dad, an ah've got kettle boiled. Is our Ernest outside in his pram? Ah'll fetch him in shall ah?" she added making for the door before her father had time to explain.

"No, he's not ere luv," replied Harold, as he rummaged in the cupboard for his mug. When he turned round Edith was staring at him, horrified. "Aw, Dad, av you tekin' im to t'workhouse, Mrs Wilson said you would, and Mrs Calton," and she began to cry noisily, large tears running down her face and loud sobs shaking her whole body.

Harold pulled her to him and held her to make her listen to what he was trying to say.

"Stop that Edi, stop it and listen to me, take no notice of them wicked auld women. Ernest has not gone to t'workhouse and never will. Nah wash thee face cos ah'm not gonna gi thee a kiss while tha's all snotty," and he pulled a face that made her laugh even while she still cried.

Herbert and Billy walked back in at that moment and stood silent, waiting for the next development

Harold had been dreading telling his children about Ada and explaining the situation, knowing as he did that children could be strict censors. In the end, he simply told them that they were moving back to Packmans Row so that Ada could look after them while he was at work.

After a quick tea, they set about packing their meagre belongings and by bedtime everything was folded and wrapped and tied up with string except the bedding and the clothes they wore.

The carter was there next morning as promised and immediately set about loading the long flat cart. By mid morning they were ready to leave. Only Edith and Sarah were allowed to ride, sitting proudly at the side of the driver. Harold and his sons walked.

By the time they arrived at Packmans Row they were all tired and ravenous. Ada made herself instantly popular by having plates of pie and mashed potatoes all ready and waiting on the oven top.

With the help of Rose and her friend Martha, all the floors had been washed, the windows cleaned and the curtains hung. Ernest lay in his pram looking happy and content. Harold looked down at him and then at Ada. "How's tha managed that? He's usually bawling his head off."

Ada just smiled at him and tickling Ernest's toes said, "Well, poor little devil ad a right sore bum, ah just bathed him and put some cream on him, and fed im. Nowt magic about that. Tell you what though, him an our Stanley don't seem to like each other. Ah put em together in t'pram but they wouldn't settle. Ah've ad to leave Stanley wi me Dad for an hour while ah help you get the house sorted."

From the beginning the children took a liking to Ada and were always trying to please her, always seeking her approval, and in return Ada heaped praise on them at every opportunity

138

Herbert and Billy kept the fires going, chopping sticks and carrying buckets of coal for William's house as well as their own, while Edith was invaluable in helping to clean and look after the babies. Ada told them truthfully that she didn't know how she would be able to manage without them. Sarah wrapped her arms around her and said she was her new Mam.

Of Winn they had heard little, only that she had gone to be housekeeper for an old man in Conisborough. On hearing that, Harold had raised his eyebrows and said, "Well lord help him, if Winn's the housekeeper it's to be hoped his eye sight's bad."

The first month was incredibly hard for Ada, going from looking after her father and one baby, to having two babies and four older children to cook and clean for.

Sometimes she was so tired she felt she would fall asleep on her feet. Her friend Martha proved again and again what a true friend she was, helping and supporting all the family. Rose came as often as she could, cheering everyone with her brisk no nonsense outlook.

Lizzie still wrote every week, telling her about Doll's progress, and promised to come over to visit as soon as she was able.

CHAPTER 12

When Harold had turned up at Ada's home that Saturday pushing a pram, most of the neighbours had been agog with curiosity. And when he left without the pram, speculation was rife as to the reason. Some of the nosier ones could not contain themselves and went knocking on Ada's door on any pretext they could think of in order to gather information. But Ada had taken the precaution of slipping the bolt on the door and refused to answer. 'Let them wait to find out,' she thought to herself, with a mischievous grin.

So when Harold arrived the next day with his family and all his possessions and moved into the empty house, the gossips had a field day, hanging about in groups watching them move in. William pushed his way through them on his way to see to Beauty, muttering about sensation seekers.

But Harold and his family were soon accepted into the close community, especially when it became known that Winn had left her children. Harold commanded much respect when it was realised that he intended looking after Herbert as if he was his own son. But it would not have occurred to Harold to do otherwise, as he loved him just as much as any of his other children.

Harold was no stranger to hard work, but the journey to and from Denaby made life even harder than before. Sometimes he was able catch a bus to Mexborough, then walk to Denaby. When he arrived at the pit he still had a long way to walk underground to the coal face. Often by the time he arrived back home he was on the point of exhaustion, and would lay down on the hearth rug in front of the fire still in his pit clothes and sleep for an hour before he could gather the strength to bathe.

No matter how busy Ada was, she always managed to have the bath water ready and a meal waiting, and wiping the black grime from his lips she would kiss him and taste the coal dust in his mouth, thinking as she did so of the place he where he spent all his working days.

Having been among miners for so many years she was well aware of the dangers all the men faced every day, and wished with all her heart that Harold could earn his living differently. But he was a miner born and bred, and his father and grandfather before him, and he knew no other life. What Harold desperately wanted was to move to Manvers Main colliery. He had been to see John Marks who was one of the deputies there and lived in the next street.

John had promised to let him know as soon as there was a chance of him joining one of the gangs who worked the coal face. That would make life so much easier Harold told Ada as she washed his hair, while he sat in the tin bath in front of the fire.

The last Saturday in March was a lovely day, so much warmer than normal that they decided to take all the family for a picnic. The children couldn't have been more excited if a week's holiday in Scarborough had been suggested and they ran around helping Ada to prepare for it.

They set off at eleven o'clock, with the two babies in the large old pram separated by a blanket as they still seemed unhappy to be close together.

Stanley, as the younger, lay well wrapped up under the hood, while Ernest, who was now sitting up, was propped against a cushion at the other end. The handles of the pram were hung with bags of food and bottles of water, and of course the football which was the pride and joy of the two older brothers.

Edith insisted on pushing the pram but by the time they were half way up Sandygate she had to accept a helping hand from Herbert.

Ada was wearing her long navy blue coat and straw hat with a blue satin band around the crown. Harold said she looked delectable. Ada replied that she didn't know he knew such long words as she slipped her hand into his and smiled at him.

Harold told her solemnly that he had learnt it at his literature class down at the coal face.

They were heading for the race course, a favourite destination for many of the miners and their families. Set on the edge of Wath on the verge of open countryside, it looked down over the Dearne Valley and the air was almost clean when the wind was in the right direction.

Herbert and Billy were keen to start eating the food the moment they found a comfortable place to sit. Ada gave them a jam sandwich each to stave off starvation, which they both insisted they were suffering from, and turned them loose with the football.

They spread their blanket on the springy turf with a grassy bank behind them to lean on. Tall hawthorn bushes overhung and protected them from the wind.

Both babies were sound asleep. Ada took off her hat and coat before sitting down thankfully, and leaned against the bank with a sigh of content.

Harold lay down with his hands behind his head and closed his eyes, then turning towards her, he gently touched her cheek and said, "Does tha remember the last time we sat on grass like this?"

Before she had time to reply, Herbert was at their side, wanting his father to play football with them. Reluctantly he rose. "Thought that resting lark was too good to be true," he said, "ah'll be back in a minute luv, ah'll just av to go and show these two how to play footie."

As they walked home in the late afternoon, with all the food eaten and the water drunk, Herbert said it had been the best day of his life and added, "Thanks Dad and Mam," and Ada realised with a happy shock that he had just called her Mam for the first time.

"That's ok son, we'll do it again soon, maybe go to Huber Stand next time," and she ruffled his hair before he charged off after Billy.

Sarah soon started whimpering that she was tired and Harold hoisted her on to his shoulders and began to run with her. Grabbing hold of his hair she giggled so much that she was soon shouting that she wanted to wee, and Harold hurridly replaced her on the ground, declaring he didn't want pee down his neck, thank you very much.

Ada took her behind a tree to relieve herself while her brothers shouted that they could see her. Sarah, ever shy, cried, "They can't see me, can they Mam?"

"No of course they can't luv, take no notice, they're just teasing," replied Ada, marvelling again at how soon the children had fallen into the habit of calling her Mam, and suddenly wondered where Winn was at this moment and if she was missing them. A cold shiver went through her as she pictured Winn turning up at the door and announcing that she was coming back.

When she relayed her fears to Harold, he put his arm on her shoulders as she pushed the pram and squeezed her to him. "Stop worrying lass, it's not goin' to happen, ah won't let it, she gone and that's it," and he kissed her ear. Billy saw them, but pretended he hadn't, and ran off with his face all pink to spread the news to Edith.

It was as they were walking back into the yard that they noticed the local bobby's bike propped against the wall. There was no mistaking it. No one else had a bike as big as that. Harold said he was probably at Shaw's, the family who lived next door but one, and always seemed to be running into trouble with the law.But to his surprise the constable was knocking on their door.

"Ah, there tha is Harold, just the man ah've been looking for," he boomed, "ah need a word in private."

Ada looked at them both anxiously as she produced the key from the bottom of her bag, but she could see that Harold was as mystified as herself.

Once inside, a quick flick of their father's head indicated to the children that they were to go upstairs, where they congregated silently on the landing as usual, trying to hear what was being said.

The constable sat on the straight backed chair near the table. "Ah think tha should sit down Harold, ah av sum bad news. Nah, ah av to ask thee first. Is Winifred Corker your wife?"

"Aye, tha knows she is," said Harold nodding.

"Well, ah av to ask thee official like, tha knows how it is. The thing is Harold, ah av to tell thee, she's dead!"

CHAPTER 13

PC Jim Smith looked from Harold to Ada, trying to gauge their reaction. Being the local bobby meant he was well acquainted with their situation, but he kept quiet and noted that that their faces registered nothing except profound shock.

He went on to explain the circumstances of Winn's tragic death. As they knew, she had gone to be housekeeper to an old man in Conisborough. The night before last she had gone to bed early, leaving the old man sitting by the fire enjoying a cigarette and a glass of beer.

It appeared he had fallen asleep, and the cigarette had slipped from his fingers and set fire to the newspaper that he had been reading, and that, in turn, had set fire to the hearth rug. It had taken no time at all for the whole room to become alight and eventually the entire house was gutted.

Winn was found in her bed, curled up in a sleeping position. The smoke had drifted through the loose-fitting floor boards, a silent deadly killer that had stolen her life away even before the flames reached the bedroom.

The old man was found in the corner of the room near the door, as if he had been overcome by the smoke as he tried to escape. They were both burned beyond recognition, and there would be no identification required, the policeman informed Harold, and he left, handing him a death certificate as he went, glad to be leaving.

Bearing news of a death to a relative was one of the aspects of the job that he hated, but there are some cases, he thought, when it could be considered a blessing in disguise for some of the people involved, although it wouldn't do to voice that thought to anyone.

As he slipped his cycle clips around the bottom of his trousers, he muttered under his breath, "Thank God I don't have the job of breaking the news to Winn's children."

Back in the house, Herbert was the first one to venture downstairs and he stood by Harold's chair, white faced and shaking. His brother and sisters were close behind him, waiting silently. Sarah looked around at everyone, thumb in her mouth and her eyes huge in her pale face.

Harold looked across at Ada and then back to Herbert. "Ah expect you all heard what the bobby said?"

Herbert nodded, and Billy prodded him from behind. "What we goin' to do Dad?"

Harold put his arm round his shoulders. "We'll just av to manage best way we can son, same as we av been doing since she left. Ada's here nah. She'll look after you kids while ah'm at work. Won't tha luv?"He looked across at her.

Ada felt moved to tears for the children, "Of course ah will. We'll manage. You av a good cry if you want."

But Herbert's lip came out, a sign they all recognised, and he said brusquely, "Ah'm not goin' to cry. She went away. So she weren't bothered about us." Wiping his nose on his sleeve, he brushed a tear away. Turning to Billy he added, "Come on, we've got some sticks to chop for t'fires."

The babies chose that moment to demand their feeds, and as Ada lifted them out of the pram she reflected on the saying that life goes on, and thought how very true it was.

News of Winn's death spread fast, and reactions among neighbours and friends were mixed.

To some, overnight, she became almost saint-like, a loving mother who could do no wrong, while others were more realistic and remembered that she had left her children. But all were agreed that it was sad and tragic. "As if," added one old lady, "there's not been enough loss of life over the last four years."

Harold borrowed a suit and shoes for Winn's funeral. The shoes were half a size too small and the suit trousers too long. Ada wanted him to buy new clothes but he was adamant that he would not lay the money out on something that he would probably not wear again for years.

Harold and Ada went shopping and managed to get a complete set of clothing for all the children from the second hand stall on Mexborough market. The clothes were all as good as new and a size too big but Harold said they would grow into them. He was dreading the funeral and several times said he would not go but Ada insisted he must for the sake of his children.

It was with great relief that Ada waved them off on the day of the funeral, glad they were all dressed decently, and thankful that it would soon be over. When she was alone she took the two babies to her father's house, intending to make him some breakfast, but he insisted she sat down and he made her a large mug of tea.

"There lass, tha looks as if tha needs that, sit down, before tha falls down."

Putting Ernest and Stanley on the sofa, one at each end, Ada sat at the table and sipped the hot tea gratefully. "That's nice Dad, you always did make a good cup of tea."

William looked at her. "How is it all going lass? Ah'm really worried about thee. That's goin' to crack up before long. Them sheets on t'line av got more colour than thee."

Ada sighed, "Well ah don't get much sleep, wi these two," and she indicated the babies on the sofa. "It'll get easier when they start sleeping through t'night. Our Stan's the least trouble, after his feed at eleven he usually sleeps till 6, but Ernest keeps waking every other hour." She yawned and rubbed her eyes. "It's so peaceful in here Dad, ah could fall asleep right now."

"Well, what about ah put yon two in t'pram an tek em for a walk, and thee av a lay down on t'sofa for an hour?"

"What's folk gonna say when they see thee pushin' a pram Dad?"

"Since when did ah bother about what folks say Ada? Ah've pushed a pram before tha knows," and with Ernest and Stanley tucked into the pram William set off, intending to walk as far as Swinton. The motion of the pram soon had them asleep and William walked along enjoying the fine weather and thinking of his daughter.

146

There was no denying, sad as it was, that Winn's death had changed things and left Harold free to marry, but it would be a hard life for Ada, taking on a ready-made family, and no doubt there would be plenty more children to come. But one step at a time he thought, with the wisdom of age. All he could do was to help as much as he could.

On the way back he stopped at Farthing's shop and bought some mint humbugs for himself and a Woman's Weekly magazine for Ada, and then four pennyworth of mixed sweets for the children. Poor souls would need a little something to cheer them up, he thought, after attending their mother's funeral.

CHAPTER 14

When William left pushing the pram, Ada had closed her eyes and breathed in the peace and quiet of the familiar room, and felt the calm wash over her. She dozed for a few moments, but, startled wide awake by the chiming of the clock, sat up and drank the rest of the tea that had now gone cold. Looking around she noticed the dust on the hearth and the sideboard and unable to rest while it stared her in the face she rose and tackled the house cleaning.

By the time William returned, Ada had the house looking clean and fresh again and in spite of not having rested she felt better, and able to cope again.

William noted the freshly polished room and sat in his chair with a sigh of content. Smiling at Ada he said, "Ah've ad a thought luv, Stanley can start and stay with me at the weekends as soon as he's weaned, that'll make things a bit easier for thee. It's not much ah know, but every little helps," and added with a cheeky grin, "as the old woman said when she piddled in the sea."

Ada laughed, "It's a long time since ah heard you say that Dad."

He took hold of her hand. "That's more like it, it's a long time since ah've seen thee laugh. It'll all get a lot easier, you'll see. It's been a bad time but tha'll manage, thee and Harold. He's a damn good worker, ah'll gi im that. Ah've noticed im comin' home from work, he looks fair knackered, but he dunt give in does he?"

"No Dad, he doesn't. It'll be a lot easier when he gets set on at Manvers. And t'kids are good, it's just tekin' a bit of gerrin' used to, avin' so many to cope wi all at once."

"Aye ah know lass, life's not easy." He got up and lifted Stanley out of the pram, and cuddled him, murmuring, "He's a grand little lad."

148

As if he understood, Ernest began to whimper and William took hold of his tiny baby hand as if he was shaking it and said, "Aye you an all Ernest, you're a grand little lad, but sad to say, tha'll never be as good lookin' as ar Stanley."

Ada shook her head at him and smiled at the comparison of Ernest's tiny unblemished hand compared to her father's rough gnarled, work-worn one.

"Come on, ah'd better get these two back home and fed. Harold will be back with the kids shortly and I've got a bad feeling that things will not have gone well at the funeral. You know what his mother-in-law's like."

William nodded sadly and opened the door for her.

Ada went quickly across the yard, relieved that there was no one about. She really didn't want to discuss the funeral with any of the gossips who were usually stood about the yard with arms folded, eyes darting everywhere, ready to scandalise about the slightest thing.

Then she realised that they had probably gone to the funeral themselves. Not because they had held Winn in any regard, it would simply be sensation seeking, something they could talk about until another event occurred that was more interesting.

As she bounced the pram over the step into the house, Ernest began chortling, showing his new front tooth that had just come through and Ada bounced the pram even more, enjoying his laughter. Stanley added to the hilarity, smiling a big gummy smile and kicking his legs.

Taking advantage that they had temporarily forgotten that it was feed time, Ada pushed sticks into the almost dying fire and piled coal on top. Giving the pram another bounce as she went past bought her a few more minutes, and she stabbed six large potatoes with a fork and arranged them in the bottom of the oven to roast. Those, together with a large dish of mushy peas and a ham shank was one of their favourite teas, and as Ada spread the cloth on the table and warmed the plates she thought as how they could all do with a bit of spoiling today.

The food-demanding chorus soon began again and Ada lifted Ernest out, first exclaiming as she did so at the sight of the leaking nappy, "Pooh, Ernest Corker, you're a little stinker. What are you?"

Receiving only a gurgle in reply, Ada laid him on a towel and quickly whipped off the offending nappy and cleaned him up.

"There you are," she said as she fastened the pin on the fresh clean nappy and placed him on the sofa. She stopped his hungry cries with his bottle and propped it carefully on a cushion while she turned her attention to Stanley.

He was in a similar state to his stepbrother and his mother opened the door to let in some fresh air, ignoring the cold wind that blew in and sent wafts of smoke puffing out into the room. "I reckon it smells better than the pong that you two have made," she told them.

As she nursed Stanley she opened the magazine that William had brought her and it was as she was admiring the knitting patterns when Martha knocked on the door and walked in calling, "You at home Ada?"

"Come in Martha, it's feeding time at the zoo again."

Laughing, Martha sat beside her and picked Ernest up to cuddle him and finish feeding him.

"I don't really like having to feed him like that, he misses out on his cuddles, but there's not much option when they both need feeding at once," explained Ada to her friend.

"Ah think you are doing marvellous. You know ah will help if ah can. Hey that looks nice, it'd suit you." Martha pointed out a pattern for a dress and jacket. It was in the latest style, a long, slender, plain dress reaching the ankles, with a high neck, and over it a shorter length v-necked coat in the same fabric, fastened with many dark shiny buttons and roulette loops. The model was also wearing a delicate brooch pinned to the shoulder and a matching cloche hat.

"Oh, that's lovely Martha. Ah'd never get the chance to wear it though, and I couldn't afford the fabric even if I could make it." Ada gave a sigh, then cheering up said, "But look, I've got Harold, these two, and the rest of the tribe, that's better than a posh outfit any day. I'd rather get something for them."

Martha agreed and turning to the knitting patterns said she would use them to make jackets for the two babies.

Ada caught her sad look and took her hand. Martha had been her best friend ever since they had moved into Packmans Row. When she had first known her, Martha had been walking out with a young man from the next street.

They had been planning to be married at the end of 1916 and Martha had adored him. He was a gentle, quiet spoken sort of man, totally unsuited to army life, but he felt it was his duty to go, and not being in a reserved occupation he had decided to join before he was conscripted. James had given Martha an engagement ring the night before he left for France. She never saw him again. He was killed almost as soon as he arrived in the trenches.

Martha was beside herself with grief and it took her a long time to come to terms with it. She swore she would never marry anyone else and had devoted her time and energy to looking after her father who was a widower. Ada and Martha had helped each other through the bad times and had developed a deep and lasting friendship.

Now, as they looked at the patterns together, Harold returned followed by the children. Martha bid a hasty goodbye and left. She always knew when to make herself scarce, thought Ada.

Harold's face was white and grim, his lips tight with tension. Edith and Sarah had been crying and Ada feared there had been trouble, but she said nothing until she had placed a mug of tea in front of Harold. Slowly she could see him relax as he sat back in his chair and closed his eyes. He let out a huge gust of breath and said quietly, "My God Ada, I'm glad that's over. What an ordeal."

"What happened luv?"

"Well, t'service in t'church went quiet enough, an t'burial were t'same, then as t'vicar said the last word, she started. Winn's muther ah mean. Started shouting across t'grave at us, said ah'd killed er daughter, then t'vicar had to stop her throwing clods of muck at me and t'kids. What an exhibition. Ah wouldn't mind, but she couldn't get rid o Winn fast enough when she were young. They never got on." He stopped for a while, unable to speak. Then he continued. "And then, tha'll niver believe it, we were just goin' to set off home, and she come to me and said Herbert should go an live wi her. Ah didn't trust mesen to answer her. Tha knows why she wants im. She's realised that Herbert's twelve nah, an it'll not be long till he's workin'. Cheeky bugger. She thinks she'll av a bloody meal ticket, the ugly auld cow. She can bugger off. She didn't want im when he were a bairn, ah'm damn sure she's not gerrin' er claws into him nah."

Ada put her arm round him. "Ah shud think not, ah don't know how she's got the nerve. She won't av any rights to claim him will she?"

"She'd better not bloody try." Harold slammed his fist down on to the chair arm. "Ah'll see her in hell first, and them bullying sons of hers. Herbert's stopping ere wi us, an that's all there is to it."

Ada hoped that would be the end of it, but two days later Harold arrived home from work looking tense and angry. It wasn't until he had washed his face that she could see the swelling at the side of his head. Gently she touched it with the cool damp flannel, and asked if he had done it at work.

He didn't reply for a moment, then said, "Ah ad a bit of a set to wi Winn's brothers, but don't worry, it won't happen again, ah've sorted it out."

That was all he would say and he began to get agitated when Ada pressed him for more information.

"That's enough Ada. Ah don't want to talk about it just nah, get me a mug o tea will tha? Ah think ah'll go an av a lay down before ah av me dinner." And she had to be satisfied with that, but knew sooner or later it would all come out.

She had to wait until the following Saturday when Harold came back from the pub with a few pints inside him that had loosened his tongue, and then he told her all the details.

Apparently he had been walking home after his shift. He had got the bus as far as Manvers, and had hoped to catch a connecting tram to take him into the centre of Wath but had just missed it, so had decided to walk. As he passed an alley way at the far side of the canal, Winn's brothers had accosted him, and said they would be calling to collect Herbert at the weekend. "Me mother wants him livin'wi us, he's er grandson, see that he's ready on Saturday."

Harold had replied, "Tha knows what thee mother can do, an yor two an all. Herbert's stopping where he is. That's what he wants. Thee mother didn't want him when he were little, she's not gerrin' im nah, so tha can bugger off, pair on ya."

The eldest brother had made a grab for Harold but he was expecting it. Harold had stepped back smartly and delivered a hard kick to his shins with his steel toe capped boot. "It alus stops em does that Ada, as long as tha can gerrin' first." Harold's speech was a little slurred due to the effects of the Barnsley bitter he had drunk, but he knew exactly what he was saying and didn't exaggerate.

"Then t'uther one rushed me an caught me a blow ere," and Harold rubbed the bruise at the side of his head. "Ah saw stars for a minute, but as he came back for another go, ah giv im one right above his eye, that put im on t'floor.Ah bet he's gor a right shiner nah. That were enough for em, they turned and went. They thought ah was still that young eighteen year old that they could push around, like ah was when ah married Winn. They'll not be back."

Ada looked doubtful, but Harold told her that as they left they were arguing with each other, the oldest one shouting, "Let him keep the little bastard and welcome," and added that his mother could fight her own battles in future.

"Tha can stop worrying lass, we'll not hear any more from them."

And time proved Harold right. They heard no more from Winn's mother, or her sons, much to Ada's relief.

CHAPTER 15

Two months later with the children settled down, Harold and Ada decided they would get married as soon as possible.

Ada felt deeply sad at Winn's death and the circumstances of it, but there was no denying the joy in her heart that Harold was now free to marry her.

They chose the fourteenth of July for their wedding, which would take place at Doncaster registry office. Ada constantly worried that she would become pregnant again before their marriage. She desperately wanted the respectability of being married when she next conceived and carried a child, and she continued suckling Stanley for as long as possible, knowing that it sometimes prevented conception.

They decided that their wedding was to be a very quiet, private affair, with only their witnesses as guests. It was this decision that caused Ada problems with the children. As soon as Edith and Sarah heard of the wedding they pictured themselves wearing frilly bridesmaids' dresses and carrying flowers. The boys had no interest in the actual wedding but Billy saw it as a chance to have a day away from school.

When it was made clear to them that they would not be present at the wedding, there were tears from the girls who saw their dreams of being bridesmaids dashed. The boys went into a sulk and Billy, for the first time, became awkward and offensive.

It caught Ada when she was feeling especially tired and stressed and when Billy refused to do his chores and disappeared to play football, Ada snapped. Her anger and agitation turned to tears, and picking up Stanley she went to her father's house and closing the door firmly behind her, lay down on the old sofa and gave way to her feelings.

She never did find out what Harold had said after she left, but within an hour the children appeared at the door with a bunch of flowers and apologies. Ada noticed a slap mark on Billy's leg and assumed that that accounted for his now subdued demeanour, and took note that it didn't take long for Harold to restore order in the house.

Ada decided she would wear the same outfit that she had worn when she was a bridesmaid for Lizzie, but Martha put new trimmings on the hat for her and John promised to make her a corsage and a small bouquet with flowers from his own garden.

Harold spent the remains of the money from the sovereign he had found on a new suit. He had told Ada he would borrow his mate's suit again but she was adamant that he must have a one of his own, so together they visited the tailor in Mexborough and chose a navy blue worsted fabric with a faint grey stripe. Within two weeks the tailor had made him a three piece suit that fitted him perfectly.

His father had given him his silver pocket watch and chain to wear for his wedding and told him he could keep it. Harold was so touched by the gift that he took it out of its box again and again, each time telling Ada that he couldn't believe his father had given it to him.

"And what does tha think Ada, he's asked me if he can come to t'wedding, and be a witness. He's that pleased we're gerrin' married. Ah've niver seen im so fussy about owt before."

"That's a good idea," replied Ada, as she scrubbed away at a pile of washing in the sink. "We could ask my Dad to be the other witness. Two Williams standing by us, that sounds just right." and she squealed as Harold grabbed her round the waist and rubbed the back of her neck with his stubbly chin. Reaching back with her wet hands she rubbed soap on his face and they collapsed laughing on to the old chair.

Early on the morning of the fourteenth of July, Rose arrived to collect the babies. Ada had been up even earlier, prepared food for them and expressed milk for Stanley. Rose kissed her and wished her the best of luck as she left with the pram loaded with Ernest, Stanley and piles of baby requirements. "Ah'm only tekin' em for today Ada. Ah'm not adoptin' em," she said with a smile, nodding at the amount of food and nappies in the pram. "Av a wonderful day luv, ah'll be thinking of you, don't worry about these two, they'll be no trouble."

Secretly though she viewed the day with trepidation. Coping with two babies plus her own infant was not a prospect she relished.

'Thank God it's only for one day,' she thought as she trundled the heavy pram through the empty early morning streets.

Ada's aunt had volunteered to come and supervise the older children for the day so she was able to devote an hour to getting herself ready for her wedding day.

Her outfit hung on the door of the wardrobe and her thoughts turned to the last time it had been hung up waiting to be worn. At that time she could never have envisaged that she would one day be wearing the clothes for her own wedding, and she remembered Winn, and how it had taken her tragic death for this to be possible.

Today it was Harold's suit that hung alongside her outfit, not Lizzie's, and it gave Ada a strange deja vu feeling.

They were all at the railway station by ten o'clock, feeling a little self conscious in their wedding finery. Harold looked young and handsome in his suit, with the silver watch chain clearly visible on the waistcoat, and a white carnation on his lapel.

Ada's outfit suited her even better this time than when she wore it for Lizzie's wedding. Happiness shone from her as she stood with her arm through Harold's.

William Dale had just met William Corker for the first time and as they warmly shook hands it was obvious they both felt great pride that they were about to witness the marriage of this young couple who meant so much to each other.

The ceremony seemed all too brief and before they knew it they were outside again, standing, all four of them, on the steps of the registry office, looking up and down the busy street, feeling conspicuous but proud in their wedding outfits.

"Well," began Ada's father, "we're going for some dinner now, that's right in't it William?" and he bent forward to look past the newlyweds to the other William.

"Aye, that's right. Come on, we've gorra couple of hours till t'train's due," and with the two fathers leading the way they walked around the corner.

For a moment Ada thought they were heading for the Danum Hotel, and gave a silent sigh of relief as they walked past the impressive steps and the brass plated doors. She knew there was no way on earth that they could afford their prices.

The haughty looking commissionaire in his royal blue uniform gave them just the briefest of nods as they were passing and then looked straight through them at the Rolls Royce that was gliding to a stop beside him.

Of course, Ada couldn't resist turning around to see the passengers of the limousine, and caught sight of the rather portly woman being handed out by the livered chauffer.

She was dressed in a tight fitting skirt and long jacket, obviously the height of fashion, and completing her outfit she wore a fox fur thrown casually around her shoulders. Ada gave a shudder of revulsion at the sight of it. The whole skin of the animal had been used with the head and tail left on. A spring clip was fixed to the underside of the fox's pretty pointed face, and glass eyes inserted into its eye sockets.

It lay around the woman's shoulders with its mouth holding its own tail, and the sad glass eyes seeming to follow people passing by.

In spite of the woman's beautiful clothes and the wafts of expensive perfume drifting across from her, Ada looked at her with disgust written on her face. The woman caught the look, and tossed her head as she walked the few yards across the pavement holding on to the arm of her escort.

Harold's father was also affected by the sight of the couple and growled in his quiet throaty voice that was so similar to his son's.

"Look at him," he said, referring to the commissionaire. "Toadying to them rich bastards.Living the high life on the sweat of the working man. You wait, there'll be some changes when the unions get some strength."

Harold shushed his father and calmed him a little, but then further enraged him by asking if he knew who the couple were.

"Course ah bloody know who they are. Yon big headed bugger owns four pits, including Denaby Main, where tha sweats thee guts out me son. Thee think about him enjoyin' hisen, when tha's down there riskin' thee life for a pittance."

William Dale nodded in agreement, but tried to lighten the atmosphere as they approached Parkinson's café, with its large bow fronted windows that were filled with fresh baked confectionaries and large piles of the famous Parkinson's butterscotch.

As they mounted the stone steps and went through the open door, the delicious smell of newly baked bread met them, and they stopped, unsure where they should sit in the large room filled with circular tables. The head waitress hurried forward to greet them and Ada's father, acting as if he was well used to eating out at restaurants, asked for a table for four, adding, "Near the window if you please."

Smiling at Ada and Harold, she ushered them to a large table close up to one of the bow windows.From there they could see the busy traffic of Frenchgate and the famous clock corner that was the centre of Doncaster.

As they seated themselves the waitress returned with the menus bound in dark green leather and asked if they had been to a wedding.

Harold charmed her with a flash of his blue eyes and replied that, yes indeed they had! Their own!

She blushed under Harold's gaze and murmured her congratulations, leaving them to decide on the food, while she went to inform the manager of their newlywed customers. In no time at all he appeared at their table and presented them with complimentary boxes of butterscotch. Harold thanked him and Ada added that the children at home would enjoy them.

The idea of newlyweds with children seemed to render the man speechless and he just nodded as he retreated.

Anxious as always about money Ada scanned the menu and chose the cheapest. As it happened it was also one of her favourites, steak pie and mashed potatoes with mushy peas! Four portions were ordered and duly arrived, the smell trying to outdo the tempting appearance of the food. Steaming slabs of golden pastry with dark squares of beef peeping from underneath and the rich gravy escaping around it. Creamy mashed potatoes topped with a round of butter and green mushy peas completed the dish.

The men made short work of theirs, finishing long before Ada was even half way through. Cups of tea completed the meal, then William called for the bill. He flinched as he saw the total and dug deep into his pocket, thinking ruefully as he did so that it would take the rest of his meagre savings. Much to his relief, Harold's father took a look at the bill and slid half the amount discreetly onto the table, holding up his hand in a sign that meant he would not accept a refusal.

There was still half an hour until the train was due, and they walked slowly up Frenchgate, admiring the imposing Guild Hall that faced on to the busy street.

An hour and a half later they were back in Wath, walking through the main street hand in hand, delighting in being married at last.

A strange feeling came over Ada as they neared home, a sense of foreboding that threatened to burst her bubble of happiness. As they walked into the yard it was clear to her that there was something wrong. As she looked around she could see all of Billy's clothes hung dripping on the washing line and his boots standing on the windowsill, turned upside down, exposing the roughly mended soles, with the rows of metal studs hammered into the toes and heels in an effort to protect the leather.

Pools of water in the small inner yard near the drain betrayed the fact that the bath had recently been emptied, and there it was, propped against the house wall and the corner of the fence that divided one house from the next.

The house inside was clean and tidy, everything in order apart from a damp patch on the hearth rug where the bath had recently been.

Ada took off her coat, turned it inside out and hung it on the back of the chair. Her breasts were heavy with unused milk and a small damp patch was appearing on the front of her dress. Taking a handkerchief from her pocket she pushed it down inside her underwear, over the offending nipple and headed for the stairs.

Harold seemed oblivious to all the signs that something was amiss, and laying his jacket over Ada's, he eased the broad elastic braces from his shoulders, and sank into his wooden armchair with a sigh of content.

His contentment, however, was short lived as Ada's aunt came down the stairs, almost colliding with her niece. Her face was flushed crimson and she looked close to tears. Her normally neat hair had escaped its pins and hung in straight grey strands around her ears.

Ada led her to a chair, and sensing that tea would be needed, pushed the kettle further on to the glowing fire,

"What's up Aunty?" she asked placing her hand over hers.

"It's that Billy," she said, her voice croaky. "T'bobby brought him home an hour ago. Wringing wet through he was. Silly little bugger nearly gorr hisen killed. Him and his daft mate ad been jumpin' on t'barges. Daring each other ah expect. Tha knows what lads are, but Billy slipped an fell in t'canal. He were lucky he didn't get crushed. T'bobby were just passing and dragged im out. Gave im a clip round t'earhole an brought im home. Eee, it's put me about summat terrible Ada. Ah gorr im in t'bath, and ah've sent im to bed." She put her hand on her forehead. "Ah'm off home nah, Ada, ah'm all in."

Refusing offers of tea, she jammed her hat firmly on her head, tucked in the loose hair and walked out, pulling on her coat as she went through the door. Ada had to run after her with the shopping bag that she had left on the table, and assured her again how sorry she was for the upset, but her aunt brushed aside the apologies and stamped away up the street, muttering to herself as she went.

Back in the house, Harold was boiling up with anger and marched up the stairs to sort out his wayward son. As Ada made the tea she could hear him shouting at Billy, his words hammered home with the sound of slaps on bare flesh.

"How many times?" Slap. "As tha been telled." Slap. "To stay away." Slap. "From the bloody canal." Slap. "Tha can stay there nah." Slap. "An there's no tea for thee." Slap, slap.

Ada had poured out a mug of tea by the time her new husband came back downstairs, but Harold was looking for something stronger. He had changed into his everyday clothes and was feeling in his pockets for beer money. Producing only a couple of pennies, he looked at them miserably.

"As tha gorr any money Ada? Ah need a drink."

Ada tipped up her purse onto the table. There was little enough there, barely sufficient to last till payday.

Picking up a shilling, Harold slipped it into his pocket. "That'll do luv, ah'll see thee later," and he left, his good humour restored by the thought of a pint and a natter with his mates down at the pub.

Rose parked the big old pram outside, lodging a brick under the front wheel to prevent it rolling backwards. Both babies were fast asleep. They had been restless and irritable on the walk back to Packmans Row, but Rose had bounced the pram so hard they had finally given up their half hearted grumbling and gone to sleep.

She opened the back door quietly and caught Ada unawares, sitting by the table, staring ruefully at her purse and the few coppers spread out around it.

Taking in the situation at a glance, Rose produced a folded ten shilling note from inside her brassiere, pushed it into Ada's purse, and kissed her sister, saying as she did so, "That's a wedding present luv, get what tha likes wi it." Picking up the teapot she poured herself a cup of tea.

Ada smiled and nodded her thanks, not trusting herself to speak for the lump in her throat.

Herbert crept cautiously into the house, knowing that Billy had been in trouble, and wore his best, 'It's nothing to do with me, I'm not involved,' expression. His relief was obvious when he realised that his father was not at home.

Edith and Sarah returned from Martha's, where they had spent the last hour helping her to wind skeins of wool into balls, ready to knit her latest project. The three children set about their chores, eagerly demonstrating how good and perfect they were in comparison to their naughty brother upstairs.

CHAPTER 16

To an outsider, it may have appeared that little had changed in Harold and Ada's lives, but that thin gold band on Ada's finger had given them respectability and turned them into a proper family.

To be addressed as Mrs Corker never failed to thrill her and fill her with a sense of security. But she quickly learned not to put all her housekeeping money in her purse at once, and squirreled away a portion for the latter part of the week, when Harold would have run out of beer money and likely to ask her if she had anything to spare for a pint. She grew more canny as the months passed and would answer, "Sorry luv, it's all gone on food."

At seven months old Stanley was weaned. At nine months he pulled himself to his feet and took his first steps, while Ernest still shuffled about on his bottom.

Despite his attempts to treat the two as equals, William couldn't hide his pride that Stanley, as the younger of the two, was the first to walk, and he took him to see Beauty in her stable, delighting when he showed no fear of the horse as he reached to gently stroke her neck.

When William lifted him on to her back, Stanley clutched her mane, and laid his face on the horse, feeling her silky fur on his lips. Soon he was demanding "Booty, Booty," every time he set eyes on his grandfather.

At two years of age, Stanley and Ernest were taken out of their baby dresses that were then the usual attire for all infants, male or female.

Ada shed sentimental tears as their hair was cut for the first time, and retrieved some of the golden curls to keep in her wooden box of memories.

Dressed in trousers, Ernest and Stanley instantly seemed to turn into boys, and developed a sort of love/hate relationship. They would play happily for hours, then for the most trivial of reasons turn on each other, fighting and shouting, rolling about on the floor and usually ending up under the table, a ball of flailing arms and legs.

Ada would pick up whoever was on top by their collars, administer sharp slaps to both their legs, and send them to bed, where they became friends again as they nursed their stinging legs.

Gradually, Stanley began to spend more and more time with his grandfather. As soon as William arrived home from work, he would find Stanley almost treading on his heels as he unlocked the door. Once inside, he would curl up on the couch, having first unceremoniously turfed off Monty, who would stand looking back at him with his tail swishing in anger at being disturbed. Of course, Stanley was totally unimpressed with the cat's anger and would point to the door saying, "Cat, go."

Monty had persistently refused to live with Ada in her new noisy home and preferred a more peaceful existence in William's house, considering it his own private domain. But when Stanley arrived he made it clear to the cat that it now took second place, and demoted it to a rug in the corner, under the sideboard.

The first time that Stanley fell asleep on the hard leather couch, his grandfather carried him upstairs to Ada's old bed, took off his boots and tucked him in. When it became a regular occurrence, William said he might as well stay with him every night, and relieve some of the strain on Ada. And so Stanley took up regular residence with his grandfather, keeping him entertained with his questions and statements.

Every weekday morning as William left for work, Stanley, all washed and dressed, would arrive at his mother's door to play and fight with Ernest for an hour or so, then grace Martha or one of the other neighbours with his presence, just biding his time until his grandfather returned from work, when he would pester him to go and feed 'Booty'.

Since Ada had found herself with a ready-made family, Rose had taken over as William's housekeeper, and came every day to clean the house and prepare him an evening meal.

Rose's daughter Hiney became more like a big sister than a cousin to Stanley, and being a full two years older than him took it upon herself to teach him all she knew.

It was not long before Ernest thought to himself that he would like to live with William too. He came knocking at the door one evening with his clothes tucked under his arm and announced his intention of moving in.

The dismay on Stanley's face at the thought of sharing his grandfather soon turned to jubilation when his half brother was taken gently but firmly back home, and Stanley stood at the window pulling faces at Ernest as he was led away.

William made it clear to Harold that although he was happy to look after Stanley, he couldn't possibly manage two boys. A few sharp slaps stung poor Ernest's legs and he retreated upstairs to sulk and plot his revenge.

As always, Lizzie wrote every Thursday, telling Ada all about Doll and their lives in Carlton. Every few months Ada took Stanley and made the journey to see her sister and daughter, usually with money her father had saved for her.

True to her word, Ada became aunt to Doll but couldn't resist cuddling her as much as possible. Her secret daughter was growing into a pretty girl with loving affectionate ways.

While Ada and Lizzie caught up with family news, the two children spent their time running about the fields, playing with the farm dogs and watching the magnificent shire horses working. The moment that Stanley waited for was to see the horses at the end of their working day when they were released into the rich meadow, and galloped about in a group, racing each other and making the ground shake as they pounded past the gate where Stanley and Doll stood watching. Acting more like young foals than sensible adult horses, they larked about kicking up their heels and chasing each other. The games usually ended with them rolling on their backs, their massive feet waving in the air.

Doll said that if they rolled right over it meant there would be fine weather the next day. Stanley listened, absorbing the knowledge, and resolved to question his grandfather about it as soon as he got home.

The visits had to stop when Ada became pregnant again, and grew pale and despondent as she endured the first few months of sickness, but this time at least she was pregnant within the safety and respectability of marriage, and Harold was able to boast to his mates that his wife was 'in the family way'.

Their baby was born on the second anniversary of their wedding. A strong healthy brown eyed girl, the image of Ada, with a pretty, pointed face and already lots of dark hair.

Harold had hoped for a son, and disappointment showed in his face as he was told he had a new daughter. The midwife, trying to make him feel better, quoted the old saying, "A son is a son till he takes him a wife, but a daughter is a daughter for all of your life."

Harold gave a thin smile, squared his shoulders and replied, "Aye well, maybe next time."

Ada, overhearing the remark, and still suffering the after effects of giving birth, bestowed on Harold a look that showed all her feelings, then slid down the bed and turned her back on him.

Realising that he had upset his wife, Harold tried his best to make amends, stroking her hair and whispering to her so that the midwife was unable to hear him. "Sorry luv, ah didn't mean owt wrong, come on, she's a lovely babby, you name her eh? Whatever you choose its ok. Come on luv, give us a kiss. Tha knows ah luv thee."

Reluctantly Ada turned to face him, gave him a watery smile and a big sigh. "Just give us a chance to ger over this one, before tha starts plotting t'next one Harold Corker, tha big lump. Tha must av been at end of t'queue were they were handin' tact out."

"Aye ah think tha's right lass, what's tha going to call her then?"

With no hesitation, Ada informed him that their new baby would be christened Elizabeth, after her sister Lizzie, but would be known as Betty.

Nodding his head in agreement, Harold patted her hand and then informed her he was just going for a pint to celebrate.

It was less than two years later that Harold got his wish, when Ada gave birth to a fine healthy son who was named after his father. There was much celebrating that night down at the Red Lion. As Ada lay on her bed recovering from the birth, she felt more than a little resentful at the thought of the cost of the beer being swilled down by Harold's mates, much of it paid for by her husband, as he stood several rounds in celebration of having another son. But Ada knew only too well that it was customary, and did her best to hide her feelings and forget about all the much needed food and clothing she could have bought with the money.

'Men will be men,' she thought, but resolved to try and make it a long time before she became pregnant again.

With the birth of baby Harold, Stanley found himself pushed further and further out of the circle of his family. Much as Ada loved him, she had so little time or energy left to give any extra to her eldest son, and so Stanley had to be satisfied with an odd word and quick cuddle now and then.

His father was more than happy to let him reside with William and paid him little attention. But Stanley was happy enough living with his grandfather, and spent every possible moment with him.

The tiny house in Packmans Row was now badly overcrowded. The new baby slept in the bottom drawer of the wardrobe, while Betty, as a toddler, had the old cot at the side of her parent's bed.

Herbert, Billy and Ernest shared the second bedroom, while Edith and Sarah slept in a makeshift room in the windowless attic.

Stanley's sleeping arrangements by comparison were almost palatial, as he had a whole bedroom to himself in his grandfather's house.

In 1922, Harold at last started work at Manvers Main, and no longer had to make the long journey to Denaby every day.

Soon after he began work there, he came home practically bursting with news. Panting and out of breath, he dumped his snap tin and dudley on the floor, picked Ada up and whirled her round till she was dizzy.

"What does tha think ah've just heard lass?" Without waiting for her to reply he continued. "They're building loads o new houses up near t'racecourse just for us colliers. Ah've put ar name down for one. Just think Ada, a new house, wi a garden."

Ada looked doubtful. "Is tha sure? It's news to me."

"It's right lass, it's been kept quiet, but they've telled us all today at a meeting, all official. Ah'll tell thee what Ada, ah were at front o t'queue to put me name down. Do ya think ah did right luv?"

"Of course tha did. Oh Harold, ah can hardly believe it. Just think, a new house! Wait till ah tell me Dad."

Work began on the large housing estate within three months, causing much excitement among the mining community and bringing much needed employment to the population of Wath.

The houses were mostly built in blocks of four. Access to the two centre houses was through an arched passage, so that there was no need for anyone to use another person's back garden to reach their own kitchen door. This fact alone was a revelation to most people who were used to living in houses with large communal yards.

Each home had a decent sized garden at the front and a larger one at the back, and even more importantly a bathroom and hot running water.

Knowing the miner's ironic sense of humour there was probably a reason why the estate was nicknamed China Town. No one ever seemed to know why it earned that name, but it stuck, and became known as China Town among all the population of Wath from the day building began.

As Harold had been one of the first to put his name down, he was among the first to be allocated a home. Theirs was to be on Oak Road, which ran in a straight line almost up to the racecourse, with open fields at the back. Other streets led off Oak Road onto Sandygate.

It became a weekly ritual on Sunday afternoons to take a walk to see the progress of the houses. On the second Sunday as they were about to leave, with the big old pram carrying the two youngest and the rest of the family tagging along behind, Stanley came running out of his grandfather's house, pulling on his jacket.

Ada saw him and called to him to come and walk beside her, but Harold looked at him sternly and snapped, "An where does tha think tha's going then?"

Stanley stared at him, the happy smile on his face fading.

"Thee stop there wi thee grandad," he continued, and as Ada began to protest, added, "We've gorr enough on wi this lot Ada, he'd only be fightin' wi Ernest," and turning round he pointed at his small son.

"Go on, ah've telled thee, tha's not comin'."

Trying to control his trembling lip, Stanley took off his jacket and stormed back into the house.

Herbert took it all in and stated that he didn't feel like going. Harold shrugged his shoulders and followed his wife, stating that that was another one less to worry about. As they disappeared down the street, Herbert went knocking on William's door. There was no answer at first, but the corner of the curtain lifted and revealed a tear streaked face peering out at him.

"Where's thee grandad? Come on, open t'door Stan."

Expecting that Stanley had gone with his parents to view the new house, William had gone to bed for an afternoon rest, but came wearily downstairs again at the sound of voices.

Upon hearing that he had been sent back, William shook his head in annoyance, muttering under his breath that Harold was a miserable, bad tempered blighter.

He sighed as he sat down in his chair. He was feeling his age today, and had looked forward to a quiet hour to himself.

Herbert spoke up. "Does tha want to go for a walk Stan? Is that ok Mr Dale? Ah'll look after him."

Relieved, William nodded, gave them a sixpence, and headed back upstairs, thankful that he could have his rest after all.

With the money calling out to be exchanged for sweets, Stanley and Herbert headed for the little corner shop that never seemed to close. After much deliberation, they emerged with a gob stopper each and a couple of sherbet dips, and still had two pence left over.

They sat on the wall of the canal bridge, dangling their feet over the side, dipping the liquorice sticks into the sherbet and enjoying the silky dark taste in contrast to the sharp lemony crystals that burst into flavour on their tongues.

They were silent at first, then Herbert said, "Ah'm startin' work next week Stan." He hardly expected a sensible answer from a three year old, but he underestimated Stanley, who was used to adult conversations with his grandfather.

After licking his lips free of sherbet, he examined the liquorice stick as he replied, "Goin' down t'pit are yer?"

"Aye, course ah am. Dad's got me a dudley an a snap tin."

Solemnly, Stanley stated, "Ah'm not goin' down t'pit. Ah'm goin' to be a farmer, and work wi t'horses. Them big uns like at Carlton." And with that he scooped up more sherbet and placed it carefully into his mouth, savouring it with his eyes closed.

Herbert laughed at him. "Thee wait, tha'll be goin' down t'pit same as rest of us."

Stanley's eyes snapped open and as he stared back at him, he replied, "No, ah won't tha knows."

In spite of his casual talk of starting work and the new dudley and snap tin, deep inside Herbert dreaded the day he would go down the pit shaft for the first time. It was made worse by the fact that he had not been able to find a place at Manvers Main, and would be starting at Corton Wood colliery instead.

He had always pictured himself going to work with his father, marching down the road early in the morning with the rest of the shift, sharing in the camaraderie of the group.

Going to start work on his own was a different matter and filled him with doubts and fears, especially when he thought of the bad reputation Corton Wood had.

CHAPTER 17

At last the house was built, and Ada held the keys to her new home in her hand. They had two weeks rent free to prepare the house, and give notice to their present landlord.

Mr Bramham, like many of the private property owners in Wath, was none too pleased to be losing tenants to the new housing estate. But of course, Ada couldn't wait to move out of the cockroach infested old house in Packmans Row and into a bright modern new residence.

At the rear of the house the entrance was through a short arched porch, with a water closet at one side, and the back door to the house at the other, which led straight into the kitchen. A large deep white sink and a wide wooden draining board stood under the window.

The copper for clothes washing was tucked away in a corner, and never again would Harold have to use it to bathe in. Not when a door at the other side of the kitchen led directly into the bathroom, with a big white bath and even a wash hand basin.

A large black cooking range took up half of one wall in the living room. The fire grate was on the left of it and the oven on the right. Behind the fire itself, out of sight, was a boiler, which, Ada had been told, would heat the water, and from there it would be piped to the bathroom and the kitchen sink.

Coal would be emptied down a shute at the side of the house, straight into the cellar, so there would be no need to struggle across a yard in all weathers with coal and sticks. Although, of course, the buckets needed to be carried up the cellar steps but Ada brushed that problem aside as she showed her sister Rose her wonderful new home.

"Marvellous,"declared Rose. "Tha'll be gerrin' one of them new fangled washing machines next."

Ada laughed. "Ah don't think so Rose. Ah can't see them catching on meself, can you?"

With just a couple of days to go before their move to the new house Ada was talking to Stanley about it, and telling him how much he would like living there, explaining to him about all the open fields at the back of the house and the racecourse jusr at the top of the road.

Her words penetrated through to Harold, who, at the time, was absorbed in his racing green newspaper.

Lowering his paper he looked across the room at Ada and said firmly,

"Oh no, Stanley's not going with us luv, it'll be better if he stays wi yer Dad." Addressing his small son said, "It's time tha went home nah, thee grandad'll av thee tea ready."

Stanley looked from one to the other, but knew better than to argue, and left, his bottom lip trembling just the slightest.

"Don't look at me like that Ada, what made thee think he'd be comin' wi us? Come on Ada, it's better he stops ere, tha knows it is. We've gorra fresh start up Oak Road. Hasn't tha thought how awkward it'd be wi is name being Dale and ours Corker? Folks would think it odd."

"What about Herbert then?" retorted Ada. "His name's Ward."

"That's different, everybody knows he were me first wife's son, and ah've looked after him, but it's not going to be easy to explain about Stanley, is it? No. He stops ere, an that's it," and Harold immersed himself in his newspaper again.

Ada was stunned by his attitude. She had always assumed that Stanley would rejoin the family when they moved. But her husband was adamant and she gave way to his will, consoling herself with the thought that her father would surely be lonely if he didn't have her eldest son to keep him company.

After his family moved to the new house, Packmans Row seemed a lonely place to Stanley. The house they had occupied stood empty with a TO LET sign stuck to the door.

Every morning he went first to the front window, then the back, pressing his face up to the glass, examining the empty rooms and picturing where the furniture had stood. Within days the steps and windowsills were covered in dust. Without Ada's constant daily cleaning routine the house soon looked dull and neglected.

Realising how much Stanley was missing his brothers and sisters, William stepped up his efforts to occupy him, and Martha often took him into her house for meals.

Then his Aunt Rose said she was planning a trip to Carlton to see Lizzie, and he could come with them if he was good. To Stanley, a visit to Carlton was better than Christmas, and for the two weeks preceding the visit was on his very best behaviour.

He only tormented the cat when he was sure no one was looking, and gave up swinging on doors altogether. He couldn't quite resist climbing on the walls that surrounded the open yard, but made sure it was after his Aunt Rose had finished cleaning and returned home.

Martha made him a new night shirt out of one of her father's old ones, and William treated him to a pair of shop bought underpants.

Stanley laid them out carefully on the bed, together with his clean shirt, and packed and repacked his cloth bag, until he was satisfied they were stacked in a neat pile.

Solemnly, he asked his grandfather if he was sure he would be able to look after Beauty without his help. Biting his lips to prevent himself smiling, William replied equally solemnly, "Well, ah'll do me best, but she'll miss thee, and so will I. Thee be a good lad for thee aunties won't tha?"

Stanley shrugged his shoulders and said, "Course ah will," as he raced off across the yard to Martha's house.

It was on the second day of their stay in Carlton that Stanley overheard his aunties talking. He was sat on the cold stone floor of the draughty scullery with Rob by his side.

He was feeling disgruntled with his two cousins, Doll and Hiney. The moment they had arrived Hiney seemed to have taken over Doll, and now they were playing houses in the old barn, and had said Stanley could only play if he agreed to be the baby.

Well, there was no way that he was going to go along with that, and he had retreated to the scullery where it was quiet and cool. He sat stroking Rob gently, stopping now and then to wait for the collie to nudge his hand back on to his head. Just as he was about to go out into the farmyard to check on the horses, he heard his Aunt Lizzie say, "How's Dad going on Rose?"

Above the chink of teacups, he heard Rose reply, "Ah'm a bit worried about him Liz, he's looking very tired lately."

Stanley had only been half listening up to that point, but his ears pricked up when he heard his name mentioned.

"Of course," said Lizzie, "it makes extra work for him, looking after Stanley, ah thought our Ada would av taken him up to t'new house wi her."

"Oh, she would av done," came Rose's reply, "It were Harold that said he should stop wi Dad. Said it wouldn't look right wi his name being Dale an rest of em Corker. Did you ever hear owt like it? Whose fault was it he's called Dale? It's a bloody excuse if you ask me. It's one less for him to feed more like."

There was a pause, and the sound of water being poured, then Lizzie said, "If it gets too much for Dad, or owt happens to him, Stanley can come to us. Me and Reggie av talked about it. Av a word wi our Ada will ya Rose? Put the idea to her, an ah'll write to her next week."

"Aye ah will. He'd be better off here than up at new house, they're overcrowded already, and to tell the truth, ah know Harold wouldn't welcome him."

Hearing footsteps coming towards the door, Stanley scuttled out quickly with Rob close behind.He went to the gate to watch the old retired horses in the field, and think about what he had overheard.

Stanley was very quiet when he returned from Carlton, and several times William looked up to find his grandson staring at him.

"What the matter? Why does tha keep lookin' at me? Does tha want summat?"

Stanley shook his head at first, then blurted out, "Ah'm worried about thee Grandad."

"Worried. What's tha got to be worried about lad?" William expected him to reply that he was worried about starting school in a few weeks' time.

"Well, ah'm watchin' to see that nowt happens to ya."

"What's tha on about?"

"Well ah heard Aunt Rose say summat might happen to ya."

William shook his head and made a mental note to tell his daughter to be careful what she said in future, especially when little ears were listening.

"Look, stop worrying lad, nowt's goin' to appen to me. Well, not just yet anyway. Why dunt tha go and see Martha for an hour, an let me av a bit of shut eye."

Then raising his voice, added, "And leave that cat alone."

"Ah think he wants to go outside Grandad, shall ah tek him wi me?"

"No! Leave poor bloody cat where he is will tha? He just wants a bit of peace same as me."

Reluctantly Stanley left Monty under the table, but promised him he'd be back to play later.

Reassured that nothing was going to happen to his grandad, Stanley turned his thoughts towards the idea of starting school.

CHAPTER 18

Stanley's Aunt Rose had said that he was a big boy now and would be starting school in the New Year. She had bought him a pair of second hand boots from her next door neighbour that were almost like new, and only one size too big. He would soon grow into them she said, and in the meantime stuffed wads of newspaper into the toes.

His grandad hammered rows of studs into the soles and heels to save wear on the leather. They made the most wonderful clomping noise as he ran up the street, and with a bit of practice he'd be able to slide in them.

He'd had a go already when no one was looking, copying what he'd seen the bigger lads do.

It looked easy when they did it. They would chose a piece of smooth concrete, then run at it fast and come to a sort of jumping stop and slide with arms outstretched and sparks flying from the metal studs in their boots as they scraped across the concrete. He was full of admiration for them.

He had had many discussions with his grandad about going to school, and found it hard to understand why he would be not be going to the same one that his brothers and sisters attended. William tried to find a reason that would satisfy him, not wanting to tell him that his father had decided it would be better that way. Harold had said it would save awkward questions about why Stanley's name was different.

Stanley was unconvinced by his grandfather's excuses and remembered the overheard conversation between his aunts. Young as he was, he knew instinctively that William was trying to save his feelings.

"Well, ah'm not bothered," he said, turning his head away. "Queen Victoria's School's better than Park Road anyway."

"Aye, tha's right there lad, ah think it is. Don't thee let it bother thee," and he ruffled Stanley's hair affectionately.

Just a few days after this conversation, Stanley had his idea. His grandfather was at work and Martha out for the day. His Aunt Rose had been and tidied the house and gone hurrying off to do her own work, leaving Mrs Hudson to keep an eye on him as he played in the yard.

But Stanley was sick of hanging about the yard.

All the older children were in school, apart from the poor lad who lived in the end house. He was known as Simple Sam and no one ever played with him.

Even Monty had slunk off on cat business, the way that cats do.

The idea came to him in a flash. He would go and visit his mother. He set off right away and within half an hour was standing outside her back door, wondering if he should knock or walk straight in. In the end he did both, knocking as hard as he could and turning the round black knob.

The warm smell of new bread met him and there was his mother working at the kitchen sink. She turned as the door opened and stared in surprise at seeing her eldest son. Pulling him to her, she gave him a hug and said, "Well, ah don't know, what a surprise, who's brought you?"

"Ah've come on me own Mam, ah thought ah'd come and see ya."

"What, you've come all this way on yer own? Yer could av got lost."

"No, it were ok Mam," said Stanley proudly. "Ah remembered t'way, can ah av some bread?"

Ada laughed. "Course tha can lad, come an get warm," and she led the way into the living room where a fire was blazing in the shining black leaded range. A large metal fireguard encircled the whole cooking range, protecting Harold and Betty who were playing on the thick homemade rug.

Harold's face lit up at the sight of his brother, and Stanley joined them on the rug, soaking in its warmth and the smell of family.

As he looked around the room he recognised the big sideboard with the mirrored back and the twisty columns on each side of the drawers as the one that used to stand in his grandfather's house. A long narrow table with two forms tucked underneath it occupied the centre of the room. Two wooden armchairs for Ada and Harold were the only other furnishings, but the room was cosy and shone with brightness, from the scrubbed white wooden table top to the gleaming sideboard. Ada tolerated no dirty corners in her house.

At the sound of heavy boots on the path outside, Stanley looked up from the game he was playing with Harold just in time to see his mother disappearing into the kitchen. Following her, he suddenly noticed how much fatter she looked than the last time he had seen her, and saw how she walked with her hand on her swollen stomach. But something stopped him mentioning it to her.

"Herbert's home," she said as she turned on the bath taps. Noticing Stanley staring at the hot water gushing out, she smiled. "What do ya think of that then?"

Stanley was almost speechless, he'd never seen anything quite so amazing. He blew out a big breath. "Phew, it's marvellous Mam," he said, as Herbert came in through the kitchen door.

Even through the black dust that coated his face, Stanley could see he looked different, harder and older, and he suddenly felt shy and at a loss of something to say.

"Come on son, thee bath'll be ready shortly, put thee pit stuff in t'bucket. Ah'll wash em later wi thee Dad's. He'll av stopped off for a pint. Now don't be long, he'll be ere soon an want his bath. An mek sure tha wipes bath out when tha's finished. Thee dinner's on t'oven top."

As Herbert closed the bathroom door behind himself, Billy and Ernest walked into the kitchen and the atmosphere changed in an instant. Sensing it, Ada patted Stanley on the shoulder and said, "Ah think tha'd better be gerrin' off now luv. It'll be dark early, an thee grandad'll wonder tha is." She called out loud, "Billy. Walk our Stanley as far as Sandygate,"

Billy groaned, "Can't he go on is own Mam? He found is own way ere. Ah've been diggin' in t'garden."

Ada's answer came loud and firm, "Don't thee answer back, do as ah've told thee. Tha's not too big to av thee earhole skelped."

With a dark look and an indication for Stanley to follow him, Billy made his way to the door.

Ada's words followed him, "And tha can tek that look off thee face, or thee Dad'll tek it off for ya."

Once outside however, Billy cheered up, and called to Stanley, "Come on young'n, gerra move on."

Falling into step together, Billy took the opportunity to boast about the fact that he would be joining his Dad at Manvers Main in three months time. Stanley nodded, but had other things on his mind.

"Billy," he said, "don't yer think me Mam's gerrin' fat?" He went on, "But she doesn't eat much does she?"

Billy let out a loud laugh and gave Stanley such a hard slap on his back that he almost stumbled.

"Why, tha soft lad, she's avin' another babby," and added coarsely, "me father's gor er in t'family way again, the randy old bugger," and he clung to a lamp post, laughing, and repeating to himself, "She's gerrin' fat!"

Then he proceeded to enlighten Stanley on the facts of life.

Stanley gazed at him in horror. "Tha's a big liar Billy Corker, me Mam wouldn't do that." And he kicked his half brother hard on the shins and ran as fast as he could down Sandygate and towards home, leaving Billy clutching his leg and calling after him that he would get him next time.

CHAPTER 19

School days, for Stanley, began at the Queen Victoria School on Doncaster Road in the first week of January 1924, just before his fifth birthday.

His cousin Hiney, being two years older than him and a pupil at the school, had been instructed to take Stanley and enrol him in the infant's class. As usual, Hiney took her responsibilities very seriously and held his hand tightly all the way, informing everyone they met that she was taking her cousin to school for the first time.

As they arrived, Stanley looked nervously at the high, stone built walls, topped by the black iron railings that raised the level of the playground high above the road at the front.

The entrance to the school was via the side road, and as they passed through the gates he clutched Hiney's hand tighter, overawed by the amount of children running about in the playground. But Hiney walked confidently through them all, straight to the arched wooden door that faced the gate.Instructing Stanley to wipe his feet on the coarse brown mat, she led him into the classroom.

The teacher looked around at the sound of footsteps, peering at them over the top of the glasses that were balanced on the end of her nose.

Hiney's hand shot up as she came to a halt. "Please Miss Sparrow, ah've brought me cousin to school, he's nearly five."

"Very good Hiney, you're a clever girl." She looked Stanley up and down, taking in the decent boots and the clean appearance of him. Noticing her look, Stanley pulled up the long socks that had escaped the bands of elastic around his knees and were now wrinkled above his boots.

His future teacher smiled. "That's better. Now, what's your name?"

Giving Stanley no time to answer, Hiney spoke up for him. "It's Stanley, miss, Stanley Dale, he lives with his grandad."

"Very well Hiney," replied Miss Sparrow, noticing the black look that her new pupil had given his older cousin. "You can go to your class now, and collect Stanley at home time please."

With Hiney gone he looked around the large room, taking in the rows of desks and the glowing stove at the front, surrounded by the high wire guard. Light flooded into the upper part of the room from the windows that were placed high, almost touching the ceiling, too high for the sunlight to reach the pupils sitting at their desks and too high for any of them to be distracted by looking out of the windows. Stanley thought how he would need a ladder to be able to see through them.

But his attention was mostly drawn to the magnificent rocking horse at the back of the room and he wondered when he would be able to have a ride on it. He was soon to find that it was never ridden. In fact, even touching it was frowned upon.

It had been presented to the school by a rich benefactor, but the school governors had decreed that it was much too good for most of the common miners children to use, and so it remained like new, its long silken mane unstroked, and its dappled grey paint unchipped. Just a glorious, glamorous toy, only for show!

Stanley adored Miss Sparrow from the first. He had never known anyone with that name, and she did so remind of a dainty bird, always dressed in a long brown skirt, with her hair drawn tightly back into a bun and her glasses perched precariously on the end of her sharp little nose. She was as kindly and chirpy as her namesake. Never having been married, she looked upon her pupils as her children and spent a large proportion of her salary every week on treats or food for children who were in need.

Stanley quickly settled into a routine. He and Hiney walked to school every morning, clean and fresh, and ran home together in the evening, pausing now and then to gaze in the shop windows with their faces pressed up against the glass.

The bakery was their favourite, with its delicious smell reminding them it was teatime, and then the distinctive aroma of fresh fruit from the greengrocers next door made them stop to admire the shiny red apples and the oranges displayed in the window. Luscious bunches of black grapes hung from hooks to be admired by many but afforded by few.

That was Stanley's favourite time of day, when he was hurrying home knowing tea would be waiting. Afterwards he would go to help his grandfather groom Beauty at the doctor's stable, all the time chattering, mostly about the wonderful Miss Sparrow, who, William gathered, was quite the most knowledgeable person in the world.

Listening patiently, William would nod now and then and declare, "Well, ah'll go to our house," which seemed an odd comment, but Stanley knew it was an expression of astonishment at the knowledge he had just received from his grandson.

On his first visit to his mother after he had started school, Stanley found that Billy had been right. His mother had produced another baby. A little sister to be called Jessie. He stared at her, shyly at first, remembering what Billy had told him. But when Ada placed her on his knee and he felt her strong grip as she held his finger, a fierce desire to protect this little being overcame everything else.

Saturday became the day he spent at the Oak Road house. He would arrive just after breakfast and take his share of the chores which Ada allocated to each of them. No matter how young, each member of the family had a job to perform.

Later in the day they would escape to run wild in the countryside that surrounded the racecourse, coming back ravenous to slabs of bread and dripping, or sometimes plates of stew, with thick crusts of bread to soak up the gravy.

Stanley avoided seeing his father as much as possible, knowing that the sight of him would bring forth the comment, "What's tha doin' ere?"

By teatime Stanley would be on his way back home to his grandad's house, glad to be going, feeling special that he was different and proud that he had the same name as his grandfather. Best of all, he had a bedroom all to himself back at Packmans Row.

He spent most Sundays with William, helping to groom Beauty in the mornings then trying to keep quiet in the afternoon while his grandfather had a well earned Sunday siesta.

And so, life was good for Stanley at that time, but of course, as we all know, things never stay the same forever, and Stanley's life was about to take a turn for the worse.

When William set off for work on the 23rd of February 1926, it was a cold damp morning, typical for that month, but he noticed the snowdrops in the gardens he passed and thought how spring was not too far away.

He'd felt so tired lately and just couldn't seem to shift the chesty cough that had bothered him since Christmas.

He was employed at the pit top at that time, labouring at various mundane jobs, which usually involved shovelling coal or the dust from it.

The closer he got to the pit, the dirtier the surroundings became, but William had developed a system for blotting it all out. As he worked, his mind would be elsewhere. As his body swept and shovelled, in his head he was out in the open fields, following the plough, with clean air filling his lungs. He chuckled to himself as he thought of the Sunday just past, and saw again his grandson as he brushed the doctor's horse, talking as if he was an adult, asking one question after another.

William pulled up his collar as the rain began and leaned on his shovel as a bout of coughing seized him. And then he saw her. His beloved Louise, surrounded by a golden glow and he smiled as she came towards him, holding out her hand for him to follow.

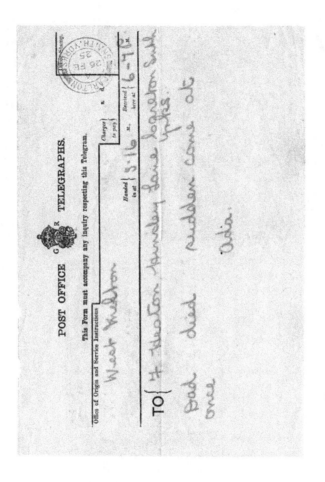

CHAPTER 20

With her three youngest children loaded on to the pram, Ada was about to set off for the shops. She had promised Harold and Betty that they could ride going down the hill, but said they would have to walk on the way back, when the pram was loaded with shopping.

The sight of a policeman walking down her garden path stopped Ada in her tracks. Putting her hand to her throat, she waited for him to reach her. The police seldom came with good news and Ada held her breath.

Betty stuck her thumb in her mouth and peered at him from around the hood of the pram, completely overawed, while Harold boldly looked his uniform up and down and admired his helmet.

PC Jones was new to the job and nervous of his present assignment. Clearing his throat, he took off his helmet and held it awkwardly under his arm.

"Mrs Corker?" he said, as he swallowed. "Mrs Ada Corker? Daughter of Mr William Dale?"

He looked at her, his eyebrows raised in a questioning manner, all the time taking in every detail, noting how tall, slim and elegant she looked in spite of having three young children.

Time seemed to stop for Ada as she nodded, and for some reason fixed her eyes on the red mark left on the policeman's forehead where his heavy helmet had rested. Without taking her eyes off the mark, she took hold of the pram handle and gripped it tight.

"Ah'm sorry to tell you Mrs Corker, that your father collapsed and died this morning while at work."

Afterwards, Ada could never remember how she came to be sitting in her living room, still wearing her outdoor clothes, holding a big mug of strong tea in her hand. The three children were rowed up on the hearth rug, staring wide eyed at PC Jones, who sat on the edge of the wooden armchair looking anxiously back at her.

"Do you feel better now, Mrs Corker? Shall I get one of your neighbours?"

Ada shook her head. "No thanks, Ah'll be alright in a minute, it were just such a shock. Ah'll av to let my sisters know," and she stood up to prove she was recovered.

Struggling to hold back tears, she gave him her father's address, and asked for his body to be taken there later in the day.

Her head began racing with things that would need to be done as she piled the children back on to the pram and set off for Rose's house. As she passed through Wath she stopped at the post office on the corner. Taking Harold and Betty in with her, she dictated a telegram to the post mistress, addressed to Lizzie, making it as brief as possible to keep down the cost.

"Dad died sudden, come at once," it read, and she handed over two shillings, thankful for the emergency ten shilling note she kept secretly tucked away at the back of her purse under the shopping list.

Baby Jessie was beginning to grizzle for her feed by the time she came out of the post office and Ada pushed a dummy into her mouth and bounced the pram vigorously to keep her from going into a full hungry bawling session.

Harold and Betty, sitting on the end of the pram, thought it great fun to be bounced about.Laughing, they clung onto the sides of the pram as their mother rushed passed the shops towards her sister's house.

Rose knew there was something wrong the moment she opened the door to Ada. The news had barely left her lips before their arms were around each other.

Shocked to see both their mother and aunty crying, Harold and Betty joined in, and not to be outdone, Jessie realised how hungry she was, spat the dummy out, and began demanding her feed.

With children to see to and hungry men folk soon due home after their shift down the pit, grief had to be put to one side and practical arrangements made.

While Ada fed the demanding baby and the children, Rose went to see Mrs Robinson, who lived in the next street. She was well known for laying out the dead and would wash William and dress him in the shroud that had been folded and wrapped in the bottom drawer of his wardrobe, ever since his wife had died.

Then together, the two sisters moved the furniture in the tiny front room of William's house in readiness for his coffin. Money would not be a problem, thanks to the life insurance policies, and fortunately the man from the Co-op was due to make his regular call that very evening. Wheels would be put in motion to close the policies and claim the money, providing them with enough to give their father a decent burial and a little left over.

It was not until Ada was leaving, with Harold and Betty again loaded onto the front of the pram, that she remembered Stanley. It was quickly decided that Rose would have to break the news to him, and he would stay with her until after the funeral.

Ada left, almost at a run, pushing the heavy pram, and worried that she would not be home in time to have dinner ready for Harold and Herbert.

William came home for the last time, carried in on a wooden stretcher by four of the men who had worked with him. Gently they laid him on the trestle table that had been set up in readiness and left him to Mrs Robinson and her helper.

By late afternoon they had washed him from head to foot, cleaned his nails, trimmed his moustache and dressed him in his shroud. With the help of his son John, they laid him his coffin and surrounded it with candles and flowers.

Rose went to meet Hiney and Stanley as they left school, and taking them to one side she quietly broke the sad news. Hiney bombarded her with questions but Stanley seemed stunned and said not a word the whole of the journey back to Packmans Row. It wasn't until he stood looking at the closed curtains in his grandfather's house that he began to cry. Rose put her arm around him and led him away, pausing to pat Monty who sat on the kitchen window sill meowing to be let into the house.

The day of William's funeral dawned as bright and fresh as mid spring, and his family remarked how it was exactly the sort of day that William loved best.

He was to be carried on his last journey by Beauty and she arrived wearing black plumes in her mane, pulling a borrowed flat cart that had been draped in black. John lead the horse out of the street, and they began the walk to the cemetery, with the long line of family and friends stretching out behind.

Stanley and his cousin Hiney should have been in school, but Rose had said they could have the day at home, although they were not to attend the funeral. William's family had discussed the matter and decided the funeral was not a suitable event for the children.

And so, Stanley and Hiney stood hand in hand, amazed at the sight of so many people dressed in black, and watched the procession make its way slowly out of sight.

As the tears plopped down Stanley's face, Hiney produced a marble from her pocket and gave it to her younger cousin. Solemnly Stanley examined it and rolled it around in his hand, admiring the green swirly markings in the glass. But, inconsolable, he handed it back and ran to sit on the doorstep with Monty.

With prayers said and the burial over, the family returned to William's home where the mourners revived themselves with large quantities of tea and fruit cake

William had left no formal will, but a single sheet of paper, carefully folded into a large brown envelope revealed how he wanted his possessions divided.

Ada was to have his one and only photograph of himself and the two china Staffordshire dogs that had been her mother's pride and joy and had stood on the mantelpiece for as long as she could remember. The wooden wall clock was for Rose, and all the brass ornaments were Lizzie's. His son Will received the double bed and all the bedding.

Everything else, including his watch, was for John.

While the rest of the family sat inside reminiscing, Ada took Stanley into the scullery and wiped his tear streaked face with the damp flannel.

Squatting down beside him, she hugged him close and said, "We're all going to miss him, aren't we?"

As Stanley nodded sadly, his eyes filling up again, his mother kissed his cheek. "Now listen love," she told him, "ah've been talkin' to yer Aunt Lizzie."

Before she could say any more, Stanley blurted out, "Yer goin' to send me to live wi Aunt Lizzie, aren't yer? Ah dunt want to go mam. Ah want ter live wi you mam."

"But Stanley, ah thought yer liked yer Aunt Lizzie, and bein on t'farm at Carlton."

"Aye ah do mam, but dunt send me away, ah want to live wi you."

It was at this point that Harold came in. Aware that other members of the family had stopped talking and were gazing at the proceedings in the scullery, he sat down on the rickety three legged stool, and looking first at Ada, then at Stanley, asked, "Nah then, what's up?"

"Well," said Ada, "ah were just putting the idea to Stanley that he might like to go back to Carlton wi Lizzie tomorrow."

Harold glanced back at the living room, and leaning forward, pushed the door shut with a bang, cutting off the audience who were listening in with interest.

In the living room, John looked around at the rest of his relatives, raised his eyes to the ceiling, gave an exasperated 'tch' sound and commented, "Ah can guess what that's about!"

In the privacy of the scullery, Harold shushed Ada as she was about to speak to Stanley.

"Nah look son," he began, "thee Aunt Lizzie and Uncle Reggie have been good enough to say tha can live wi them. So tha's goin', and that's all there is to it. Nah be a good lad and behave thee sen."

That was just about the kindest speech that Stanley could ever remember his father making to him, and he sniffed as he nodded and rubbed his sleeve across his eyes.

His mother gave him a tremulous smile and hugged him close. "Ah'll come to see thee love, and Aunt Lizzie'll bring thee over to visit."

Harold stood up, patting Ada on the shoulder. "Stop bloody pampering him, tha'll mek im as soft as shit. Come on, it's time we were off, ah'm on early shift tomorra."

Ada followed him after giving her son a final hug. As she did so, she whispered in his ear, "Go to Aunt Lizzie's, but if tha dunt like it ah'll fetch yer back, OK?"

Stanley nodded again, reassured, and waved his parents off, almost managing a smile.

Early next morning he was at the railway station with his aunt, waiting for the Doncaster train. John had walked with them, using a borrowed hand cart to carry their baggage but had said goodbye to them on the platform and gone rushing off to return the cart before he set off for work.

On all his previous trips to Carlton, Stanley had been filled with excitement, but today there was a black cloud of melancholy hanging over him. Lizzie held his hand and tried to cheer him up with tales of what they could do once he was settled in, even promising that he could help Reggie with the shire horses, but poor Stanley was inconsolable and sat on the edge of his seat clutching his cloth bag with all his belongings in it. All he could think of was that he would never see his grandad again and that his mother had sent him away.

By the time they arrived at Snaith station it was well past midday, and to Lizzie's relief they were just in time to catch the carrier to Carlton and were able to sit on the flat cart amid the boxes and bundles destined for the village shop.

Stanley soon realised his Aunt Lizzie was in a very bad mood when they eventually arrived at the cottage. He had thought that the house looked fine, but evidently he was wrong, as was made clear by the way Lizzie slammed around the room declaring that Reggie had left it like a pig sty.

He could see her point when he looked at the fireplace and noted that the fire was out and the hearth filled with cold ash. A fine film of dust coated every surface and even the piles of unwashed dishes on the table.

Lizzie stormed around the house, cleaning the fireplace and rolling up the hearth rug to be shaken outside. Stanley brought the basket of wood from the scullery and set it down beside her without saying a word.

As Lizzie looked at his woebegone face she held out her arms to him. "Come on love," she said as she held him. "Tha'll be alright, me an Uncle Reggie will look after yer."

He felt a little better after that and helped her to polish and tidy the room before he sat down by the now glowing fire and ate toast and dripping for his belated dinner.

Doll burst into the room at teatime, first throwing her arms around her mother, then coming to Stanley, sat down beside him and laid her arm around his shoulders.

"Are you alright Stan?" she asked, scanning his pale face. "Let's go see the horses." Holding his hand she led him outside, but even his joy at being with the horses couldn't chase away the hollow black feeling deep inside himself, and his face remained solemn.

The grief really took hold of him that night as he lay in bed with nothing to distract his thoughts, and he sobbed until he fell into an exhausted sleep.

When, at the end of the week, Stanley was no happier, Reggie and Lizzie despaired and agreed they would have to take him back to his mother.

"He needs his mam," said Reggie. "This can't go on. Look, he's nowt but skin and bone."

"Ah know," Lizzie replied. "He's hardly eating, poor lad. There's no time to write to Ada, it's Friday today, she wouldn't get a letter till Monday. Do yer think ah should send her a telegram to say ah'm tekin' him back?"

"No Lizzie, we've had enough expense, what wi train fares and one thing an another. Just tek him back tomorrow and then come straight home."

Lizzie hated being told what to do, but she had to agree. They couldn't keep him here, she decided, he was so unhappy. She'd done her best, but all she could get from Stanley was that he wanted his mam.

So early next morning Lizzie and Stanley were once again stood on a station platform waiting for a train. She was feeling none too pleased that all her efforts to make her nephew settle in had failed, and Stanley stole glances at her to gauge her humour and wisely kept quiet.

Doll had been left at home in tears, partly because Stanley was not staying and partly because she was missing out on a train ride. As her mother had told her impatiently as she pulled on her outdoor clothes, "We've spent enough money on train fares lately, so shut up and stop that bloody crying, ah've heard enough of it."

Once they were on the train, Stanley's spirit began to lift and as he slipped his hand into his aunt's he told her he was sorry.

Her heart melting as she looked into his blue eyes, Lizzie squeezed his hand, kissed the top of his head and told him not to worry, it would all be ok.

Privately she had great misgivings about their reception at the Oak Road house. Not from Ada, but from Harold, and she steeled herself to have a showdown with him, determined to let him know what she thought of a man who couldn't be bothered with his own son.

As it happened she had prepared herself needlessly for a confrontation.

She found Ada looking pale and tired hanging out washing, the pit clothes contrasting with the snowy white nappies blowing on the line.

She put the last peg in her husband's work shorts, and hoisting the line high with the long wooden prop, she gathered up the wicker clothes basket and hurried back up the garden path, exclaiming at the sight of her sister and young son.

"Well, ah dunt know, what a surprise. What's up Liz?"

Taking Ada to one side, Lizzie explained how Stanley had been and how she had felt she had to bring him back.

Ada sighed, gave Stanley an exasperated look and scolded him. "Ah thought tha promised to be a good lad," she said. "Ah dunt know what thee Dad's goin' to say to thee."

194

"Don't ger on at him Ada, he's little more than a babby, an he's lost his grandad, who were more of a father to him than his own has ever been. Talking of his Dad, where is he? If he's goin' to mek a fuss, ah've got summat to say to him."

"There's no need to be like that Lizzie, dunt start a row. Ah can't cope wi it just now. Harold's out, gone down to t'Oak Tree for a pint wi his mates. Come an have a cup of tea luv, tha looks tired."

"Me look tired!" exclaimed her sister. "Ada, tha looks shocking. As tha looked in t'mirror lately? Dunt tell me tha's expectin' again?"

Ada shook her head at her sister. "Ah dunt know, tha dunt change does tha Lizzie? Don't wrap it will tha, just come right out wi it." She added as they walked into the house, "No ah'm not expectin', well not at the moment anyway, but ah guess it's only a matter of time. Sometimes it seems Harold only has to hang his trousers on the bed post for me to be in the family way again."

"Ah'll tell yer what Ada," quipped Lizzie nudging her sister, "tha'll have to get Harold to tie a knot in it."

It was then that they realised Stanley was standing right beside them taking in everything they said and Ada sent him upstairs to take his bag away.

"Put it at t'side of t'bed. Yer'll have to sleep wi Ernest and Harold. They're playin' up on t'racecourse, tha can go an find em when tha's put t'bag away."

Stanley dashed up stairs with his bag, full of excitement at the thought of sleeping with his brothers. He stood for a moment at the door, surveying the room. Two double beds took up almost all the floor space. It was certainly going to be cosy, sharing the small room with four others.

But Stanley's immediate thoughts were on finding his brothers and he tore down the stairs with barely a second glance at his mother and aunt.

As he reached the sandy path that ran parallel with the racecourse he could hear the sound of voices among the thicket of bushes. They silenced as he drew close and Stanley stood still, looking around until a movement caught his attention. Then his younger brother Harold's unmistakable voice called out, "Hi, Stan, we're here."

Stanley dropped to his knees and crawled through the thick grass and under the low branches to find Harold, Ernest and four other lads hidden in a small hollow clearing.

As he crouched down beside them, Stanley grinned. "Hi, this is good, is it a den?"

"Who's tha?" demanded the tallest of the group.

"He's our brother," stated Ernest and Harold in unison, "he's our Stan."

"Oh, so tha's Stan Corker is tha?"

"No ah'm not," stated Stanley firmly, "ah'm Stanley Dale."

"Well tha can't be their brother then, else tha'd be a Corker."

"Yes he is our brother," retorted Ernest.

"Aye ah am," said Stanley proudly, "but ah'm still a Dale not a Corker."

As Lizzie was on her way out, she met Harold who was just returning from his lunch time drinking session at the Oak Tree inn. He was feeling in a convivial mood and greeted his sister in law warmly.

"Nah then Lizzie, it's good to see thee again so soon, how's me favourite sister in law?"

Lizzie gave him the brief account of why she was there, and watched how quickly his mood changed.

"Why the maungy little bugger, ah've told Ada she pampers him too much, he wants his arse skelpin' a few times."

He received no agreement from Lizzie, who scowled at him and retorted,

"Aye, well ah expect poor lad'll get plenty of that now he's under your roof," and without another word, she turned her back on him and walked away, leaving Harold staring after her.

With his happy weekend mood completely gone, he entered the kitchen, intent on having strong words with Ada. But as he closed the door behind him his wife met his eye, her face set in the way she had at times that said she would take no arguments. Speaking with quiet determination, she said, "Our Stanley's come home and he's staying here!"

With a shrug of his shoulders Harold gave in and settled in his chair, picked up the paper and uttered not another word for the rest of the afternoon, by which time he had come to the conclusion that one more in the house would make little difference.

By the time he pulled his chair up to the table at tea time, and prepared to enjoy the meal that Ada had put in front of him, his good humour had returned and he contemplated his evening session at the British Legion Club with pleasure.

Picking up the longest stick of celery out of the tall glass jug, he dipped it into the mound of salt on the side of his plate and took a crunchy bite, relishing the taste he loved. He could hear the sound of the children's voices in the kitchen and Ada's telling them to settle down and get their hands washed before tea, and knew she would hold them back until he had finished his, but being once more in a genial mood he called for her to let them come in straight away.

Under their father's stern gaze they filed in and took their places on the long forms with Stanley among them, hoping to avoid drawing attention to himself. But his father sought him out as he surveyed his offspring and caught his eye. "Nah then, Stanley," he said, "if tha's going to live here tha'll av to behave, does tha hear me?"

"Yes," said Stanley, and lowered his eyes.

CHAPTER 21

His brothers and sisters welcomed Stanley and drew him into the circle of the family. Edith, his eldest half-sister, mothered him as she did all her younger siblings, while his younger brother Harold followed him like a shadow. As usual he was alternately best friends and worst enemies with Ernest. With Herbert, in spite of their difference in ages, he felt a special kinship, perhaps because, like himself, Herbert had a different surname to the rest of the family.

It was three days after Stanley had taken up residence at Oak Road that he developed a great admiration for Herbert. As he entered the house one dinnertime, the strong smell of kippers frying met him, and his mouth watered as he watched his mother cook them on the single gas ring on top of the little whitewood table in the corner of the kitchen.

Carefully Ada slid one kipper on to a dinner plate and carried it through to the living room, placing it in front of Herbert who sat at the table, freshly washed following his shift down the pit.

Picking up a thick slice of bread, Herbert transferred the kipper on to it, liberally sprinkled it with vinegar and squashed another slice of bread on top. Seeing Stanley eyeing the fish, he lifted the top slice, pulled off a chunk of the smoked fish and handed it to him with broad grin. While Stanley picked out the bones before eating it, he stopped and gazed in fascination as his step brother began eating his giant sandwich. Bones, head, tail, the whole of the kipper was crunched and devoured.

"Too good to waste," explained Herbert through a mouth full of bread and fish.

The sleeping arrangements were not a part of family life that Stanley enjoyed. Being used to having his own room, it came as an unpleasant shock to have to share a bed with Ernest and Harold. Frequent fights broke out between himself and Ernest, usually resulting in their father doling out a few blows that settled the argument. In the end, Ada insisted that Stanley move in with Herbert, while a very disgruntled Billy was transferred to sleeping with his younger brothers.

Since they now had their own water closet in the porch Ada came to the decision that chamber pots would be banished.

"Ah'm not emptying any more jerries," she declared firmly. "If anyone wants to pee in the night they can go downstairs, and make sure the doors are locked again after you've been, and that includes you an all Harold," she added to her husband. Harold groaned.

"Good God woman, ah'll be up and down like a bloody yo-yo when ah've had a few pints."

"Well, tha'll have to have a few less then, won't tha?" retorted Ada, determined to have her own way.

Stanley soon slipped into the routine and became a part of the family life, but while his siblings attended the Park Road School, Stanley was sent back to the Queen Victoria at the other end of Wath, where he made a point of correcting anyone who assumed that his surname was Corker.

Stanley's stubborn insistence on making sure that everyone knew his name was different to the rest of the family's did little to forge any bond between himself and his father, who had no desire to draw attention to the circumstances of his son's birth.

Lizzie and Ada still wrote to each other every week, exchanging news. Ada was always hungry to hear every detail of her eldest daughter, and Lizzie brought her to visit as often as she could, but never for a moment did they disclose Doll's real parentage. Ada's visits to Carlton were few and far between now.

As the size of the family increased so did their financial hardship, and there was little enough money to put food on the table and provide clothes for the growing children; certainly none left over for bus or train fares. Stanley, like his brothers, had to reline his boots every morning with fresh pads of newspaper in an attempt to cover the holes in the soles.

Their poverty worsened year by year, and although more than enough of Harold's wages passed over the bars of the local pubs, Ada accepted it as a being inevitable. It was part and parcel of a miner's life to enjoy a few pints with his mates after spending so many hours slaving underground in the dangerous conditions.

What Ada did resent was Harold's growing love of gambling on the horses, and it was the cause of many bitter arguments whenever Ada suspected that more money was being wasted down at the illegal bookies.

The highlight of the year for all the family, and the children in particular, was the trip to the seaside in midsummer organised by the British Legion Club. Money was collected little by little throughout the year until by June there was usually enough in the kitty to hire several coaches to transport the excited families to either Cleethorpes or Bridlington. Every coach would be packed with passengers and crates of bottled beer to help sustain the thirsty miners on their way home, just in case they had not managed to drink sufficient in the pubs at the resort.

On Stanley's first trip they were headed for Bridlington, and he could hardly contain his excitement at the thought of seeing the place that Herbert had described to him with such enthusiasm.

Each child was given two shillings as spending money, which seemed like a fortune to Stanley and his brothers and sisters, but unfortunately, the money usually found its way into their father's pockets to fund his drink for the day, plus a bet or two on the horses. Harold reasoned that as he had contributed every week towards the trip, he was entitled to the money, and what were the kids going to do with it anyway? Spend it on donkey rides and ice creams no doubt.But to salve his conscious he gave Ada a little of it back to get them a treat.

The singing on the coach began almost as soon as they set off. Beginning with, 'It's a Long Way to Tipperary' and continuing through to, 'Old Macdonald had a Farm' with loud moos and grunts in all the wrong places. 'Ten green bottles' was a great favourite and sung with gusto several times until Ada thought her head would burst if she heard it once more.

By the time they reached the half way stage, many of the passengers were looking decidedly green and sickly, and were begging the driver for a toilet stop. A mad scramble for the door began as soon as the coach drew to a halt, and a race began for a discreet place to relieve themselves.

While the men rowed up behind the sparsest of hedges and watered the undergrowth, the women were forced to go further into the bushes to hide their modesty. It was a cause for much hilarity as the ladies picked their way among the long grass and nettles, inspiring witty comments from their menfolk.

"Careful tha dunt nettle it love," followed by, "bring a dock leaf love, an ah'll rub it for ya."

All loaded aboard once more, the singing resumed as the engine coughed into life and prepared to tackle the steep hill up on to the Yorkshire Wolds. They dragged slowly up the hill, the coach struggling valiantly, and the driver changing down the gears with loud revs of the engine.

Shouts of, "Shall we get out and push?" went up, and cheers as they finally made it to the top with steam coming out of the radiator.

There were even louder cheers later on at the first glimpse of the sea, and the singing halted as arguments erupted as to who had been the first to spot the blue water on the horizon.

Pulling up beside the harbour in Bridlington the driver opened the door, relieved that they had arrived safely, and gave instructions for them all to be back on the coach by 6pm.

"Think on," he called, "6pm. Anybody who's late will be sleepin' on t'sands, and don't be gerrin' bloody lost. No excuses, this old bus has to be back in t'yard before t'boss locks up for t'night."

Ada stood anxiously at the side of the harbour, counting heads and telling them all repeatedly to keep away from the sheer drop at the side, imagining one of her tribe falling in. Stanley gazed about in awe, looking at the fishing boats and breathing in the salty air. Harold shepherded them all in front of him to the nearby south beach and left them to settle on the sands while he headed to the nearest pub with his mates to sample the local beverages.

Claiming a half moon shaped circle of beach close to the sea wall, Ada paid for four deck chairs and settled the family in for a full day on the beach.

Stripping off their boots, Stanley and Ernest ran down to the sea, gasping at the coldness of the water and began splashing each other, grinning with delight.

They were quickly joined by the rest of the family. Even Ada removed her shoes and stockings, and lifting the skirt of her long navy blue coat, paddled at the edge of the sea, exclaiming that she could almost feel the salty water doing her feet good.

Returning to her chair Ada sat back, closing her eyes for a moment and wriggling her toes in the cold sand.She breathed deeply, savouring the rare relaxation of a day out. She blinked as she opened her eyes, holding up her hand to extend the shade given by the brim of her hat and stared at the figure in front of her.

For one surreal moment she thought it was her father, William, until she recognised Mr Smithson, an old neighbour from Packmans Row. He had been good friends with her father and they had spent many a night playing dominos down at the Red Lion.

Realising he was all alone, Ada insisted he join them. Lowering himself carefully into the rocky deckchair, he smiled at Ada, displaying his large loose fitting dentures beneath the bushy moustache. As he made himself comfortable he confided in a loud whisper that he might have to take his teeth out later.

"They're a bit too big, you know love. Ah got em off ar Charlie. He had em made but couldn't wear em, so he give em to me. Well he's me brother, so they should fit, but by heck, they aren't half painful, it's no wonder ar Charlie give em away."

Ada nodded in sympathy and looked away as he pushed the bottom dentures out of his mouth and wriggled them about. It was a little later on that she noticed the bowler hat he was wearing. She'd never seen him in a hat before. There was something familiar about it. It reminded her of her father's hat that he wore when he drove the doctor about in his pony and trap. Seeing her look, Mr Smithson took off the hat, and turning it upside down, showed the inside of it to Ada.

"Hey, look here Ada," he said, "it's your Dad's hat. Your Rose give it to me after he passed on, it's a bit small, but ah can manage."

Ada, lost for words, bent over and began rummaging in the picnic bag, unsure whether to laugh or cry.

It was a matter of pride to Ada that she dress her family as well as she possibly could and they had all set out that morning in their Sunday best, and had even managed to arrive at their destination still looking good, apart from a droopy sock and limp hair ribbon here and there. But by 4pm, after a day spent on the beach, they were all beginning to look decidedly grubby.

Harold turned up after his beer sampling tour, slightly unsteady on his legs and full of alcoholic good humour, but Ada by this time was tired of coping with the hungry children and sick of sitting in the not too comfortable deck chair. Her neck was aching and all she wanted was a nice cup of tea.

Of course, Harold was in much too good a mood to notice the warning glare she gave him and proceeded to plant a kiss on her cheek, breathing beery fumes all over her as he did so.

Slowly lowering himself into the deck chair nearest to his wife, he also failed to notice that Ada had kicked the back rung of the deck chair out of its socket, and Harold found himself falling flat on his back with his legs in the air.

The children laughed so much that they forgot their hunger and cold wet feet, and the sight of Harold flailing about on top of the collapsed chair caused poor Mr Smithson to lose his loose fitting dentures as he threw back his head and laughed till tears rolled down his face.

Harold sat up, looked around at his audience and declared in his husky voice, "What's tha lot bloody laughing at?" Then rolled back on to the floor and pulled Ada on top of him in spite of her protests that everyone was staring at them.

Not caring who was looking, Harold gave his wife a long lingering kiss, the kind he usually saved for the privacy of their bedroom, before he released her and gave her a push to help her up. On her feet again, Ada dusted down her clothes and pulled the brim of her hat lower to hide her blushes.

"Harold Corker," she exclaimed, "tha gets dafter," but she couldn't help a smile as she said it.

Harold held out his hand. "Give us a pull up lass, will tha, ah've got summat to show thee."

Shaking her head and tutting, Ada helped him up and stood waiting as he searched his pockets and produced a piece of crumpled white paper. He proceeded with irritating slowness to unravel it. Impatiently Ada took it from him and as she smoothed it out she gasped, "Harold, it's a five pound note, where did tha get this?"

"It was a lovely little horse, love. Romped in first she did. Everybody said she hadn't a chance, but ah knew she could do it. Ah put a dollar on her at 20 to 1. What does tha think of that? Come on, ah'm gonna buy us all fish and chips wi it, an tha can av what's left as long as tha gives me some beer money."

Stanley and Ernest had stood together on the edge of the group and joined in the laughter, but Stanley in particular didn't really know what to make of it all. He was not used to seeing his father and mother like this, in a happy carefree mood. He certainly understood the five pound note though, and the mention of fish and chips started his stomach rumbling.

Nudging Ernest to help him, he began gathering up the shoes and socks belonging to his younger siblings and urged them to put them on.

Within half an hour they were sitting on a bench near the harbour, holding newspaper cones full of steaming chips and scraps of fish. Stanley had sprinkled his liberally with salt, and so much vinegar that the fumes rising with the steam made his eyes sting.

Turning to his mother, he said it was the most delicious meal he had ever eaten. Giving him a fond look, she leaned over and kissed him on the top of his head. That completed the day for Stanley and he filed the memory away to think of many times over the rest of his life.

CHAPTER 22

Less than two weeks after their seaside trip, Edith and Sarah left home to begin work. They were both to go into service at two separate large houses in Lincolnshire. Edith, as the eldest, tried to put a brave face on, although inside she was quaking with nerves and tension at the thought of setting off for a place she had never seen. Lincolnshire, to both of them, might have been at the other side of the world for all they knew about it.

Most of the family trooped down to the station to see them off on a rainy Friday afternoon. They would both be sadly missed, although the extra space in the house with two less would be welcome. Edith was like a second mother to all the family and Sarah never failed to cheer them all up with her happy disposition and constant chattering.

Ada was a bag of nerves, worrying in case they got lost out in the wilds of Lincolnshire and also concerned about how on earth she was going to cope without their help.

Stanley and Ernest were the next in line age wise and their older sisters' work was soon delegated to them. Scrubbing the steps and window sills was to be one of Stanley's regular Saturday jobs, and he tackled them with the thoroughness that was to become his trademark, even brushing and applying yellow donkey stone to the surrounds of the grates and cellar opening.

As he proudly surveyed his work he challenged everyone in the family not to walk on them and woe betide anyone who did.

He had quickly learned to keep out of his father's way whenever possible, knowing from bitter experience that he was more likely to receive a blow or a tongue lashing than a word of praise or encouragement.

Until, that is, the Whitsuntide of 1930 when Harold discovered that Stanley was a good runner and a favourite to win in the children's section of the race that took place without fail every Whit Monday.

Encouraged by his brothers and sisters, Stanley had entered the race and in an ancient pair of plimsols began training. To his surprise he suddenly found himself the centre of his father's attention for the first time.

On a borrowed bicycle Harold rode alongside him shouting instructions and urging him to go faster. At the pub each evening he boasted that his son was a favourite to be the first across the line and took bets from many of his drinking mates.

Whit Monday dawned bright but bitterly cold for May and Stanley shivered as he stood on the start line dressed in a pair of well washed but very baggy pit shorts belonging to Herbert and a much too large vest. The pimsols had holes in the soles and Stanley examined them anxiously hoping they would last out the race. Most of the competitors were no better dressed than he, but none of them lacked enthusiasm or determination to win.

The five pound prize money was a great incentive and there was not a single entrant that did not dream of winning it.

The runners jostled into position at the starting line in the centre of Wath, and accompanied by loud cheers and applause they were off. It was to be a long run, up West Melton and back again, through the shopping centre, up Sandygate, then down into Doncaster Road, ending up opposite the post office.

The race quickly separated into two groups, with the adults at the front and the children following behind. By the time they reached West Melton both the adult and children's groups had been depleted as one after another gave up and dropped out of the race. Back down into Wath they came, all running hard and panting heavily. Stanley was tall for his age and not an ounce of spare fat on him. As more of the runners dropped out, the groups split again as they tackled the steepest part of Sandygate, with Stanley and two of his rivals leading.

To Stanley's dismay, his father appeared alongside of him as he drew level with New Road, riding the borrowed bicycle. At first he rode at the side of him shouting encouragement, but soon fell back and stopped, out of breath as the strain of pedalling uphill took its toll on his miner's dust- filled lungs.

Stanley couldn't resist a smile as he bounded up the hill, leaving his father behind and concentrated on keeping up with his rivals.

They picked up speed as the marshals directed them down Burnham Road, running with longer strides now that they were going downhill. As he ran Stanley began to realise there was something wrong with his shoes and glanced down as his right foot came forwards and saw that the sole had parted company from the flimsy canvas top.

Gritting his teeth he altered his stride to try and make the flapping sole make contact with the tarmac before his bare toes did.

Tony Kirby, who was Stanley's strongest rival, grinned as he saw his predicament and gasped, "Got ya Daley," as he ran.

By the time they were on the homeward stretch along Doncaster Road Stanley had dropped back into third position and was concentrating hard on maintaining as much speed as he could while coping with the flapping shoe. To add to his problems his father reappeared, having cut down the side street and shouted at him to get a move on.

With the pain of a stitch in his side and a foot sore from scraping on the tarmac, Stanley put all he had into catching the two leaders and although he kept pace he just couldn't find the strength to overtake them.

Tony Kirby reached the finish line first, closely followed by a lad from Mexborough, while Stanley came in at third. As he passed the line he came to a stop on the pavement and leaned on the blackened stone wall at the side of the road. Herbert had been waiting at the finish line and cheered him across. Patting him on the back he praised him. "Well done Stan, tha's got third."

Stanley looked up, thrilled at the praise but his face fell as his father muttered, "Useless bugger, what good's third," and rode off.

"Take no notice of him, Stan, he's a miserable old sod sometimes," consoled Herbert. "And besides don't forget tha's won a pound for third prize, ah should go an collect it before ar auld fella finds out about it."

Stanley's face lit up at the thought of the pound and shot off to the red velvet covered table that had been set up for the officials to sit at.

The minute the money was in his hand he set off home, wanting to catch his mother alone. He found her bringing in the washing. Taking the basket from her he followed her into the kitchen. "Here mam, ah've got summat for ya," he said as he held out the envelope.

Ada looked him up and down and shook her head at the sight he made in his makeshift running clothes, and then saw his toes poking out of his shoe.

"Just look at the state of thee Stanley," she grumbled as she tore open the envelope.

"It's for you mam," he said proudly, "ah won it for you."

Ada sat down and put her head in her hands, completely overcome and lost for words

"What's up Mam? What yer cryin' for? Ah thought yer'd be pleased."

Ada lifted her head, smiling with a tear running down her cheeks. "Oh, ah am pleased love, and does tha know what's the first thing ah'm going to buy wi it?

Stanley shook his head.

"A new pair of running shoes for thee!"

"Ah. That's good, then next year ah'll be able to get first prize!"

Ada laughed at his confidence and warned him to say nothing to his brothers and sisters, and especially nothing to his father.

With Herbert and Billy now fully fledged miners and contributing to the housekeeping, they were excused gardening duties on the allotment and the job fell to Stanley and Ernest. They had so many fights about it that in the end Stanley told his half brother to clear off. Which Ernest did with great relief.

Left in full control of the piece of land, Stanley was in his natural element and gradually organised it. He was soon producing such a plentiful supply of vegetables that even his father gave him a nod of approval as he stood at the gate and surveyed the orderly rows of produce.

In late October that year Stanley planned to have a day out alone, away from the noise and tension of a large family living in a small house. He said nothing to anyone and rose early one Sunday morning in mid October. He slid out of the bedroom with barely a sound, carefully avoiding the creaking floorboard near the window and eased the door open an inch at a time.

Harold turned over as he passed, his eyes flickered and Stanley held his breath, crossing his fingers that he wouldn't wake up, but Harold gave a little snore, snuggled further down the bed and went back into a sound sleep.

Stanley gave a sigh of relief; as much as he cared for his younger brother, he didn't want him or any of the others tagging along today. Ten minutes later he was leaving the house, his face and hair still feeling damp from his hasty wash. As usual he left via the back garden and through the allotment, admiring his straight rows of carrots and swedes as he walked quickly down the path.

He glanced back at the house half expecting to be called back to perform some task, or take the younger children out with him, but the curtains were still closed and he blew his breath out with a big relieved sigh and set off up the lane. He'd left a note for his mother propped against the kettle telling her he'd be back at teatime but had said nothing about where he was going. No doubt he'd be in trouble when he got back, but Stanley thought it would be worth it.

He took a short cut over the race course and headed towards West Melton. His destination was the village of Wentworth where he intended to see Hoober Stand which was a famous folly, well known in the area. It was said that it was a hundred foot high and Stanley wanted to see it for himself.

It had been barely light when he set off and there was a sharp almost frosty feel to the air, but by the time he had been walking for half an hour the sun had risen and it promised to be a beautiful day.

With sixpence in his pocket he had enough to treat himself to a hot pie for his dinner, and he felt so carefree he began to sing his favourite song out loud. It took him till late morning to reach the folly, and he stood for minutes gazing at it before he ventured through the gate and right up to the door set deep in the brickwork.

From this angle the tower seemed higher than ever and Stanley could well believe that it was a hundred foot high. He would have loved to climb to the top and view the surrounding countryside but the door was firmly locked. A sign nailed there informed him that the tower was closed for repairs but would be open next spring.

As he continued his walk he took notice of the countryside, admiring the farm stock grazing and the newly ploughed fields. One had been harrowed and sown with winter wheat. Guarding it against the crows and land gulls was the best dressed scarecrow that Stanley had ever seen. It stood in the centre of the field, slightly tilted, with its arms outstretched, wearing a brown tweed overcoat. Glancing about to check there was no one around Stanley jumped the dyke and scrambled through the hedge. Then with a further check to left and right he was off, racing across the field, his long legs taking large strides. His feet sank into the soft newly turned soil, leaving large footprints. As he reached the scarecrow he could see its body was a straw filled sack, the top part rounded and formed into a head shape. An old cap had been tied on top and a garish face painted, with a wide grinning mouth and two black eyes. A stick had been tied to its arm in an effort to fool the birds into thinking it was a gun.

But there was no time to admire the farmer's handiwork and Stanley quickly unfastened the coat, rolled it up and retraced his steps, leaving the scarecrow toppled over, now just a bag of straw with the cap beside it on the floor.

He waited to examine the coat until he reached home, entering as he had left that morning, through the back gate of the allotment and let himself straight into the garden shed.

As he unrolled the coat and shook it straight he held it against himself, then slipped his arms into it and felt the comforting weight of the fabric cover him. The sleeves were too long, but he tucked them up and reassured himself that his mother would shorten them for him if he chose the right time to ask her.

First though, he would have to think of a satisfactory explanation as to how he had acquired it. In the meantime, he hung it up carefully behind a few lengths of wood out of sight.

In the end, he told his mother the truth, but he had to wait almost a week in order to catch the right moment. It was on the following Friday afternoon when she was nursing her youngest baby, Cyril, while Herbert's girlfriend, Mavis, pinned up her hair in metal curling rods. Ada had recently had her long hair cut shorter and now wore it the tight waves and curls that were more fashionable.

Stanley hovered about in the kitchen, willing Mavis to hurry up and finish. Herbert looked at him over the top of his newspaper as he sat on the stool in the corner.

"What's up wi thee Stan? Tha's like a cat on hot bricks."

"Nought," replied Stanley as he went to the sink and turned on the tap. Bending over he drank straight from it. "Ah just want a word wi mam, on me own."

Herbert sat up, stretching his arms behind his head. He was obviously in a teasing mood. "Mmm," he said. "What's tha been up to? Not got some lass into trouble, has tha? Is tha gunna have to get married quick?"And he grinned as Stanley threw a pretend punch at him.

Mavis came through just in time to stop it developing into a wrestling match. Straightening the ruffled mats she picked up her handbag and demanded that they set off on their date.

Thankfully Stanley waved them off and, taking a deep breath, went to explain the new overcoat to his mother.

"Tha's got what?" she asked. "An overcoat? Where did tha get that from then?"

"Well, ah sort of found it."

"What does tha mean, tha sort of found it? Was it at side of t'road or summat?"

"Well, actually, it were on a scarecrow," explained Stanley, his face colouring up.

Ada hesitated, taking in what he had said.

"What? Tha pinched off a boody scarecrow?"

"Yes mam, cos ah thought ah needed it more than he did."

"Ah dunt bloody know, tha'll get sent down t'line before tha's done, pinching a bloody scarecrow's coat." Her lips twitched in spite of her stern words. "Ah reckon tha's right though, tha does need it more than him. Let's av a look at it then."

As Stanley ran to the shed for the coat he reflected on his mother's words and the expression she had used about being sent 'down the line'. For years, when he was younger, he had visualised someone being sent to a little hut somewhere along the railway lines, until one day it had dawned on him that it meant being sent to prison.

As Ada looked at the overcoat and exclaimed on its good quality, she cross examined her son. "Is tha sure no one saw thee?" she asked repeatedly.

Then she promised to shorten it, on condition that he shared it with Ernest.

He nodded in agreement, but silently resolved that Ernest would never get the chance to wear it.

Stanley was growing up fast. By the time he was twelve his playing days were well past. The long summer days of running wild with his brothers and mates faded into the distance. He thought with affection of his mother, standing at the bedroom window and shouting them all in for dinner, her voice echoing up to the racecourse as she shouted their names out loudly one by one.

She still called them in but his name was not among them, now he was twelve going on thirteen he was almost old enough to start working, and as he dug the allotment he decided it was time to go and look for a job.

CHAPTER 23

Stanley began his farming career at 6am on a Saturday morning in the autumn of 1931. Before his brothers were awake he was walking into the farmyard in Sandygate feeling nervous but excited.

As he reached the cowhouse door he could hear the fast regular swish of milk hitting the metal pails and smell the unmistakable aroma of cows in a confined space.

He could see his new employer, Mr Downing, at the far end of the building, wearing a brown overall with the sleeves rolled up and a trilby pulled well down over his eyes.

He acknowledged Stanley with a nod of his head, and then with another nod indicated for Stanley to come over to him. The two men already at work gave him a curt, "Nah then," in unison, then bent their heads down again, concentrating on the milking. One of them whistled tunelessly, and Stanley jumped as Mr Downing bellowed out, "Stop that bloody whistling, will tha? It's enough to turn t'milk sour; tha's giving poor cows a bloody headache."

Stanley flinched, wondering what sort of reception he could expect. But as he reached him he gave Stanley a kindly glance and almost smiled, then handed him a brown smock that had seen the inside of the wash tub many times and been repaired many times too. The top pocket had been removed and used to repair a large hole in the middle of the back, which looked a little odd, but Stanley put it on and wore it with pride.

"Nah then son," his employer said as he handed him a small three legged stool. "Sit thee sen down same as Eric and Ben over there and hold t'bucket between thee knees. She's nice and quiet is this one, but watch out for her tail, she's gorra habit of cloutin' thee round t'earhole wi it."

Stanley sat down gingerly and positioned the bucket with care between his knees.

"That's it son, tha's a natural, nah ger hold of her teats, just the two nearest to thee for a start, seeing as tha's only got two hands. Nah, pull and squeeze, pull and squeeze, gentle but firm like."

Straight away the milk began to flow and Mr Downing almost danced about in his praise of Stanley.

"Hey, look at this lads, ah told thee, he's a natural. Yor two ad better buck thee ideas up, else you'll both be out of a job."

Stanley fairly glowed at his words and hardly noticed as the cow's tail hit him twice. With the pail almost full, he stood up, carefully shielding the milk with a damp cloth.

As he backed out of the stall the cow turned her head towards him and looked him in the eye, her mouth grinding methodically.

Patting her rump, Stanley just managed to step out of the way as she arched her back, and let forth a stream of wet brown liquid from her rear end that splashed as it hit the floor.

Thankful that she had missed the bucket of milk, Stanley proudly placed it alongside the churns, and waited for instructions. His next task was to turn the cows loose and take them to the field.

"Nah then, Stan me lad," announced Eric, "gaffer's gone for his breakfast. We've to get these auld girls out into t'pasture, and then we'll get t'muckin' out done. Thee turn em loose, startin' wi Daisy near t'door, and watch thee feet. She thinks it's funny to stand on thee toes."

Cautiously, Stanley edged his way between the two cows in the first stall and unfastened the chain from around Daisy's neck. Easy enough, he thought, and he ran his hand over her silky fur and touched her horns briefly. As the chain clanged down on to the floor Daisy began to reverse, her splayed hooves skidding on the wet stone floor. He breathed in as her warm bulky body pressed him up against the neighbouring cow. She moved over and gave her head a toss, impatient to be free. Wasting no time he slipped the straight metal bar through the ring on her chain and skipped out of the way before she had even moved.

214

"That's right lad, tha's learning." He looked up to see Eric nodding with approval. "It pays to ger out of t'way fast, if tha don't want thee feet squashing."

Stanley moved more confidently now, elbowing his way between the animals and standing well back as they filed along the centre of the cowhouse, jostling to be first through the door and out into the field at the top of the farm yard.

As he followed them over the rough cobbles, carefully avoiding the trail of steaming wet cow pats that they left, he looked them over, already feeling affection for them, and knew with complete certainty that this was how he wanted to spend his life.

If he'd had a choice Stanley would have stayed at the farm working all day and never set foot in school again, but he consoled himself with the thought that he would be back for the afternoon milking and set off for home at a fast run, eager to tell his mother all about his first day at work.

The days soon fell into a pattern. He would wake at 5am and by six be at the farm ready and eager to start work. After two hours helping with the milking he was on his way home again with just enough time to wash and eat a hasty breakfast before he set off for school.

When it came to farming he was a quick learner, and soaked up everything that Mr Downing and his two employees were willing to teach him.

He was not such a willing pupil at school however and desperately wanted to leave and begin work full time.

Mr Downing, impressed by Stanley's aptitude, had offered him a full time job. With his thirteenth birthday in January Stanley hoped that the authorities would allow him to leave school at Christmas, but they were adamant that he would have to stay on until the end of the next term which was Easter.

Even Mr Downing's appearance at the school requesting that they waive their ruling as he was willing to employ him did no good. He was met with a firm refusal and Stanley had no alternative but to grit his teeth and abide by their decision.

In the meantime he continued to work two hours before school and another two hours after. Every week he became more skilled at looking after the livestock and more absorbed in the running of the farm.

Everyday it seemed there was something new to learn and Stanley was happier than he had been for a long time.

Ada was pleased to have another contribution to the housekeeping and at last was able to buy her tall lanky son his first pair of long trousers. With the threepence he was allowed to keep each week Stanley bought himself a piece of strong leather to repair his boots with. He set about repairing them, sitting cross-legged in the yard just outside the kitchen window using the cobblers last that had belonged to his grandfather. As he worked he thought of him and how he used to sit in exactly the same way repairing all the family's footwear.

He also thought of the boots he had seen at the farm, lying abandoned in a corner in the granary, covered in dust and cobwebs. The very next day he got his chance to examine the boots more closely when he went up into the granary to collect corn for the hens.

Picking up one of the boots, Stanley turned it upside down and banged it on the floor, dislodging a large spider that had made its home in there. As he squashed the spider he looked inside the boot and wiped away the thick net of cobwebs, shuddering a little at the touch of them. Satisfied that it was now free of residents he slipped his foot into the boot and tested the size of it. They were just a little too big but Stanley thought to himself as he admired them, 'These are going to be mine'.

Two days later when Mr Downing had left to deliver the fresh milk to his customers, Stanley fairly flew up the stone steps to claim the boots, and was soon on his way home with them tucked under his arm.

Taking the cinder covered path between the allotments, he let himself into the garden via the rear gate and slipping into the shed he tucked them away in his usual hiding place until he could find the time to clean them.

Half expecting to be challenged about the boots when he returned to work that evening, Stanley felt quite guilty and was exceptionally quiet, but nothing was said and he thankfully assumed that as the boots had been abandoned up in the granary they must have been forgotten about.

Later, with work over for the day, he locked himself in the shed with an old cloth and a tin of dubbin and set about transforming the battered old boots.

Thinking that no one could possibly recognise them now that they were polished and shining, Stanley wore the boots for work the next day.

As he walked up the driveway towards the farmhouse, MrDowning appeared. He bid Stanley a good morning and looked him up and down, his gaze lingering on his feet. He gave a little smile, nodded at Stanley and patted him on the shoulder, and Stanley realised he knew, but nothing was said.

The following month he was called to the farmhouse door as he returned from taking the cows to the field. Alarmed that he had might have done something wrong and was about to be sacked, Stanley stood waiting in the porch while his employer went inside. When he emerged again he was carrying a large brown paper parcel.

"Ah'm very pleased wi the way tha's worked Stan, here tha is, ah reckon tha can use these. They should fit."

Stanley unfolded the paper to find a brand new pair of boots. To his embarrassment he almost burst into tears, and unable to speak was forced to just nod his thanks, his face contorted by his efforts not to cry.

"It's all right son, thee gerroff home nah, and don't be late for t'afternoon milkin'." He waved as he closed the door and walked down the long passage with a lump in his throat as he thought of Stanley's face.

The house was full of family when Stanley arrived home. They were loudly discussing Ernest's new job, while Ernest sat on the long form, basking in his father's praise. Stanley had opened the door briefly, but his presence had not been noticed and he backed out again and sat in the kitchen listening.

He soon gathered that his half brother had decided to follow his example and go for a farming life instead of mining. He had evidently managed to get a job on a farm near the racecourse in Doncaster, and of course would be living in. As he listened, he heard the conversation turning to what Ernest would need.

"We'll have to get him a couple of pairs of long trousers," he heard his mother say, "and some boots!"

Stanley froze at these words, and his eyes fell on the brown carrier bag with his new boots inside.

"Oh no," he said quietly to himself, "Ah know what'll come next, and he's not aving em." And picking up the bag, he quietly left the kitchen, ran down the garden path, through the allotment and into the shed where he hid the boots away, until such a time as Ernest was kitted out and on his way to his new job.

Also stashed away in the shed was the bike his uncle John had given him. He had walked to Bolton the month earlier and practically carried it all the way home due to the front wheel being buckled.

He examined it now, feeling pleased with the progress he had made with repairing it; all he needed now was a new wheel.

It was as he was racking his brains to think of a way to obtain one that he heard voices and footsteps approaching the shed. Checking that the new boots were well hidden he opened the door to find his brother Harold and his cousin Jack.

"Hey up Stan, ah've got summat for thee." Jack gave a grin and produced a wheel from behind his back. "What does tha think of that then?"

Stan took hold of it. "Eeh just what ah need, where did tha ger it from?"

"Nah then, ask no questions, Stan. It'll cost thee two bob, but," he added seeing the look on Stanley's face, "tha can pay me a bit at a time, but say nowt to me dad, will tha?"

Stanley examined the wheel closely, holding it by its spindle and spinning it round to check that it ran true.

"Erm, ah'll tell thee what," he said, "ah'll give thee one and six pence. That's all ah can manage, and ah can give thee a bob now and a tanner next month."

"Well, alright then," said Jack tutting, "but ah want t'buckled wheel in part exchange."

Before he had time to change his mind Stan dug deep into his pocket, produced the shilling and handing it over then set about fitting the wheel.

As Jack left half an hour later carrying the old wheel he pointed at Stanley and reminded him, "Think on," he said, "say nowt to me Dad."

When he had gone, Harold turned to his brother.

"Stan," he said, "what does tha reckon ar Jack wants wi a buckled bike wheel?"

Stanley looked at him. "Well," he said slowly, "Ah've got a feeling that somebody, somewhere, is going to wake up in the morning and wonder how the hell his front bike wheel comes to be buckled when it was ok the night before."

Owning a bicycle made a huge difference to Stanley's life. Getting to and from work was of course much easier and quicker, but best of all it made it possible for him to see the countryside and villages outside of the Dearne Valley.

Every Sunday he was off. With a bottle of water and a roughly wrapped hunk of bread and jam strapped to the back of his bike, he explored the countryside in every direction.

One Sunday he arrived in Hooton Pagnell at midday and stood admiring the stone built cottages and listened, entranced, to the famous church clock play its melody.

He began to think that perhaps he could ride as far as Carlton to visit Doll and his aunt Lizzie. If he set off at dinnertime on a Saturday when he finished work he could just make it before dark and stay there overnight. What a surprise they would get when he turned up he thought!

But his mother had other plans for his weekend rides. Ernest was now away working on a farm near the Doncaster racecourse. He was living in with food provided, but the farmer's wife had made it clear that she was not prepared to do his laundry.

So Ada came up with the idea that Stanley, seeing as he now had transport, could cycle to Doncaster every weekend, taking Ernest his clean clothes and bringing back the dirty ones.

Stanley accepted the plan, reluctantly at first it has to be said, but eventually came to look upon it as a challenge and a bit of an adventure.

He had no map and no idea how to get to the farm where Ernest worked, so initially, he followed the Doncaster bus route out of Wath, through Mexborough and Denaby to Conisborough; and from there he watched for and followed the signposts until he arrived hungry and tired on the outskirts of Doncaster.

Leaning his bike against a low wall he walked up and down, trying to relieve his aching legs and saddle sore bottom. He re-tied the parcel of clean laundry on the back of his bike and tested the tyres. The front one was much softer than it had been when he had set off, and Stanley sent up a little prayer that it would last until he met up with Ernest. He remounted to make the last leg of his journey, with his bread and jam in one hand and his bottle of water rammed firmly into his pocket.

His instinct was to go right and he set off down the long wide road lined with newly built houses. Stanley admired them, noting the big bay windows hung with expensive curtains and stored the picture firmly in his mind, planning to describe them in detail to his mother.

Just as he was beginning to think he was lost, the white post and railed fences of the racecourse came into view, and then there was the grandstand whichwas awe inspiring to Stanley who had never seen it before. He thought about the racecourse back home in Wath and realised this one was in a different league altogether.

From there it was easy to find his way to the farm where Ernest worked and as he pedalled slowly up the incline, he could see him waiting at the gate.

They very nearly had a fall out before Stanley had even reached him when Ernest called out for him to ride faster. "Is that the best tha can do? No wonder tha's late."

But Stanley was in no mood for his comments and almost threw the parcel of clean clothes at him, got back on the bike and began to free wheel down the hill towards Doncaster.

Ernest left the parcel where it had fallen and ran after him. "Wait Stan," he called, "ah were only kidding, don't be like that. Ah'm sorry."

Stanley stopped and turning around was shocked to see that Ernest was almost in tears. "What's up ar kid?"

Ernest swallowed a few times before he replied, "Ah hate it here Stan. Gaffer's a right slave driver and t'other lads are a nasty bunch. Ah'd pack it in if it weren't for what me father'd say."

"Come on Ernest, it can't be that bad. It's better than going down t'pit int it? Tha'll get used to it."

He put his hand on his brother's shoulder briefly as they walked down the rough track that led to the farm, and for a while they were best mates.

Ernest showed him his sleeping quarters and changed into his clean clothes while Stanley looked around the bare rooms above the barn that was home to the five other lads who worked on the farm. Ernest was the youngest and had been the butt of their crude jokes since he had begun.

As he told his brother about it Stanley thought that it was no wonder he was unhappy and was more than thankful for his own job at Downing's farm.

"Tha'll have to stand up to em Ernest," he urged him. "Pick on one that tha can beat and give him a leathering as soon as he starts. That'll make t'others respect thee a bit more."

Ernest nodded doubtfully, thinking that if he did that they would likely all gang up on him.

"It's all right for thee to talk Stan, tha dunt have to stand up to em. They're all out at t'pub nah, and they'll all be canned up when they get back and worse than ever." He looked close to tears again and Stanley felt sorry for him in spite of their past differences.

"Well pack thee bags nah, and we'll set off home, we can take turns at riding t'bike."

"Nah Stan, ah can't do that, tha knows what me father's like, he'll av me down t'pit staight away."

Stanley knew he was right and that Ernest had no choice but to try and stick it out and hope that things improved.

He said as much and added that he should start looking for another job, little thinking that that advice would cause problems for himself in the not too distant future.

But for now they spent the next hour walking around the farm, which Stanley, on noting the dirty cow house and the grass growing between the cobbles in the yard, declared with all the wisdom of someone with just a few months' experience, that it was very badly run and a disgrace.

They were unable to fix the slow puncture in Stanley's bike wheel due to neither of them having a puncture outfit. Ernest did go very nervously to the door of the farmhouse and asked his employer if he could borrow one, but was sent away empty handed and with a stern reminder that it was Sunday. "Don't tha know it's Sunday," he said. "Tha should keep the Sabbath holy,"and he slammed the door in his face.

Stanley thought it made no difference to his bike tyre, it was going to go flat whatever the day was, and he could visualise himself walking most of the way home.

He pumped the tyre up again and set off, promising to return the following weekend, while a very miserable looking Ernest waved him off and watched until he disappeared from sight.

It seemed a long way home with many stops to inflate the tyre, giving Stanley plenty of time to resolve that he would always carry a repair kit with him in future.

He rode to Doncaster again on the next two weekends, by which time the novelty of the journey had definitely worn off, especially as it rained all the way home on both of the trips.

He arrived home wet through and thankful to see a good fire glowing in the living room, and stood in front of it shivering, grateful to be soaking in its warmth. But he soon found that the comfort of the fire was to be short-lived when his father came downstairs from his Sunday afternoon nap and told him to clear off into the kitchen.

Stanley dared to protest. "Ah were just getting warm Dad. Ah got wet through riding home from taking our Ernest his clothes."

However, there was no sympathy coming his way as his father jeered at him, "What's up wi thee, ah thought all you farmers were hard and could stand a bit of cold weather?Go on, gerroff into t'kitchen out of t'way while ah av me tea."

Stanley went, still wet and full of resentment, and sat on the stool in the corner of the kitchen to eat the cold dinner that had been sitting on the table since dinnertime.

Harold followed him with Cyril practically treading on his heels and they stood at the side of their older brother while he ate and gradually dried out and entertained them with stories of his bike ride and the famous racecourse at Doncaster.

By the time he set off on the fourth Sunday with the parcel of clean clothes Stanley was feeling pretty fed up with the whole business of being Ernest's personnel laundry deliverer. His old bike creaked and protested with every turn of the pedals; the brakes were almost non-existent and as he rode he day dreamed about owning a new one.

Then it came to him in a flash of inspiration! He'd buy himself a new bike!

He had just over ten pounds hidden away in his secret hiding place in the shed. He had been adding to his savings bit by bit, by any means that he could. Although he still gave his mother his wages and received just a small amount pocket money from them in return, Stanley figured that overtime money was his, and said nothing to anyone about it. He sold any spare cabbages from the allotment and moved loads of coal for anyone willing to pay him. It had all added up and with every penny he saved he felt more independent.

The thought of a new bike excited him and lifted his spirits. And then he had what he thought was his best idea yet. He would sell his old bike to Ernest! And then he could ride home himself every Sunday and collect his own laundry! Yes, thought Stanley, elated by his idea, he would charge him £1 for the old bike. That seemed like a fair price. But Ernest never had any money to spare, and he doubted he would ever pay him back if he let him have the bike before he got the cash.

He pondered the problem as he rode, and it was just as he came within sight of Conisborough castle that the solution hit him. He'd get the £1 from his mother, and then she could deduct it from the pocket money that was due back to Ernest from his wages, which, like Stanley's, went to swell the family finances.

He felt sure that his mother would agree to it and he sang out loud all the rest of the way.

For once his plans fell into place, and by Wednesday he had spotted just what he was looking for in Sammy Bowley's shop window. There it was, a dark green Raleigh that had been pawned and not collected. At £12 it was just above his limit but with some hard bargaining he was able to buy it for £11. That cleared all his savings, but as he rode it home proudly and listened to the characteristic tick tick from the Raleigh free wheel he felt it was worth every penny.

Ernest arrived home on Saturday night for the first time in six weeks and was treated like a returned hero by his brothers and sisters who listened to his stories about his experiences.

He was pleased to have Stanley's old bike as a means of transport, until that is he saw the new Raleigh and the green eyed monster of jealousy reared its ugly head and he couldn't help asking in a surly voice, "How's tha managed to afford that then?"

Stanley grinned, "Cos ah worked for it and saved me money instead of wasting it."

Ernest couldn't think of an answer to that and went into the house to complain to his mother about how unfair it was, but he got short shrift from Ada who told him abruptly to stop trying to cause trouble and added that it was time he was setting off back to Doncaster.

CHAPTER 24

Ernest was not the only one to be unhappy away from home. Edith and Sarah had both obtained posts in two separate houses in Lincolnshire.

The two houses and employers couldn't have been more different.

Edith found herself living in a tall three storey town house in the centre of Gainsborough.For the first time in her life Edith had a room to herself, a smart uniform to wear, plenty of food and a little money of her own. Her employer was a strict but kindly woman, who expected hard work from her staff but treated them with consideration.

Poor Sarah on the other hand had drawn an unlucky card and found herself living on a farm in an isolated area of Lincolnshire with miles of flat countryside stretching out as far as she could see. The farmer's wife, Mrs Brown, was mean to the point of being miserly and put so little food on the table that Sarah, who had always been slim and dainty, was soon looking half starved and feeling thoroughly miserable.

She kept it all to herself, not wanting to complain, until Edith, suspecting there was something wrong, made the long journey out to visit her sister on her day off. Shocked by Sarah's appearance she wasted no time in writing home to Harold and Ada, telling them in great detail how distressed her sister was and how badly she was being treated.

Harold read the letter three times before looking up from it, his face bright red with anger and said, "Ah'm fetching ar Sarah home tomorrow Ada. Here, read this," and he passed the letter over to her. "Ah'm not avin' ar lass treated like that. Just bloody wait till ah get there, ah shall av summat to say to that mean old bugger."

Ada nodded, she could hardly bear the thought of their happy, cheerful little Sarah being badly treated.So Harold, early next morning looking impressive in his best suit, caught the train to Gainsborough.

His face and mouth were set into that look that said he was going to stand no nonsense from anyone. As he strode down the street towards the station, Ada commented to her younger daughters that she would like to be a fly on the wall when their Dad came face to face with the farmer's wife.

It was for certain that she was going to get an unpleasant surprise when she opened her door to find a very blunt Yorkshireman on her doorstep.

As it happened, it was Sarah herself who opened the door and was so surprised to see her father there that she was speechless. At a glance Harold saw how pale and drawn his daughter looked and he reached out his hand towards her. "Nah then lass, tha didn't expect to see me did tha?"

Sarah shook her head and a tear trickled down her cheek and she stepped towards him.

It was then that Harold became aware of someone behind him and he turned swiftly to find a woman striding across the yard. She was wearing a pair of men's tweed trousers and a dirty trilby hat on the back of her head. As soon as she spoke he realised that this was the woman he had been preparing himself to meet, and he drew in his breath and waited.

"What's all this then? Sarah, why aren't you scrubbing the dairy floor? Get on with it." She took a grubby handkerchief from her pocket and blew her nose loudly before addressing Harold, who she evidently mistook for a salesman. "If tha's trying to sell summat tha's come to t'wrong place so bugger off, we don't need owt."

As she pushed past him Harold caught a whiff of stale body odour mixed with animal smell.

"Well, what's tha waiting for, ah've told thee to clear off,"she said. Then turning her attention to Sarah who was stood with her back against the wall, she raised her hand in a threatening gesture. Harold was between her and his daughter in a flash.

"Ah wouldn't do that if I were thee," and even as he spoke he had a quick vision of Ada nodding with approval that he had kept his temper.

Leaning towards Mrs Brown he said very quietly, "That's my daughter tha's threatening, and tha'll not be doing it any longer, she's coming home wi me nah, and by God if tha were a man, ah'd smash thee face in for t'way tha's been treating her. Look at state of her, tha bloody cruel auld bitch."

Turning to a white-faced Sarah he told her to get her clothes packed quickly, and she needed no second bidding. Within five minutes she was back downstairs with her few clothes pushed into her cloth bag.

If Mrs Brown thought that was the end of it she was mistaken. Harold demanded, and got, Sarah's wages that were owed to her and as they left he gave her some advice. "Tha needs a bath Mrs, tha stinks worse than them pigs."

It was late evening by the time Harold returned home with his exhausted daughter following close behind.

Ada was shocked at the state of Sarah and would not have believed that her health could have deteriorated so much in just a few short weeks. What hurt her more than anything else was that Sarah began to cry and said she was sorry her Dad had had to fetch her home. Putting her arms around her, Ada was not far away from tears herself but held it all inside and told her not to be silly, it was not her fault, and everything would be alright now she was safely back home.

Her brothers and sisters stood around her, not sure how to treat their Sarah who had changed so much.

For the next few days she was the centre of the family's attention and slowly her smile came out again and she ate everything that Ada put in front of her.

Stanley picked her up every day and pretended to weigh her, declaring that she was getting fat, while Sarah giggled and shouted at him to put her down.

After three weeks she was back to her usual self, with her wide toothy smile and sunny nature, but still stick thin as she always would be. Edith arrived home with the news that there was a job going at the house where she worked and said it was Sarah's for the asking.

Harold was reluctant to let her go. Sarah had always been special to him. But she pleaded so long that he agreed in the end, reassured by Edith that she would be safe there.

So Sarah set off again for the wilds of Lincolnshire with Edith as her minder, and they worked happily together, returning to Wath only for weekends and holidays.

CHAPTER 25

With his transport and weekly laundry delivery problems solved, Stanley turned his attention to his sleeping arrangements. He hated having to sleep with two of his brothers. Three in a bed was two too many in Stanley's opinion and he determined to do something about it. But with two double beds in a small bedroom, the only floor space left spare was a narrow area at the end of one of the beds.

Stanley lay down in it and stretched his long body full length. He smiled to himself as he thought that it would do.

The very next day he searched the upstairs barn at the farm until he found two hessian sacks that looked cleaner than the rest, and measured them end to end. He estimated that they would be just over six foot long when he sewed them together.

Instead of going home when work was done, he set about joining them using the large needle that they used for repairing the sacks. Once his giant bag was made, he filled it to the brim with soft oat straw and carried it home on his bike, pushing it up Sandygate and into China Town.

Unsure what his mother would say to a huge bag of straw being taken upstairs,he concealed it in the shed for the time being.

Harold stared at it. "What's that for Stan?"

"It's my new bed," came the reply and was rewarded by an incredulous look from his younger brother.

But Stanley was not ready to put his new bed in place yet. He needed bedding, and went to visit Samuel Bowley again.

As he entered the shop Sammy recognised him. "Here tha is again me lad," he called, adjusting his fingerless mittens. He gave what passed for a smile and continued, "Tha's one of me best customers, what can ah do thee for today?"

Stanley looked around. "Ah want a couple of blankets. How much are they?"

Sammy gave him a sidelong glance. "Well now then, how much have you got to spend young man?"

In his pocket was the ten shillings he had saved since he had bought the bike from this very shop, but Stanley had no intention of letting Sammy know exactly how much he had. "Eight bob," he replied.

Sammy pursed his lips and sucked in his breath through his teeth, "Eee that's not going to buy thee much ah'm afraid. Blankets have gone up in price recently."

Stanley's face showed nothing. He was learning the art of bargaining fast. He wandered around the shop until a bundle caught his eye. There was at least one blanket and a sheet all wrapped around by a green satin eiderdown and tied up with brown string.

"Can ah have a look at this one?" he asked.

"Eee, ah can't sell thee that lot for eight bob. Here have a look at it. Tha can see it's quality is this one. Tha's got a good eye lad." And he pulled the bundle apart and rolled out the bedding. A damp musty smell rose up from it and Stanley bent over and sniffed at it.

"Phew, it pongs a bit Mr Bowley, how long's it been in t'shop?"

He had hit a sore point there. It had been left wrapped up in a wardrobe at the back of the shop for almost two years, and mould was beginning to grow on the innermost part of the rolled up sheets.

Pulling a sad face Sammy informed his young customer, "Well seeing as you're a regular customer, ah can let you have it for ten bob," and he sighed.

"Ah'm sorry Mr Bowley ah can't afford it. Ah only have eight bob, ah'll have to leave it," and he turned and walked away.

Sammy waited until he was about to close the door after him on the way out.

"Wait young fella," and he almost groaned as he continued, "go on, just this once. Tha can have it for eight bob. Your bloody family will bankrupt me. Tha knows ah'm selling this at a loss don't tha?"

"Aye, ah know Mr Bowley these are hard times aren't they?" Stanley very carefully extracted eight shillings from his pocket and placed it in Sammy's hand, and smiled all the way home with his bedding balanced on his handlebars.

As he walked into the kitchen at home he could see that his mother was in the middle of her regular Saturday afternoon job of washing the men's pit clothes so that they would be ready for wearing on Monday morning.

She lifted her head and glanced at him, noting the bundle under his arm.

Stanley thought how pale and tired she looked.

"Now what's tha up to? What's tha got there?"

Stanley took the clothes posher from her; it always reminded him of an upside down colander attached to a pole. "Ah'll finish this mam, sit down a bit," and he attacked the clothes in the tub, pushing them up and down vigorously till the water turned black with the coal dust that was embedded in the cloth.

Ada sat down with a weary sigh and waited for his explanation. As he worked he told her of his plans for his own bed, and waited for an ear bashing, but none came. Instead she unpacked the bedding and examined it closely.

"It bloody stinks Stanley. Tha'd better get some clean water when tha's finished them and give this lot a good wash, ah'm not having them upstairs till ah know they're clean, and don't use all t'hot water. Kids need a bath tonight." Stanley nodded and took the pit clothes out to hang on the line before he refilled the tub and set about his own washing.

By Monday evening his bed was ready and he squeezed into the narrow space and pulled the eiderdown up to his chin, delighting in the soft satiny feel of it.

Apart from the narrowness of his bed, the only other two problems were firstly, the straw in the mattress that creaked and rustled everytime he moved, and secondly, the fact that being on the floor meant he had a his eyeline was levelwith the chamber pots under the beds and even worse, the full view of his brothers using them! Ada's insistence when they moved in to Oak Road that the chamber pots be discarded hadn't lasted long at all, and she'd had to relent for a bit of peace.

So Stanley turned his face to the wall and slept every night on his side, but on the whole he reckoned it was worth a few inconveniences in order to be able to sleep on his own.

He was not the only one to love that satin eiderdown. His mother's cat, Monty, also loved the new bed and spent most afternoons curled up on it fast asleep. Stanley tolerated the cat sleeping on it, but came upstairs after work one day to find that the cat had used the centre of his precious eiderdown as a toilet, and left there a large pile of offending mess.

The cat sat on the windowsill by the open window casually washing itself and gave Stanley that disdainful look that all cats have perfected.

Stanley looked from the mess, to Monty, and back again. Almost speechless with rage he picked up the cat he hurled it through the open window.

Ada was in the kitchen at the time washing pots and gazing down the garden, when Monty flashed past and landed on the ground in front of her with a loud meow, before jumping to his feet and darting across the grass to hide under the thick hawthorn hedge.

Panicking that the cat might be hurt Ada rushed outside still clutching the tea towel. Her daughters were playing in the garden, and Betty, who had witnessed the whole thing and feeling full of importance called out, "Mam. Ar Stan threw Monty through t'window, ah saw him."

At that moment Stanley appeared at the kitchen door, carrying the soiled eiderdown. Before he had time to speak Ada set about him with the tea towel, lashing out at him as he ran down the garden path and leapt over the gate, leaving his mother shouting loud enough for all the street to hear.

He didn't stop until he reached the shed at the bottom of the allotment and opened the door to find Cyril and Harold sitting on the floor sorting out their large collection of marbles.

Harold looked up. "What's up Stan?"

There was an incredulous silence for a moment after he had given them the whole story, until Cyril, still sitting cross legged on the floor said, "Well, ah know Monty's been wanting to learn how to fly!" Then a big grin broke out on his face as his brothers laughed.

"It's not funny though Cyril, ah shouldn't av thrown him out of t'window, ah were just that mad. He's not hurt though. Well, ah don't think he is. Me Mam'll never forgive me. Ah'll have to leave home."

And he sat down with a big sigh and said, "Bloody cat."

Half an hour passed before he could bring himself to begin cleaning the quilt. As he unrolled it a foul aroma filled the air and Cyril ran outside gagging and retching. Harold shook his head at him and called him a big ninny, but was forced to put his hand over his nose as he brought in scoops of water from the rain barrel outside, using an old tin pan.

Stanley scraped away the mess and gradually washed it clean, cursing the cat every minute and swore he would have drowned it if it had been there at that precise moment.

Harold and Cyril went in for their tea but Stanley thought he had better lay low for a while longer. Eventually however, hunger drove him indoors and he realised just how angry his mother was when he found that she had left him no food.

But support came for him from an unexpected quarter. His brothers had obviously told their parents what the cat had done and he heard his father say quite clearly, "Well ah have to tell thee Ada, if that cat had shit on my bed, ah'd have done the same. Keep it out of t'bedrooms in future."

CHAPTER 26

With every week that went by Stanley became more involved with the running of the farm and more absorbed in learning the skills that were passed on to him by Eric and Mr Downing. Every day it seemed there was something new to learn and he applied himself with an enthusiasm that he had never shown at school.

He was fortunate that his employer was a good teacher who patiently showed him and explained the right way to do each seasonable job. Knowing that Stanley had a great liking of horses he put him in charge of Punch, a huge giant of a horse with a glossy black coat and mane. Mostly, Punch was a gentle giant, providing he was handled with care. If Stanley was nervous of his new charge he did his best to hide it and spoke calmly and firmly and rewarded him with treats from his pocket.

From the first day Punch took to his new young horseman and responded to his every word. There was no prouder lad in Wath than Stanley as he rode on the back of his horse out to the fields to begin the day's work.

His first assignment was to plough the small field at the rear of the farm and Stanley slid from the horse's back and harnessed him to the plough. He looked up and down the field, sizing it up, and began by striding out equal distances at each end of the field and drove in stakes as markers. These were essential to ensure that he ploughed a straight furrow.

Confidently he manoeuvred Punch into position and manhandled the heavy plough into exactly the right place. It was crucial that his first furrow was straight, or every one would be wrong. Taking a deep breath he gave a couple of loud clicks with his tongue and gripped the handles of the plough firmly as the horse stepped forward and the share sank into the ground.

As Punch plodded forward Stanley fixed his eye on the stake at the far end of the field and kept the plough in a straight line. In spite of the cold day he was sweating by the time they reached the end of the field, and he turned the horse to the left and swung the heavy plough around ready to repeat it all over again.

Looking down the length of the furrow he noted with pride that apart from a slight kink at the beginning of the row it was straight and true. As usual when he was happy Stanley began to sing, and Punch twitched his ears, and plodded steadily up and down the field.

By evening half the field was ploughed and the soil lay fresh and rich, still slightly damp and shining and Stanley was more tired than he had ever been in his life. Thankfully he unhitched the plough and climbed on to Punch's back, sitting side-saddle as the horse carried him back to the farm.

Exhausted though he was, there was still work to be done.

He unharnessed the horse and brushed him down as he munched his evening feed. With a final pat he said, "See thee in t'morning auld lad," and Punch shook his head and blew oats out of mouth as he munched.

That evening Mr Downing, or Teddy as his employees called him (behind his back, you understand, never to his face if they valued their jobs), made his regular evening walk around his land and checked on the work that had been done that day. He stopped and leaned on the gate of the field where his youngest employee had been ploughing.

Leaning his arms on the gate he rested his chin on them and stared up and down the length of the field. His vision was good and he could see the long rows of turned earth and the odd wisp of the old wheat stubble poking out here and there.

Satisfied that the work had been done well, he gave a nod and smile of approval.

His next stop was the stables to check on the horses; Punch was stretched out full length in his stall but rolled over onto his haunches and turned his head to look at him reproachfully as if to say, don't disturb me. Teddy smiled and bid them all goodnight as he fastened the bottom half of the door but left the top half open for fresh air.

As he walked across the yard to the farmhouse a robin sang its last song of the day and Teddy Downing thought about Stanley and what a good and promising worker he was. There was no doubt about it, Teddy had a soft spot of affection for his youngest employee but that didn't prevent him from being hard a taskmaster and expecting a lot from him, as Stanley was to find out the very next morning.

Morning milking was over and Stanley and Eric were enjoying their pint mugs of tea before setting off for the fields, when Teddy walked into the barn. He had a smile on his face which Eric noted with trepidation. Stanley was younger and more naïve and returned the smile as he rose to his feet respectfully and bid his boss. "Good morning."

"Nah then lads, ah've got a right nice little change for you two tomorrow."

Stanley and Eric waited expectantly while he continued. "Ah want you to walk them four bullocks," and he indicated with his thumb at the cattle that were at that very moment leaning over the fence as if listening.

"Ah want you to walk em to a field just at the other side of Askern, ah've sold em to Massey's and he wants em delivering."

Eric's jaw dropped and Stanley waited, looking from one to the other, wisely deciding to let Eric, who was ten years older, do the talking.

"Askern?" he queried. "But that's miles away."

"Nay, it's not far, not for a couple of fit young blokes like you two. It's maybe four or five miles. It'll be a nice little change for you. And ah'll come and pick you up and give you a ride home in my nice new Wolseley. Ah should have enough petrol. How's that for a treat? Be here an hour early tomorrow morning."

Without waiting for an answer he turned and left, leaving Eric and Stanley speechless.

236

Eric was the first to break the silence. "Four or five miles? More like twelve," he stated indignantly.

They started out early the next morning when it was barely light, hoping to get through Wath and out into more open countryside before most of the town was awake. Each of them carried a long walking stick and an ex army haversack with a bottle of water and chunk of bread packed away inside.

The first mile as they headed down New Road and along Doncaster Road rapidly turned into a test of Eric and Stanley's running ability, as the bullocks took off at top speed and were only prevented from charging straight on to the railway line by a group of miners who were just leaving the colliery after the night shift.

Linking outstretched arms they herded the four bullocks into a tight corner between the Manvers Arms and the railway fence. White teeth lit up the miners' coal blackened faces as they joked about being cowboys in their spare time.

As Stanley and Eric finally caught up with their cornered cattle, calls of "Where's thee hosses then?" rang out.

Panting they leaned on the wall and gathered their breath.

"Bloody hell, Stan it's to be hoped they settle down, ah can't keep this up for twelve miles. If there's any more of it I'm walking away and Teddy can take t'bullocks to Askern hisen,"said Eric.

Overhearing him, one of the miners turned to his mates. "Did tha hear that lads? These two daft buggers are walking all t'way to Askern wi these cows."

"Well ah'd rather them than me," came the reply from several of them at once, spoken as if in a chorus.

Nodding in agreement Stanley and Eric were preparing to set off again when disaster almost struck.

A loud whistle and rumble from an approaching train threw the cattle into a panic, and it was only due to the miners herding them back into the corner that prevented them from being crushed under the wheels of the heavy trucks loaded with coal.

As the last truck rumbled away into the distance they urged the nervous cattle across the railway line, past the pit yard and the steaming coke ovens. The miners' steel-tipped clogs and boots echoed as they helped to herd them safely through the railway arch and into quieter countryside heading towards Adwick on Dearne.

Now on their own again with the cattle, both Stanley and Eric were relieved that their charges seemed to have settled down and plodded on at a steady pace, just stopping now and then to snatch a mouthful of grass from the hedgerows.

Eric had gone to the front to lead them and with Stanley driving them from the back they soon covered the distance to Adwick on Dearne.

The only directions they had was a list that Teddy Downing had given them of villages they needed to pass through, and Eric called back to Stanley that they needed to head for Hickleton next.

Eric strode out using his stick as a walking aid, matching it to his stride, and even began to whistle a variety of tunes which were mostly unrecognisable, but the cattle seemed to like it, although a passing cyclist called to him that he'd heard squeaky wheelbarrows make a better noise.

They were soon passing the stone built walls that surrounded the Hickleton Estate and Stanley was fascinated by the magnificent stone statue of a deer among the trees.

As they approached the crossroads Eric ran ahead and stood with arms outstretched in the middle of the road, like a policeman on point duty, until they were all safely across. Just a hundred yards further on was a stream and they stopped, allowing their charges to drink and graze while they lay on the slightly damp grass and stared up at the clouds.

When Stanley asked how much further they had to go, Eric produced his list.

"It's a long way yet Stan. Look, it's Brodworth next, then Adwick le Street, then Carcroft. Ah'm sure he's sending us a long way round."

"We'd better get on our way then," said Stanley, prodding one of the bullocks that had decided to copy them and lay down.

"Come on old lad, tha can't get comfortable, we've a long way to go."

Turning to Eric he prodded him lightly too.

238

"That goes for thee an all, Eric me lad," he said, doing a fair impersonation of Teddy Downing.

Having tasted the lush grass near the stream the cattle were reluctant to continue the journey, until Eric took a handful of feed laced with molasses from his bag and offered it to the one nearest to him. Smelling the molasses the rest of the group gathered around him, but Eric set off up the road at a brisk pace teasing the cattle into following him.

Stanley's boot was beginning to rub his heel, and by the time they had passed through the picturesque village of Brodworth he knew that a blister was developing, and he was grateful when they stopped for a rest as the Brodsworth coal mine came into view.

Like most of the mines it looked totally out of place in the green, gently rolling countryside. The mountain of black waste piled high was a dirty blot on countryside that would otherwise have been as pretty as a picture.

As the cattle bent their heads to graze, Stanley sat on the grass verge and took off his boots to examine his feet.

The left heel was every bit as bad as he thought it would be, a large blister had formed and burst as he pulled off his boot, leaving a red raw wound.

"Bloody hell Stan, that looks a mess. Tha needs summat on that," Eric commented at the sight of his heel.

Stanley nodded and pulled a grubby cloth from his pocket and padded the back of his boot with it.

Eric looked on with concern, "Tha wants to get theesen some socks Stan, it'll be a lot more comfortable and stop thee gerrin' blisters."

"Aye, ah know, they're on me list. Ah haven't had any socks for years," Stanley replied.

Pulling a dock leaf he laid it across his raw heel. It felt cool and soothing and in answer to Eric's questioning look he stated that if dock leaves worked for stings, why not use them for blisters?

But the truth was they did no good at all and with every step his heel became more painful.

The bullocks were tired now and it was difficult to keep them moving in the right direction. Even the smell of molasses seemed to have lost its attraction.They plodded slowly on, leaving a trail of sloppy cow pats behind them.

The next hazard was the Great North Road which they had to cross on their way to their destination. There was, of course, no way around it, and they both viewed the prospect with trepidation.

Quite a large, fairly new housing estate spread out to their right as they approached the busy road.Obviously mine workers' houses thought Stanley, judging by the style of them. And there leaning on the wall near the bottom of the hill was just the help they needed.

A small crowd of retired miners watched their progress.A cheer went up as the leading bullock suddenly found some energy and tried to veer off to the left. Stanley brought it back into line but winced at the pain in his heel.

"Nah then lads. Where's tha rustled them from?"

Eric grinned and shouted back, "Can somebody watch the traffic for us? We need to get these across."

One of the men whipped his cap off and stepped out on to the road, waving it at the oncoming traffic with no regard for his own safety. With the traffic halted, Stanley and Eric soon had the cattle safely across to other side and gave thanks to their helpers.

From there it was a short walk down the hill to Adwick le Street, and then on to Carcroft. For the rest of the journey Stanley just concentrated on putting one foot in front of the other and he could hardly believe it when Eric shouted that they had reached Askern.

Askern was a mining town but distinguished by the large lake in the centre surrounded by grassy banks; it was obviously a popular playground for the local children.

As they slowly drew level with the lake they were soon surrounded by a large group of children of varying ages. They all looked poorly dressed and some of them none too clean. A few had no shoes and at that moment Stanley quite envied them and seriously toyed with the idea of taking his boots off and carrying them.

The children were in a state of excitement at the prospect of a diversion to their usual games and bombarded them with questions.

"Where you come from mister?" one of them called out.

When Stanley told them Wath on Dearne, they were so much in awe that he may as well have said Africa.

"That's a long way mister, me dad went there once. He went on t'train."

Stanley nodded. "Aye, ah wish we'd come on t'train."

"Where are ya going mister, can we come wi ya?

Eric had led the cattle on to the grass and they rested while they consulted their directions. Speaking to Stanley, Eric said that he thought Massey's field was just down a road to their right.

But of course there were a dozen ears listening in and as a chorus they all shouted, "We know where Massey's field is mister, we'll show yer. It's not far."

Glad of their help, Stanley roused the cattle again and managed to persuade them to follow Eric. Half the children, skinny as rabbits and almost as quick, ran in front and had the gate wide open ready for them. The four weary bullocks made no argument about going through the gate. As Stanley closed it after them he looked at Eric and instinctively they shook hands, before they both sank down on the grass.

Their helpers hung around a while, obviously hoping for some reward, and when none was forthcoming they soon headed back towards town and the lake.

Eric shrugged his shoulders and commented to Stanley that he couldn't give them anything as he had nothing to give.

To which Stanley replied, "Aye, ah know, same here," and he thankfully eased his boots off and buried his feet in the long cool grass.

For the first ten minutes they were only too glad to lay back and rest, but soon hungry stomachs called for food. Sitting up Stanley checked his bag, hoping to find a few bits of left over bread.

Eric looked up. "Is yours empty an all? Mine's like old Mother Hubbard's cupboard."

"What time did he say he'd pick us up?" asked Stanley.

241

"He didn't say a time, just said he'd be here.If he's much longer ah shall go and rob that bakery. Did tha smell that bread as we were coming past it?"

Stanley pulled a handful of leaves from the hawthorn hedge, rolled them all up together and pushed them into his mouth. "We used to call this bread and cheese when we were kids. It tastes nowt like it does it?"

Eric didn't answer. He'd climbed the gate and was stood on top of it, hoping to catch sight of Teddy Downing's car coming to collect them.

But it was another half an hour before he was rewarded by the sight of the shiny black Wolseley coming down the lane.

Teddy got out of the car and gave them a slight smile before going to check on the four bullocks that were all now lying down.

Looking them over he commented, "What have you been doing to em? Poor beasts look exhausted."

Eric didn't trust himself to speak, but his expression said it all.

Nodding his head in the direction of the car, Teddy laughed."Only kidding lads. Come on, you'd better get in t'car and ah'll give you a lift home. It's a good job ah came to fetch yer both, or you'd av been in a right pickle."

The moment Stanley slid into the car he forgot his tiredness, forgot his sore heel, forgot his hunger; everything went by the board as he touched and smelt the leather seats and admired the highly polished dashboard. As the engine purred into life he was lost for words and he began to daydream about owning a car like this.

He was still taking in the attributes of the Wolseley when Teddy casually informed him that his brother Ernest had been to the farm asking for work that very afternoon.

Fortunately Teddy was too preoccupied in winding down his window and signalling that he was turning to hear Stanley mutter, "Sneaky bastard." As soon as the turn was negotiated Downing continued, "Well, ah've set him on. We're a bit short handed at the moment, but he'll have to frame himself. Let's hope he's as good a worker as thee Stan."

Stanley's cheeks flushed, partly from the rare compliment but mostly from anger at the thought of Ernest working alongside him every day.

By the time he arrived home he was very tired and very hungry. His heel was sore and he was in a rare old temper.

CHAPTER 27

The first person he saw as he walked around the corner to the rear of the house was Ernest. There he was, sitting on the kitchen chair in the back yard with his feet on the fence and the chair tilted onto its back legs.

He had a cigarette in his mouth and as he saw Stanley he removed it with his finger and thumb and blew a smoke ring.

"Nah then Stan," he said, with such a smug expression on his face that Stanley completely lost his temper and kicked the chair from under him.

The resulting loud crash and shout brought Ada rushing to the door. Ernest was picking himself up as his mother took in the scene and he immediately began holding his head.

Ada sighed, "Nah what's yor two up to this time?"

"It's him Mam, he kicked t'chair on to t'floor."

Before any more could be said Harold and Cyril came running down the garden path.

"He's lyin' mam. We saw him. He tilted chair too far back and fell over. He nearly broke t'chair Mam." Harold delivered his speech then turned to Stanley and gave him a wink.

Ada swiped at Ernest with her tea towel. "A've told thee before about swinging on that chair. Nah, fetch it in. Tha's not too big for a clout across t'earhole tha knows," and she flicked it again with great accuracy before she turned and went back into the kitchen giving a weary sigh.

Ernest had flinched as the teatowel stung his ear and he glared at Stanley.

"Thee wait," he said as he carried the chair back indoors.

"Oh aye, ah'm trembling. Ah'll give thee a pasting any day, tha sneaky bastard."

"Ah well," called Ernest from just inside the porch, "ah got the job didn't ah? So tha can like it or lump it."

Stanley made no reply to that, but picked up the packet of Woodbines that Ernest had dropped and threw them over the high fence into the neighbour's yard. He felt a lot better after that and went down to the garden shed whistling.

Monday morning came and feelings had calmed a little but not completely.

Stanley was washed and dressed and about to leave for work when Ernest came downstairs, his hair standing on end and obviously just out of bed.

"Wait for me Stan, ah'v gorra puncture in me front tyre.Can tha gi me a croggy on thee bike?"

Stanley looked at him and grinned. "Tha must be joking, not likely," and he left and arrived at work a good fifteen minutes early.

By the time Teddy Downing entered the cow house Stanley had given each cow its feed and was just about to start on the milking.

"By tha's up early this morning," he said, nodding with approval. "Where is tha brother?"

Stanley shrugged his shoulders. "No idea," he said, and carried on with the milking.

Teddy gave him a sharp glance. "Ah, it's like that is it?"

Before the conversation had chance to go any further Ernest ran into the building, red faced and sweating, and he looked with dismay at his new employer.

Teddy took out his watch and studied it. "Well tha's only just made it on time young man. Ah hope tha's not going to be a bad time keeper. Ah can't do with that tha knows. Nah, put that overall on and help Stanley to get the milking done. Ah'm a man short today and there's work waiting to be done in t'fields."

With that he turned and left them to it, informing them that he would be back shortly.

Ernest dragged the overall on while Stanley kept his head tucked into the cow's side and concentrated on the milking. He resented Ernest being there and decided to ignore him as much as possible.

Sensing his brother's mood Ernest wisely said nothing. Placing his stool by the side of the large black and white Friesian near the door he sat down, held the bucket between his knees and began. The cow turned her head towards him as far as the chain around her neck would allow and swung her tail, catching him at the side of his head with considerable force.

"Why you nasty auld bugger. She did that on purpose, did tha see her Stan?"

Stanley hid a smile. "Oh aye, ah forgot to warn thee about her."

Ernest stood up. "Ah'll tie her tail to her leg, tha'll stop her little games."

"Ah wouldn't do that if I were thee Ernie. Mr Downing wouldn't like it. Tha'd be sacked before tha'd even started."

"Oh hell Stan, will tha milk this one then? Tha'll be more used to her than me."

"Oh go on then, tha big ninny, thee start on t'little Jersey over there, and be gentle wi her, she's t'boss's favourite."

Ernest had the good grace to mumble a thank you, and reflected to himself that his first day had not got off to a very good start.

Stanley had often marvelled at his employer's ability to turn up at the exact moment that they had finished a job and today was no exception. No sooner had the last churn been filled and the cleaning up finished, than Teddy appeared in the doorway.

"Well done lads, all spick and span, that's how ah like it. Nah then, t'missis has put two mugs of tea out in t'porch for ya. Too soft hearted she is, she spoils ya. Get it down yer quick and then ah need a word with you both."

In addition to the mugs of tea there were also two sandwiches, made with thick brown bread and filled with very salty fat bacon; fried until it was crisp and brown.

Always hungry, Stanley and Ernest made no attempt at any conversation, but matched each other bite for bite until the last

246

crumb was gone. As they drained the last drop of tea Ernest gave a sigh of contentment. "By ah needed that Stan, do we get it every day?"

Before he had time to reply Teddy Downing was back on the scene.

"Nah Stanley, ah've got a nice little change for you."

Stanley waited, feeling apprehensive; the last time he had heard those words from his boss it had been just before the expedition to Askern.

Not noticing the tension in Stanley's face, he continued, "Ah want you to learn the milk round. Starting this morning. You can come with me and if you frame thee sen ok," and here he stopped and gave a rare smile before he continued with the air of someone bestowing a gift. "If tha frames theesen, tha can do it on thee own regular. Nah then, what does tha think to that?"

Stanley's face lit up, eager to meet the new challenge, but was not quite so pleased to hear that Ernest would be finishing the field that he had been ploughing.

"Ah think Ernest will be able to manage Punch. He seems to have settled down since you've been working with him Stanley."

It had taken Stanley weeks to get Punch quietened down and working well, and he had become quite possessive about the horse. He tried to tell Ernest how to handle him, but of course the advice was not welcome.

Before an argument had time to develop Stanley walked away and began to harness Jacky, the horse used for the milk round.

"That's right Stanley," commented Teddy when he saw him talking to the old horse, "Jacky knows the round better than ah do, he knows every customer."

And he was right. Jacky stopped at every house on the round and waited patiently while Stanley carefully poured out the required amount into each customer's jug.

He was welcomed by the customers, all of them glad to see a good looking, energetic young man delivering their milk every morning instead of Teddy, who was often grumpy and inclined to be stingy with the measurements. Stanley was soon running the milk round like clockwork, flirting with the ladies young and old, but quick to put anyone right who tried to take advantage.

Just one month into his new job, Stanley knocked on the door of the cottage third from the right of the farm.He stood there willing Mrs Bramham who lived there to hurry and answer the door. It was a cold morning and he was anxious to get the milk delivered as soon as possible. He lifted the latch of the door and opened it slightly, calling as he did so "Milko, Mrs Bramham."

But it was not Mrs Bramham who came hurrying through from the scullery as he expected, instead her daughter came with the blue patterned jug in her hand, looking at him shyly with the darkest brown eyes he had ever seen. Of course he had noticed her before, usually walking up Sandygate with her mother, but never face to face, this close. As he poured the milk his hand shook a little and he filled the jug almost to the brim.

"That's too much," she said quietly, "we only have half a pint."

"It's ok. Ah've got some spare today," and he turned to go tripping over the step. "Ta-ra."

His next stop was at Mrs Ashton's who unfortunately had been born with a cleft palate and as a consequence spoke in a strange echoing sort of way and could not pronounce words correctly, which often made her difficult to understand.

But she was very astute and after observing the stumble and the look on Stanley's face she said, "Ou et oris en? Iiy irl." As she also suffering from a hearing problem she said it in an extra loud voice and repeated it several times without Stanley being able to understand, until her neighbour came out and translated for him.

"She says you've met Doris then? She's a pretty girl."

Mrs Ashton nodded vigorously and gave him a twisted smile and patted his arm.

Stanley grinned. "She certainly is," he said into Mrs Ashton's ear. "How old is she?"

She held up ten fingers and then four and her neighbour added with a wink, "She's fourteen in March."

As Stanley clicked to the horse and moved off, the two women exchanged glances, the way that only women do. A look that said all they wanted to say without speaking a word.

Teddy Downing owned the cottage where Doris lived with her mother. Stanley made what he thought would be interpreted as casual remarks and questions about them to Teddy. But of course his employer was no fool and soon figured out that it was the beautiful young girl he was asking about.

He smiled to himself as he passed on the information that Doris and her mother had lived there alone for the past ten years. He went on to add that Doris's father was Larrett Bramham, son of Arthur Bramham, the well- known plumber and property owner who lived in the large imposing house in the centre of Wath. Stanley remembered him. He had been the owner of Packmans Yard where he had spent his early years.

"Oh aye," went on Teddy, "Larrett's problem was that he had a bad memory," and he gave a smile. "Aye, he went away to work in Scunthorpe for a while on a contract that his father had taken on, and he got into bed with the landlady's daughter and clean forgot that he had a wife and child at home. Now that's what I call a really bad memory."

Apparently there had been a huge argument when the news got out and Larrett's wife Edith had taken Doris and left him. They had lived in the cottage in Sandygate ever since and Doris had no contact whatsoever with her father or paternal grandparents.

Stanley instantly felt sympathy for Doris, but not just that, he could not get her out of his head and it brightened up his day whenever he set eyes on her.

At home it was no secret that Doris felt the same way and she came in for much teasing from her mother and maternal grandmother. Although her grandmother urged caution, reminding her that she was too young to be thinking about courting. Not that any heed was paid to their words. Doris mostly did whatever Doris wanted to do.

Stanley's training on the farm continued and his next lesson was to sow the winter wheat. Under Teddy's close supervision he walked up and down the field with a large oval shaped metal hopper full of seed strapped to his body.

Fully loaded it was a considerable weight, but Stanley managed to stop his knees buckling and picked up a rhythm, striding up and down taking long paces and flinging the grain out in regular handfuls that flew through the air and landed evenly.

He glowed with pride again as his employer commented, "Well done lad, keep that up, tha's doing a grand job," and left him to it.

Less than a quarter of a mile away Ernest was not doing so well. Punch had reverted to his old ways and was making life difficult. The more Ernest shouted at him the more the horse refused to cooperate and even bit him whenever he had the chance. Ernest had still not learned that he worked best with rewards, and refused to listen when his brother told him to carry treats in his pocket for the horse.

"Ah've just had enough of this Stan," Ernest said. "Ah thought it'd be easier ere but it's worse. Ah could earn four times as much down t'pit."

"Aye tha could, but tha'd av to spend all thee workin' life underground. Thee please thee sen Ern, but it's not for me, ah want to be able to look up at t'sky an hear t'birds sing."

By the end of the month Ernest had asked his father if there were any jobs going at Manvers Main.

"Well that's a turnaround. Ah thought tha wanted to be a farmer?" said Harold with a grin.

"Well Dad, it pays a lot better than farming, ah've ad enough of slaving all week for old Teddy Downing for a starvation wage."

Within a week it was all arranged. There were vacancies, and as Harold was now head of a gang down the mine no objections were made to his son joining the hard working Corkers. He began the following Monday morning.

When he had handed in his notice at the farm Teddy accepted it with relief.

"Well tha's given me this just in time lad. It saves me sacking thee. T'missis will give thee tha wages tonight," and he turned on his heel as if to leave, then stopped. "Tha can make up rest of t'day mucking out t'fold yard," he said, giving Ernest a tight little smile.

Later that day he spoke to Stanley just as he was cleaning his boots in readiness for the bike ride home.

"Ah hope tha's not planning on becoming a miner an all Stanley."

"Not likely Mr Downing, ah'm going to be a farmer. Ah couldn't work underground."

"Ah'm very pleased to hear it son." To Stanley's astonishment he added, "There'll be an extra sixpence a week in thee wage packet starting from next pay day."

Stanley went home that night in high spirits, well pleased with the way things had turned out.

CHAPTER 28

Despite the distance that separated them, the bond between Stanley and Doll remained strong over the years.

Since the revelation four years ago that they were brother and sister, nothing had been said by way of explanation. Whenever Stanley tentatively tried to touch on the subject with his mother, she simply turned away tight-lipped and ignored him. As for asking his father about it, well, that was unthinkable.

Aunt Lizzie(who Doll considered her mother) was a little more willing to talk and what information she was able to gather, Doll passed on to him.

Ernest, being the same age as Stanley, seemed to be just as much in the dark and as their relationship was always stormy, they seldom discussed much of anything.

Stanley was especially fond of his younger brothers, Harold and Cyril, who treated him with almost hero worship, meeting him from work and hanging about wherever he happened to be. At weekends they joined him at Downing's farm to help with the milking.

Cyril was rapidly turning into the comedian of the family and never failed to have them laughing with his comic tales and original quotations.

Ada had continued to produce children and Iris and Laura were the latest editions to the Corker family. Stanley viewed all his young sisters, Betty and Jessie included, with a mixture of pride in their beauty and intense irritation at their constant chattering and ability to always be in the way. But for all his irritation he would have defended each one of them to his last breath.

There had never been any love lost between Stanley and Billy. Since Stanley had grown up he was now a good six inches taller, and he would no longer put up with Billy's teasing and tormenting. After coming to blows on several occasions they now, by unspoken agreement, kept out of each other's way as much as possible.

Herbert and Stanley were as different in every way as it was possible to be.

While Herbert was short, dark haired and sturdily built, and happy to be a miner, Stanley was tall, fair haired and slender as a whippet, and could not think of nothing worse than working underground. And then of course there was the big difference in their ages.But in spite of all that they had great affection and respect for each other.

Being the eldest, Herbert remembered his own mother Winn, and shared what little knowledge he had of events around the time of Stanley's birth, but so much had been shrouded in secrecy that he could only surmise what had happened and Herbert was reluctant to talk about it.

"It's in the past Stan," he said, "leave it be." He preferred instead to talk of Mabel, who he was engaged to. Like many of the men of Yorkshire he referred to her as 'our lass' and he said it with great affection.

It was to Stanley that he had confided in when he thought of asking Mabel to marry him.

"What does tha think Stan? Ah'm thinking of getting wed to Mabel."

"Mabel getting wed?" Stanley replied absent mindedly. "Who to? What does tha mean?" As soon as the words were out he realised what a silly thing he had said.

Herbert turned to him with a grin and punched him on the arm. "Me of course, tha idiot, who does tha expect she'd be marrying? Bloody dustbin man?"

Stanley laughed, "Ah didn't mean it like that," he hesitated, "and talkin' of expecting, she's not, is she?

"No she's bloody not," replied Herbert indignantly. Then he said. "Well, it's not for want of me trying, but Mabel says there's to be none of that till we're married. More's the pity. Ah'll just av to wait. Mind you, she might be a bit more willing if we're engaged."

Stanley nodded, not quite sure what to say next. Then after a moment's thought he commented that he liked Mabel and he wouldn't go far wrong with her for a wife.

"Well, ah'm glad av got thee approval Stan. Ah'll break t'news to me Mam an Dad next week. Don't thee say owt to em will ya?" and he went off to work whistling.

Herbert believed in doing things properly, and Mabel was soon wearing a dainty ring with a tiny sapphire in the centre of a cluster of semi precious stones, acquired as usual from Sammy Bowley's pawn shop.

Harold and Ada received his news of marrying Mabel with mixed feelings. Not that they had anything against her. On the contrary, they both liked her and thought the couple well suited. It was the loss of Herbert's substantial contribution to the housekeeping that was the problem. It would certainly make a difference, thought Ada, but she was reassured when Herbert told her that they wouldn't be getting married straight away.

Two months later Herbert shocked the whole family again when he informed them that he would be moving into lodgings.

Noting how Ada's face fell, he quickly added, "Ah need me own bedroom Mam, ah'm sick of sharing with five others, fed up to t'back teeth of it. Ah've got a room on Barnsley Road and Mabel can move in wi me when we get wed."

Ada laid the trousers she was mending to one side. "But Herbert, what about yer dinners an yer washing?"

"Well," Herbert put his hand on her shoulder. "Ah were just going to say, maybe ah could still have me dinners here, and maybe you'd still do me washing. Until we get wed that is."

Harold broke into the conversation. "It sounds as if tha's gor it all worked out. Tha could have said what tha were up to."

"Don't be like that Dad, ah'll never forget what you an Mam av done for me, an ah'll still be tipping some money up every week." Then he hastily added, "Until me an Mabel get married of course."

He left them then and walked down the garden path and into the allotment where Stanley was busy working among the vegetables.

Their eyes met and Herbert blew out his breath. "Phew, that wasn't easy."

"You told em then? How did it go?"

"Ok ah suppose, got it sorted ah think. Mam's a bit upset about it, but she'll get used to it." He sighed. "Ah can't wait for me and Mabel to get wed an be on ar own."

"Not long now Bertie," said Stanley and dodged as a large clod of soil sailed past him.

"Ah'll give thee bloody Bertie, tha cheeky little bugger."

Stanley drew himself up to his full height and looked down at Herbert.

"That's good, thee calling me little."

"Aye tha's right Stan, ah don't know what me Mam's feeding thee on but tha's gerrin' like a bloody drainpipe. When's tha going to stop growin'?"

Herbert squatted down and lit the stub end of a Woodbine that he had been keeping in the brim of his flat cap. As he blew out a cloud of smoke he nodded at Stanley.

"Carry on lad," he said. "Don't let me stop yer, tha's doin' a good job. Ah'll just stop a bit an see tha don't start slackin'." He grinned, his natural good humour restored.

Stanley looked at him resting in a squatting position. "How does tha manage to rest like that?It makes my knees ache just looking at thee."

"Aye well, ah ain't got such long lanky legs as thee, and ah spend hours like this workin' down t'pit tha knows."

"That's another good reason for me not to be a collier int it?"

"Tha's right Stan, ah don't think tha's cut out for it. Thee stick to farmin', and when tha's a rich farmer ah'll come and stop wi thee for me holidays."

While Herbert smoked his Woodbine, Stanley leaned on his hoe and they relaxed in the late October sunshine, soaking in the unseasonable warmth.

A week passed before they saw each other again and the weather had changed from mild and warm to bitterly cold. They walked together down Sandygate and as Stanley pushed his bike he thought he had never felt so cold before and grumbled to Herbert that he was shivering so much he could barely stop his teeth from chattering.

But with his wedding only a week away nothing could dampen Herbert's spirits, and as they parted company at Downing's farm he called out, "See thee next week Stan, don't forget to wash behind thee ears when tha comes to t'wedding, and put thee best suit on."

As Stanley turned into the farmyard he glanced at Herbert striding out down the road with his dudley and snap tin slung over his shoulder.

"See thee Herbert," he called, but his stepbrother was whistling and heard nothing but the tune in his head as he walked briskly to catch up with a group of miners who, like him, were on their way to the afternoon shift at Cortonwood Colliery.

It was dark extra early on Wednesday the 13th of November 1935. Ada had closed the green chenille curtains that had once hung in her father's house and noticed the frayed hem and the small holes that were appearing where she gripped them every day to open and close them and she made a mental note to try and repair them. The fire was glowing bright, making the room feel cosy and she silently gave thanks for their free allocation of coal that arrived every month.

Harold sat in his chair looking totally relaxed with his green sporting newspaper in front of him. Young Harold and Cyril lay on the floor under the table sharing a comic.

Due to the cold weather, Ada had lit a fire in the small grate in the kitchen and Stanley and Ernest huddled close to it playing cards on the tin tray.

Betty and Jessie were at the sink washing the dishes from tea time while Iris and Laura shared a bath in the bathroom that led just off the kitchen. Ada could hear them laughing and the splash of water and called out to them to hurry up and not to make a mess.

She looked around at her family; for once they all seemed to be in harmony. Billy was out, probably chasing some girl, she reflected. Then she thought of Edith and Sarah working together in Lincolnshire. That only left left Herbert and she thought about his marriage next week.

What a gathering that was going to be. Mabel came from a large family too.

There was still so much to do in the way of preparation for the big day.

The wedding was to be at the parish church followed by tea in the village hall. Ada had promised to bake some of her famous bread buns to go with the ham that Mabel's mother would boil, and then of course all the family were to have new clothes.

The four girls' dresses were still to be finished and Ada took the first one that was hanging on the picture rail and laid it on the table. The fabric was blue satin and with her sister Rose's help she had cut the dresses out and sewn them together by hand. She had found the cloth on a stall in Mexborough market and had paid the stall holder in instalments, a little each week until she had enough to cover the cost.

She sighed happily as she looked at the dresses. How lovely the girls would look with their long blonde hair plaited and blue satin ribbons woven into the plaits.

Nudging Harold with her toe she held up the dress. "What do you think Harold?"

Without looking up from his paper he said, "Very nice love, they'll look like fifty bob hosses in em."

Ada tossed her head and gave a 'tch' sound as she threaded her needle.

"Men!" she muttered and smiled.

The knock came loud and clear on the front door, disturbing the peaceful atmosphere.

"Who the hell's that at this time of night?" grumbled Harold. "And at t'front door an all. Go an see who it is lads, and if it's them young buggers from across t'street playing silly devils again, tell em ah'll tan their hides for em."

Ada was distracted by the loud squeals coming from the bathroom and without waiting to see who was at the door, laid down her sewing and hurried to investigate. As she passed her husband she patted his shoulder.

"Well t'peace and quiet didn't last long did it?" she said.

In the bathroom she found Iris and Laura fighting over the ownership of an old rubber doll. Administering two sharp slaps sorted out the argument and Ada told them to get out of the bath and get dried and dressed right away. Betty and Jessie were instructed to finish the pots and get into the bath.

Ada left them to it, shaking her head in exasperation. "Now you lasses behave yoursens," she called to them, "ah've got to get these frocks finished or there'll be no wedding for any of you."

As she placed her hand on the door of the living room she heard an unfamiliar voice and a sense of foreboding went through her. Pushing open the door she took in the scene.

The policeman stood just inside the room, looking huge in his uniform and thick cape, with his helmet tucked under his arm.

Harold sat in his chair, his normally rosy complexion deathly white. As she entered the room he rose quickly and went to her, putting his arm around her shoulders.

"It's bad news luv, it's ar Herbert. There's been an accident."

Ada looked at the policeman. His face was full of sympathy and even in that awful moment she recognised him as the constable that had come to tell her of her father's death all those years ago. She found that all the hairs on the back of her neck suddenly felt as if they were trembling and felt so cold that a huge shiver went through her.

Harold pulled her towards the chair and insisted that she sit down.

"An accident?" she asked, dreading the answer. "Is he hurt bad? Oh my God, he's not-" and she stopped, unable to say the word.

"I'm afraid, Mrs Corker, that it was a fatal accident. I'm very sorry to have to bring you such bad news."

He looked as if he was about to break into tears himself, and he took out a large white handkerchief and blew his nose.

Ada looked at the dresses hung on the picture rail and the one on the table and touched it almost reverently. "But Harold, he can't be. He's getting married next week." And she put her head in her hands, struggling to cope with the shock.

In moments Harold was in the kitchen, pulling on his still damp work shorts from the line that was strung across the ceiling. He said not a word but his face was set in a mask of determination that hid his grief. With his work boots on he returned to the living room. "Has tha got transport?" he asked the constable.

"Aye, t'black van's outside. Come on ah'll get thee there quick as ah can."

He opened the door and led the way out into the dark evening glad to have something constructive to do.

Harold said not a single word on the way to the colliery. His teeth were clamped together so tightly in an effort not to allow the sobs to escape that it felt as if his jaw would crack.

A large crowd had gathered around the gates to the pit but they parted like a wave when Harold was recognised. "Move aside folks let t'lad's father come through." And as Harold walked the last few yards hands patted him in silent sympathy.

Afterward Harold could never actually remember getting into the cage or the descent down into the mine. He was on unfamiliar territory down in the Cortonwood Colliery but the darkness and the dust and the smell and the sense of being enclosed in the bowels of the earth were the same as any other mine.

He followed the deputy down the ever narrowing spaces into the area where Herbert lay trapped. With all his years of experience Harold could see there was no chance that his son could have survived. He knew it only too well, but deep in his heart there was a tiny little hope that maybe, just maybe, he could be safely enclosed in a pocket beneath a rock.

There were already a team of miners working to clear the extensive fall. Experienced men who knew exactly what to do. Harold joined them, digging as he had never dug before, silently willing Herbert to still be alive.

But it was to be twenty four hours before his body was finally retrieved and carried reverently up to the surface and Harold gave way to the tears he had been holding back.

Herbert's funeral was held on the 22nd November 1935 following the inquest four days previously on the 18th.

The cause of his death was given as multiple injuries including a fractured skull sustained by an extensive fall of roof, following a weight bump underground at Cortonwood Colliery, Brampton. There was no post mortem.

His body was so crushed that it was only possible to identify him by the tags that he wore around his neck. It was said by many that his death would have been instantaneous, but that was little consolation to his family and friends, and in particular to his fiancée Mabel who had been counting the days off joyously to her wedding day but instead found herself attending her husband to be's funeral.

All she could think of was his fit 28 year old body crushed beyond recognition beneath the tons of coal; his life extinguished in an instant.

Harold felt icy cold every time he thought of Herbert trapped in the narrow tunnel and wondered if he had heard the rumble of the roof fall before it reached him. He kept remembering Herbert as a child, and just could not get the memory of him out of his mind and heard his voice as if it was yesterday, telling him that he wanted to be a miner and have a dudley and a snap tin to take to work.

The church was packed for his funeral service, filled to capacity by family and friends. Outside the church waited dozens of his fellow workers, some of them just as they had left their shift down the pit, still covered in the grime of their job.

Silently they stood with their helmets held in their hands, some of them with tears leaving trails down their coal-blackened faces.

In an industry as dangerous as coal mining, Herbert's death was not unique, or unusual, and every death brought the community closer, bonded by the danger they courted every single day of their working lives.

There was not a man there who didn't thank the Lord that it was not them in that coffin or a woman who wouldn't worry more about their menfolk going down into the depths of the earth every day.

Each of Herbert's family handled their grief in a different way. Ada, almost as if she refused to admit that he was gone, set his plate and chair out at mealtimes. Harold tried to drown his sorrow with extra pints of bitter and the companionship of his mates, while Stanley sought some solace from his work and toiled ceaselessly, trying to rid his mind of the loss of his stepbrother.

Teddy Downing could see his suffering and in an effort to offer him some comfort he put his hand on his shoulder, but Stanley brushed it away and tried to hide the tears in his eyes. Teddy walked away and left him, realising that it was solitude he needed.

For a while Mabel continued to visit, but her presence was too painful for everyone and gradually she faded out of their lives.

Her mother sent a message to Ada telling her that Mabel had found a job in service and had left Wath.It was to be many years before their paths crossed again.

CHAPTER 29

The highlight of Stanley's day was delivering milk to the cottage where Doris lived, and he began turning up for work with his hair combed even more carefully than usual and with an extra shine to his boots. It had not gone unnoticed by his work mates. Nor had the fact that Stanley seemed to take longer to deliver the milk to that one cottage than all the rest of the row put together, especially when it was Doris who answered the door.

Doris's maternal grandmother lived in a cottage that ran at right angles to Sandygate, just a little higher up the road, and occasionally Doris somehow managed to be there when the milk delivery was due.

One Saturday morning as Stanley approached the open kitchen door he could hear voices. It was Doris's grandmother, who, being a little deaf, sometimes spoke loudly and Stanley could hear her words clearly.

"Now then ar Doris," she said, "don't you go making eyes at that nice young man. Ah've seen you, an ah've told you before, you're too young to be courting, so no more of it. You understand?"

Before the conversation could go any further, they both looked up to see Stanley stood at the open door, milk churn in his hand and his face bright red with embarrassment.

Doris blushed and ran out of the room and up the narrow staircase. Mrs Morriss instantly weighed the situation up. Putting down the enamel bowl that she was holding she looked directly at him and said in her stern way, "Ah'm sorry you had to hear that young man, but it had to be said. Our Doris is still at school and far too young to be courting. You remember that."

Stanley poured out the measure of milk and could think of nothing to say apart from, "Yes, Mrs Morriss," and he left, his cheeks still burning.

If only he could have heard the conversation that followed between Doris and her grandmother. Doris had stormed back into the room and stamped her feet in rage. Much as she loved her grandma she shouted in anger, "What did you do that for? I'll never be able to look at him again. You've shown me up, grandma. He'll think ah'm just a little school girl."

Mrs Morriss's lips tightened. "Well that's just what you are young lady. You can mind your manners and behave yourself. Ah'll be avin' words with your mam when she gets home."

Doris tossed her head. It was an empty threat. She knew very well that she could twist her mother any way she wanted and so did her grandmother.

"You want your legs slappin', you are a right little madam these days. Get off home. Ah've had enough of your cheek today."

Without another word Doris picked up her coat and left, slamming the door behind her, and so bad was her mood that she totally ignored Mrs Chapel who lived in the next house and who had always doted on her.

"Wonder what's got into Doris today?" she asked her cousin Polly who lived with her. Polly heaved her considerable weight over to the open door and peered short-sightedly down the uneven path.

But Doris was already out of sight, heading for home, walking as fast as she could without actually breaking into a run. Once safely inside she climbed the stairs and threw herself onto the narrow single bed in her tiny room, punching her pillow as she shed tears, more of anger than sorrow. Soon remorse began to creep in as she thought of how she had shouted at her beloved grandmother, and by the time her mother returned from work Doris had been back and made amends, kissing her grandma and charming her back into a good humour.

Stanley, on the other hand, was still smarting from what he saw as an unfair telling off, and was exceptionally quiet for the rest of the day.

As he rode slowly home that evening he was overtaken by Jim Alsop who lived in the next street. They had been good friends since school days. Jim gave Stanley a quick glance. "What's up Stan? Tha dunt look very happy. Are things bad at home?"

"Well they're never good are they?" replied Stanley as he battled up the hill against a strong head wind. He said nothing else until they turned off Sandygate and on to the street where Jim lived. Now that they were riding on the level and out of the wind they were able to talk easier, and Stanley related the exchange he had had with Mrs Morriss. It had been burning him up all day and it was a relief to tell Jim about it.

"Who is this then that tha's got thee eye on? Do ah know her?" asked Jim as they drew to a halt outside his house. Stanley told him Doris's name and added, "Keep it to thee sen. Ah'm not goin' out wi her, she's still at school."

Jim thought for a while then gave a whistle. "Ah know who tha means. She lives near Downing's farm wi her mam. Her Dad's Larratt Bramham. He lives over t'brush wi that woman from Scunthorpe. She's got legs like tree trunks."

Stanley grinned at his description, while Jim continued. "By she's a bonny lass is that Doris Bramham, no wonder tha's after her. Ah see her walkin' home wi that Maisie Law, she's turnin' into a right cracker an all."

"Aye she is Jim, an tha's welcome to try thee luck wi Maisie, but keep thee eyes off Doris. Ah'm only waitin' till she leaves school. She likes me, ah know she does."

Somehow he felt much better for having talked to Jim and was just setting off home when he had an idea. Turning around quickly in the narrow road he called Jim who stopped and waited until Stanley got back to him.

"Hey, av just ad an idea Jim. Seeing as t'weather's pickin' up a bit, how does tha feel about avin'a long bike ride on Sunday?"

Jim nodded. "Alright, ah'll see thee tomorrow an fix a time. Ah'll come round to thee shed after work."

True to his word Jim arrived the next day, just as Stanley had piled up all the garden rubbish and set fire to it. Standing beside it, enjoying the warmth, they took turns to stir the bonfire and add more dried grass and roots to the flames.

As their cheeks began to glow from the heat they discussed their plans for the next day. Hooton Pagnell was a favourite with both of

264

them, so that was their planned destination with Uncle Jack's at Bolton as an alternative if the weather was bad. Having made their arrangements Jim walked away calling, "See thee," as he opened the gate.But before he could walk through it he collided with Cyril, who dodged under his arm and tried to go straight past his brother.

Stanley grabbed him by his shirt collar and pulled him back.

"Where's tha goin' in such a hurry?" he said and laughed, then stopped as he saw the state of his little brother.

"Nah then, what's up wi thee Cyril? What's tha been up to?"

Cyril's face was tear streaked and his hair damp. He wiped his runny nose on his sleeve and tried to tug his clothes into place, but that only drew attention to the fact that his jumper was on back to front and his trousers inside out.

Stanley stared at him. "What's tha been runnin' for? Tha's wet through wi sweat." Then he sniffed. "It's not sweat is it? It's chlorine ah can smell. Has tha been to t'baths?"

Calming down, Cyril nodded. "They threw me in t'water Stan, ah nearly drowned, but ah got out and ran outside. Ah'm not goin' there again." He sniffed as he rubbed his eyes, tears brimming over.

"Well did tha go on thee own?"

"Nah Stan, ar Harold went an all, but ah left im there."

"And who was it who threw thee in then?"

Cyril hesitated until Stanley shook him. "Go on, tell me. Who threw thee in?"

"It were Tom and Harry Law. Is tha gonna gerrem Stan?"

Stanley looked at Jim and pulled a face. "No, ah'm not gonna gerr em. They've got four big brothers. Has tha seen t'size of em? They'd make mincemeat of me. But ah'll think of summat, don't thee worry. Gerroff into t'house nah and get thee sen dried."

"Don't tell me Mam, will tha Stan."

"Nah, ah'll not tell her, but ah think she's going to notice when she sees state of thee."

Ten minutes later Harold turned up and told them the whole story.

They had set off to go to the swimming baths in the late afternoon. Cyril had been excited about learning to swim and as they walked

Harold had demonstrated how he should move his arms and legs in the water.

Of course, Harold was something of an expert as he had learnt to swim nearly three weeks ago.

As they had walked down towards the swimming baths they had been joined by a large group of other lads, all about the same age, all from China Town and all good mates together.But then the Law brothers had arrived and tagged along.

There was a history of trouble between the younger members of the Corker and Law families and straight away both Harold and Cyril had begun to feel nervous, but neither of them wanted to lose face by backing out of the swimming trip.

Harold had whispered to his younger brother to keep quiet and stay away from them.

Once inside the baths, Harold and Cyril had stayed near the shallow end of the pool and tried not to attract attention to themselves. For a while it seemed to work. The Law brothers were both good swimmers and powered up and down several times, until Tom spotted Cyril sitting alone on the side of the pool. Signalling to Harry they both popped up in the water directly in front of Cyril, who was sat with his arms wrapped around his skinny frame trying to pluck up courage to slide into the cold water.

Jumping out, they grabbed poor Cyril by his arms and dragged him backwards towards the deepest part of the pool.

Once there, one took his arms and the other his legs and amid loud cheers from many of the other children, they swung him back and forth before letting him go, which sent him flying through the air to land right in the centre of the pool.

Harold was held back and forced to watch until his younger brother somehow managed to reach the steps. The minute his feet touched firm ground he grabbed his clothes and ran outside.

From what Stanley could gather he had set off home as fast as he could, dressing himself as he went. By the time Harold was able to leave the baths, Cyril was just a small figure in the distance and disappearing fast.

"Ah didn't know he could run like that," said Harold.In an attempt to lighten the moment he added, "We'll av to enter him in t'Whitsuntide race."

Stanley was furious that his little brother had been so cruelly treated and he racked his brains to think of a way to get even with Harry and Tom Law.

But as it happened, retribution was about to be dealt out to them from within their own family.

When Cyril suffered nightmares three times in a row, and woke the whole house with his screams, his father decided to take a hand in matters. Harold knew Alf Law very well, both at the pub and also as part of his working gang down the pit.

At that stage in Harold's working life he held considerable influence in who worked where down at the coal face, and Alf had no wish to lose out on pay by being put to work on a poor coal seam. All it took was a few quiet words between the men and Alf took the belt to his two sons.

Tom and Harry were both subdued after their punishment and steered clear of the Corkers for quite some time after it.

The matter was then considered closed, and Cyril gradually returned to being the bright, funny little comedian of the family. But the incident left him with a lifelong fear of water, which he was never able to overcome, and he never did learn to swim.

CHAPTER 30

Over the next few months Jim and Stanley became close friends and spent many Sundays cycling out into the surrounding countryside. Once out of Wath the scenery changed. Dust covered trees and roads were replaced by gentle rolling hills and cleaner air that lasted for a few miles until they reached yet another mining village, with stereotype houses and blackened walls in long, grimy streets.

They marvelled at how similar every community seemed to be. Streets full of children playing and groups of women wearing the uniform of turbans and pinafores standing with folded arms chatting outside their homes.

No matter how poor the home, almost every one had shining windows and yellow donkey-stoned steps that were cleaned every day, almost as a gesture of defiance against the constant dirt that the pit spewed out.

Not to conform meant instant condemnation by their neighbours. Only the old and sick were excused, and keeping the front of their houses clean was then the duty of family or an obliging next door neighbour.

Each village had its fair share of public houses from where, through open windows, the smell of beer and tobacco wafted out. The main customers were the miners of course, and they all had a favourite local where they enjoyed the banter and camaraderie for a few hours whenever they had money in their pockets.

In the course of this camaraderie it was usual for several pints of beer to flow down their throats in an effort (or so they said) to quench the thirst brought on by the coal dust and the working conditions.

Every village also had an area of land given over to allotment plots, each one divided by a motley collection of fencing, ranging from bits of wood to old metal bedsteads.

Sheds of all shapes and sizes were built on the plots of land. Like the fences, they were constructed with ingenuity, using whatever materials were available and free. Old doors and windows were highly prized and nailed together haphazardly to form walls and roofs. The more elaborate ones sported a chimney and a stove of some sort.

Here and there were tall pigeon lofts with white painted railings on the roof that served as land marks for the birds when they were flying home. They usually stood higher than all the other sheds and were kept immaculate. Pigeon keeping was a serious business to many of the miners and competition keen.

Saturday evening gave Stanley a chance to wear his newly acquired suit. It was a time to go walking around the town, eyeing up the girls who were also out walking, usually in pairs, eyeing up the boys.

But much as Stanley enjoyed showing off his new clothes and flirting with the girls, he was well and truly smitten by Doris and no one else compared to her. He lived for their chance meetings and waited impatiently for the day she would leave school.

In the meantime he set about charming her mother, Edith Bramham, and while doing so he found himself charmed by Edith. He had never met anyone quite like her, with her easy going ways, generous nature and friendly smile.

Edith often gave the impression of being slightly scatty but she was thrifty and careful with her money. She worked at a variety of jobs and always seemed to be dashing about from one place to another.

When Stanley offered to tidy her garden she accepted but insisted that she must pay him.

Of course Stanley was delighted, not just about the extra money, but because it gave him the perfect opportunity to see Doris more often.

Winning her grandmother over was more difficult but he persevered, pouring out her measure of milk every morning without spilling a drop on her spotless steps.

One day as he made his way back to the farm at the end of the milk round he spotted her familiar figure, dressed in her long black coat, walking slowly up the hill carrying two shopping bags.

As he came alongside her he pulled the horse to a stop and offered her a lift. Taking the bags from her he held her hand as she stepped up on to the milk cart. Giving him a smile she said, "My word, this brings back good memories, it's a long time since a young man gave me a ride in a pony and trap."

After that it seemed he could do no wrong. But, friendly as she became with Stanley, she had a sad look about her that no chatting or jokes could completely banish. It was rumoured that there had been some tragedy in her past and he resolved to ask Doris's mother about it when the time was right.

There was also some mystery about Doris's uncle, William Morriss, who, it was rumoured, had served a prison sentence a long time ago, but no one seemed to know what his crime was. Doris referred to him as Uncle Willie and there appeared to be no chance of charming him. He was in a permanent glum and grumpy mood until the day that Stanley asked him about his garden.

With a sideways nod of his head he indicated for Stanley to follow him up the four wide uneven steps into his garden.He proudly showed him around and talked at such length that Stanley became worried about being late with his milk deliveries.

"Ah'll have to go nah Mr Morriss," he said, "ah'm gonna be late."

At his words Willie fell silent and his face assumed its normal gloomy expression, until Stanley called as he ran down the path that he would come again and learn how to look after raspberries.

"Aye thee gerroff lad," answered Willie, "else auld Downing'll be on to thee. Come back when tha's finished work."

Jackie was stamping his hooves, impatient to be off, and began walking almost before Stanley was aboard. He practically ran between every house he delivered to in an effort to make up the time, but decided it was worth the effort if he had got on good terms with Doris's grumpy uncle.

Over the next few weeks he began to like William Morriss, until the day he heard him shouting at his mother and arrived at the open door just in time to see him hurl his plate of food into the hearth.

He would have backtracked and pretended not to have witnessed his action but Willie looked up.Catching sight of Stanley's shocked expression he simply dragged his chair around until his back was to him and uttered not one word.

Doris's grandmother struggled to keep her face composed as she held out the milk jug for the measure of milk to be poured into it and said nothing, but tears were not far away and Stanley touched her hand briefly. His instinct was to comfort her, but knowing that there was nothing he could do he said goodbye and walked away.

He avoided Willie after that and never forgot the incident. The garden conversations were over and Stanley developed a lifelong dislike of William Morris as he gradually learned that it was not unusual for him to take out his irritations on his mother.

CHAPTER 31

By 1937 Stanley's sister Betty had begun work in a local factory and young Harold was about to join his father at Manvers Main.

With more money coming into the house the grinding poverty had eased, and Ada was able to relax her tight housekeeping budget a little.

She also dared to hope that her childbearing years were over. Only once since Laura had been born had she feared that she might be pregnant, and for a month she sank into deep despair at the thought of going through it all again.

She was filled with delight when the end of the month brought evidence that she was wrong, and to celebrate she arranged to go to Carlton to see her sister Lizzie and Doll.

Edith was home from Lincolnshire on one of her rare weekends off and agreed to look after the family.

It felt strange to be waiting on the station platform alone with no tribe of young children to keep in control, and she felt a strange kind of guilt at doing something just for herself. So much so that she almost abandoned the trip, but the arrival of the train decided her and she stepped aboard and settled in a seat near the window.

As the whistle blew and the train began to move, her thoughts went back over the years. She closed her eyes and was again that young woman running to hide her pregnancy at her sister's house in Carlton.

And then she thought of Doll who had been born there and of how she had left her with Lizzie to be brought up as her daughter.

Now there was an awkward atmosphere between Doll and Ada, her natural mother.

Ada knew that Doll was aware of the circumstances of her birth, but she found it impossible to speak of it. Again and again she rehearsed the words in her head, but somehow it was all locked deep inside her and resisted all her efforts to bring it out into the open. But Doll was a perceptive girl and had an understanding and wisdom of a person much older.

When the train finally pulled into Snaith station, Doll was waiting on the platform and in her loving way she wrapped her arms around Ada, kissed her cheek and whispered in her ear, "I love you Mam."

Ada kissed her back and simply replied, "I love you too Doll." There were no explanations and no more was ever said.

The weekend away had refreshed Ada and she returned feeling optimistic. With more money coming into the house she determined that she would replace the shabby furniture and curtains.

She had spent the journey home on the train planning what she would save for. There were to be no second-hand sofas that smelt of other people's houses this time. No, the new shop in Mexborough would be her destination, just as soon as she could get the money together. Gritting her teeth she made a resolution to cut back Harold's gambling. Too much hard earned cash was finding its way into the pockets of the illegal bookies, thought Ada, already picturing her newly furnished living room.

Ada was not the only one to be making plans. Stanley had his eye on a Royal Enfield motorcycle that was for sale outside a house on Doncaster Road.

The moment he sat on it, with the engine running, he knew it had to be his. Every day he stopped to admire it and spent hours scheming how he could get his savings up to the £25 asking price.

The vendor was a young man in his early twenties whose wife had produced four children in five years and was soon to present him with another. He had clung on to the motorcycle as long as he could, but as his wife had told him, food was more important than running a motorbike and he would just have to walk to work like everyone else.

If he had not been so anxious to sell the machine he would probably have lost patience with Stanley's dithering several days ago, but as there were no other buyers in sight he had held his tongue.

It came to Friday and Stanley had just been paid. As he handed his mother his pay packet, Ada began telling him about her plans for a new sofa and table.

Warning bells sounded in Stanley's head. Any savings he had were very likely to be commandeered for the new furniture, and much as he loved his mother, he saw no reason why he should contribute any more to the family finances.

So, retrieving his whole savings of twenty pounds from his hiding place he walked down to Doncaster Road and struck a deal for the motorbike, for exactly that amount.

After brief riding instructions Stanley kicked the bike into life and set off, shakily at first but soon gaining confidence and by the time he reached home he felt able to ride down the narrow path to the back of the house.

He had intended to arrive discreetly, but the engine had other ideas and backfired twice, sending out sounds as loud as gunfire. His younger brothers and sisters were out of the house and circling the motorbike almost before he had it propped up on its stand.

By the time his mother appeared, Betty and Iris were seated astride it. Ada looked from her son to the bike and back again and shook her head.

"Now what's tha done Stanley. Them things are a death trap. Ah dunt want thee ridin' about on that thing. An don't thee be tekin' ar Harold and Cyril out on t'roads on it."

Stanley glanced up at the neighbouring fence. All the children from next door were peering over the top of it. Betty and Iris stuck their tongues out at them and a face pulling contest developed until Ada gave them one of her steely glares and the disembodied heads dropped out of view.

In spite of her scolding there was a large part of Ada that was proud that her son had acquired a motorcycle. After all, it was bound to raise their standing among the neighbours now that her son had motorised transport. Stanley's father did not share her pride however.

The back firing of the engine had disturbed him from his afternoon rest and that did nothing to improve his temper.

Sensing Harold's mood, the younger children made themselves scarce, leaving Stanley to face his father. Ada stood to one side, hoping to calm the situation that she could see developing.

"An what's this then? Who told thee tha could av one o these things? Where did tha get t'money from?"

Harold moved toward Stanley, belligerent and threatening, but Stanley stood his ground, his chin jutting out and his blue eyes meeting his father's.

He uttered one word quietly, "Don't."

Harold stopped, turned away and waving his arm said, "Serve thee bloody right if tha kills thee sen on it."

Ada and Stanley exchanged glances but said nothing. She gave a deep sigh and followed her husband back into the house, while her son placed his hands on the seat of the motorbike, and relaxed with relief that the confrontation was over. He had triumphed this time, and knew instinctively that his father would never lift a finger to him again.

Strangely, this incident seemed to mark a change in their relationship.

Harold's attitude to this tall gangly son of his began to soften, and even a small degree of respect crept in.

Stanley, starved of his father's affection for so long, revelled in this change and went out of his way to please him, even offering to take him to work early one morning on the back of his motorcycle when Harold was feeling the effects of the previous night's drinking.

Harold had come out of the bathroom looking pale and older than usual, muttering about the beer he had drunk being off. Privately Stanley thought it was the quantity he had consumed, not the quality, but knew better than to voice those thoughts, and instead said, "Do you want a lift to work Dad?"

As he said it Harold was sitting with his head in his hands, but looked up at the words and stared hard at his son trying to bring his eyes back into focus.

"Aye," he said slowly. "Ah could do wi a lift. Ah'll be ok once ah get down t'pit. Ah'll work it off."

It was Harold's first time on a motorbike and he clung tightly to Stanley who reflected that it was the closest contact he could ever remember having with his father.

As they arrived at the pit gates the engine gave its usual backfire, drawing the attention of a group of Harold's workmates who were walking towards them.

In front of them, Harold climbed off the pillion as if it was something he did every day. He patted Stanley's shoulder and loud enough for his mates to hear, he said, "Thanks son."

Just two simple little words, but they made Stanley's heart swell with pride as he revved the bike and roared off back into Wath to begin work himself.

The day had begun well, and was to turn out to be even better later on

With all the milk delivered he turned Jack around and clicked to him to signal their return to the farm. His last call had been at the far side of Wath and both he and the horse were looking forward to breakfast.

Having completely missed out on even a cup of tea that morning due to taking his father to work, Stanley was particularly hungry and looked forward to the fat bacon sandwich that Mrs Downing had promised him.

In his younger days, Jack would have broken out into a trot at this point, eager to reach the waiting oats in his comfortable stable followed by a quick grooming before he was turned out into the field. But he was older and steadier now and content to take the return journey at a gentle pace.

As they passed through the centre of Wath, Stanley spotted a familiar figure. He would have recognised those shapely legs and shiny black bobbed hair anywhere, and he pulled Jack to a halt beside her.

Hastily, he smoothed his own hair and wiped his hands on a damp piece of towelling that he kept beside the seat.

"Morning Doris," he called, "do you want a lift?"

276

Doris looked warily at the horse and trap crowded with the empty milk churns. There was barely enough room for Stanley, let alone herself and her shopping bags. But Stanley quickly moved the churns and pulled himself as tightly up to them as he could.

"Plenty of room, look, you can stand here beside me."

Doris smiled at him and nodded ok, and Stanley's heart seemed to be behaving in the most peculiar manner. Taking her bags he carefully lodged them among the churns and then held her hand as she climbed gingerly on to the step and then into the narrow space that he indicated. He held on to her hand as long as he could, and had forced himself not to stare at her neat ankles on display as she climbed aboard.

The horse was none too pleased at the delay in getting back to the farm and turned his head around as far as the harness would allow, then shifted his feet and moved forward slightly, causing the cart to rock. Stanley could have kissed the horse right there and then for his action as Doris gave a little cry and gripped his arm tightly.

"It's all right, you're safe," he reassured her, feeling ten foot tall. Picking up the reins he positioned himself so that he was standing behind Doris and encircling her with his long arms. As he gave a couple of clicks with his tongue the horse shook his head and gave a snort as if to say, "About time too," and leaned into the shafts to take the weight.

Lifting his tail he blasted out an explosion of wind, and Doris giggled and relaxed while Stanley shook the reins and shouted, "Jack, tha's showin' me up." Doris held her nose as the smell wafted around them and any tension that had existed between them vanished.

As they left the centre of Wath and started up Sandygate, Stanley placed the reins in Doris's hands, then putting his own calloused hands over hers, he instructed her on how to handle the horse.

As he stood behind her looking down on her dark shining hair, he wished that Sandygate was ten miles long, but all too soon the farm was in sight and Jack, with his thoughts on the waiting food, was picking up speed in spite of the extra weight aboard the cart.

With fifty yards to go Stanley decided that this was the right time, and bending his head to Doris's ear he asked her if she would go for a walk with him on Sunday afternoon.

There was still a month to go until she left school, but he could wait no longer, and Doris said yes almost before the words had left his lips. And so it was arranged. Their very first date! Stanley would call for her at three o'clock on Sunday afternoon.

Doris's mother was peering into the tiny round kitchen mirror, patting Ponds Powder onto her face when Doris burst through the door.

"Mam, he's asked me to go out with him on Sunday, we're going for a walk. It's ok, isn't it Mam?"

"Well is this Stanley we're talking about?"

"Course it is," Doris tutted as she answered impatiently.

"And ah expect you said yes?" Edith hid her expression as she examined her face in the mirror for signs of her face powder showing.

"Course ah did. Can ah have some new shoes Mam? Look at these, they're a mess and so ugly."

"Now hang on Doris, ah haven't said you could go yet have ah?" But she smiled as she said it. Both of them knew she could deny her daughter nothing. "But," she added with a sigh, "ah don't know what your grandma's going to say when she hears about it."

As it happened, Grandma had already heard about it.

Stanley and Doris's ride home had been observed by Mrs Ashton, and she had lost no time in trying to enlighten her of every detail when she met her in the Co-op shop.

Unfortunately, due to Mrs Ashton's severe speech impediment, and Grandma's increasing deafness, the conversation had been both loud and difficult.

Thankfully, few people could understand much of what Mrs Ashton said. Which was just as well, seeing as she was doing her best to turn it into a juicy piece of scandal.

Doris was still pursuing her case for a new pair of shoes when her grandma opened the door. She was out of breath and looking harassed as she dumped her shopping bags on the floor and sat down in the nearest chair.

She looked hard at her granddaughter and grabbing her hand she held it tight. "Right Doris, look at me, ah want to know what you've been up to this morning."

"What do you mean Grandma?"

"Don't play innocent with me young lady. Mrs Ashton's been trying to tell me something's been going on wi you and Stanley."

Edith interrupted. "Well she would try to cause trouble mother," and she went on to explain, shushing Doris with a shake of her finger when she was about to break into the conversation. She went on to add that Doris was going to walk out with Stanley on Sunday afternoon.

Grandma digested the speech and considered the firm voice her daughter was using, and knew when she was beaten.

"Well, you're Doris's mother not me," she said, her lips tight with disapproval. "Ah just don't want her getting into trouble, she's far too young to be courting, as you should know Edith."

Doris looked from one to the other. She knew she had won. Kissing her beloved grandmother she picked up the shopping bags.

"Stop worrying Grandma, I won't get into no trouble, you can trust me. Come on, ah'll carry these home for yer and make you a cup of tea."

When Doris returned home her mother had gone out, leaving a note on the table to say she would be back by nine thirty. She was not surprised. Edith was popular and had a wide circle of friends and plenty of social life.

Doris picked up her book and sat down on the hard leather sofa that was her mother's pride and joy. She kept it shiny and well-polished, but it was certainly not designed for comfort. The long narrow arms were studded with raised round headed nails to hold the leather securely in place, and, supposedly, to look decorative. The back was cold and unyielding, so Doris took every cushion in the room and padded them around her and settled among them.

Opening the book, she prepared to lose herself in the story. Three pages into the book she realised that not a word she had read made any sense at all. Her head was full of Stanley and the walk on Sunday, interspersed with the style of shoes she hoped her mother would buy for her.

Restless, she walked around the tiny room, replacing the cushions as she did so. Finally, she could stand it no longer, and making sure that the spark guard was securely in place in front of the fire she put on her coat and set off to see her best friend Maisie. She just had to share her news.As she walked she counted out the days until Sunday and then began mental calculations as to how many hours there were up to that day.

Stanley was in a similar state. He had told his mate Jim about his date and also his younger brother Harold, but had made him promise to keep it to himself, although it was obvious to anyone who knew him that he was burning up with happiness and anticipation.

He serenaded the cows as he milked them and even laughed it off when the bad tempered Friesen caught him a nasty blow at the side of his head with her tail.

Teddy Downing observed his happy humour and commented to his wife at the dinner table that he thought young Stanley was in love.

"What makes you think that Ted?" she asked as she placed the large portion of meat and potatoes in front of him.

"Well, ah only have to look at him. Ah reckon it's Edith Bramham's lass that's caught his eye. Ah've seen him. Every time she passes by he goes into a trance. Tha'd better give him an extra spoonful of sugar in his morning tea love. He'll need it if he's going to start courting."

The week passed slowly, but at last it was Saturday. Doris had persuaded her mother that the new shoes were essential. Edith would have liked a few extra minutes in bed, but knew she would get no peace until the shoes were chosen and bought. So they were on their way to Mexborough in record time, with Doris practically bouncing with excitement.

For Stanley, Saturday was a working day. He started at the usual time, but finished at one o'clock then returned in the late afternoon to do the milking and stock feeding.

Harold and Cyril volunteered to help with the Saturday afternoon work and so Stanley wheeled his trusty Raleigh out of the shed. He figured that as it was mostly downhill to the farm the bike could carry them all.

Cyril perched precariously on the handlebars with his knees drawn up and his feet on the mudguard; he kept insisting that he was going to fall off, but his brothers gave him no sympathy, apart from telling him to shut up and hold on. Harold sat on the luggage rack at the back. He gripped the rear of the seat and as soon as Stanley set off he raised his legs and held them outwards away from the wheels.

Stanley stood up in the pedals and concentrated on moving forwards. It was hard going until they reached the corner and turned into Sandygate, then it was downhill and they soon gathered speed. By now Cyril was half laughing and half screaming with exhilaration, and he gripped the handlebars behind him so tight that Stanley was barely able to apply the brakes.

Their speed rapidly increased and even Cyril went quiet; all they could hear from him was a sort of long drawn in, gasping breath.As they approached the farm Stanley risked a quick glance behind which caused a serious wobble but he regained control and shot across the road and up the slight incline into the yard. Sliding his feet along the ground they came to a halt and Cyril jumped off. His face was pale and his hair stood on end but he grasped his knees and bent over laughing. "That were good Stan, can we do it again?"

Mrs Downing opened the kitchen window and shook her head at them.

"Have you come all the way like that Stanley?" Without waiting for an answer she went on to warn him, "If t'bobby sees you there'll be trouble."

Stanley managed to look sheepish and nodded but made no comment.

Propping up his bike against the wall he beckoned to his brothers and they set to work. With three of them working the milking was soon done and the animals fed and bedded down for the night. As they walked the cows back to their pasture, Cyril pointed to the sturdy piebald horse alongside of Jack in the next field.

"Is that a new horse? Ah like him, he's got fur like patchwork."

Stanley raised his eyebrows and tutted at Cyril's description.

"Patchwork! Tha's a right comic," he said, making a cuffing gesture towards Cyril's ear.

"He's a piebald, Boss gorrim off them gypsies down near t'canal. He's called Roman. He's goin' to tek over from Jack on t'milk round when we've gorrim trained. Jack's gerrin' a bit tired, int tha lad?" and he stroked Jack's neck as the horse leaned over the gate, sniffing in Stanley's pocket hoping for a treat.

The new horse joined them at the gate and jostled to get to the handfuls of sweet grass that Harold and Cyril were offering.

"Can tha ride him Stan?" asked Harold.

Without answering, Stanley climbed on top of the gate and slipped on to the back of the handsome piebald horse. A tremor passed through the horse and he shook his head and stamped his feet.

Harold stared in admiration. "Can tha ride him like that, wi no saddle Stan?"

"Well t'gypos don't have saddles. He's used to it."

But for all his bravado Stanley was a little nervous as he held the horse's mane and pulled his head around to face the open field. With a couple of clicks and slight movement of his heels they were off, trotting slowly round the perimeter of the meadow.

Gradually as he gained confidence, Stanley urged the horse to go faster, and moving with the animal he bent low over his neck, talking to him and gripping with his knees.

If only he had carried on like that all would have been well. But the low mound of gorse tempted him and he steered Roman towards it, expecting him to jump over it. Possibly the horse himself intended to jump over it, but at the last moment changed his mind and swerved sharply off towards the left. Unfortunately, Stanley carried straight on and sailed over the gorse. He landed with a thump and rolled to a stop where he lay, stunned.

When he opened his eyes he was looking directly into Harold's.

"Ah thank God. Bloody hell Stan, ah thought tha were dead. Is tha ok?"

282

Stanley raised his head and waited until the scenery stopped spinning. Slowly he got to his feet and checked himself over. Roman was five yards away munching grass and glanced innocently at him as if to say, "It's nothing to do with me!"

Cyril spoke up then. "Tha's gorra big bump on thee head Stan. Bet it hurts."

It did. A large swelling just above his right eye was rapidly rising and Stanley's first thought was what a sight he was going to look for his date with Doris. He groaned and prayed that it would go away.

Of course his prayers were unanswered. Nature took its course and he awoke next morning to find he had a huge lump on his forehead and an eye of many colours. He cursed his stupidity and wondered what Doris's reaction would be.

At home he had been greeted as he expected, with jokes and comments that assumed he had been in a fight. Even Harold and Cyril's attempts to put forward the facts had been ignored. Most of the family preferred their version of how he had acquired the black eye.

Even his mother had quipped that she hoped the other chap looked worse, but at least she had given him a pat of butter to smear on the lump, and told him to bathe his eye in cold water.

Neither of these remedies were any help. And it was a very self-conscious and apprehensive young man who put on his best suit on that Sunday afternoon.

As he stepped out of the gate at 93 Oak Road he adjusted his jacket sleeves and the brim of his cap. If he pulled his cap down low over his forehead and kept his head down the black eye was barely visible.

Although he had not admitted it, he still felt shook up by the fall, and his head pounded but he walked at his usual brisk pace.He was soon at Doris's door.

Taking a deep breath and crossing his fingers he knocked. Doris had been waiting for that sound. She had intended to walk slowly to the door in an attempt to appear casual and not too eager, but all those intentions vanished at the thought of actually going out on her first date.

She smoothed her dark hair and tapped across the floor in her new grey suede shoes with the leather straps that fastened around her ankles. A blush coloured her cheeks as she opened the door.

Edith watched her daughter from the kitchen where she stood washing the Sunday dinner pots. She smiled proudly and thought how lovely her Doris was, and today she had never looked prettier.

Stanley thought he had prepared himself for Doris's reaction, but her sharp intake of breath at the sight of his injured face left him uncomfortable, and he began to say he was sorry, that maybe she wouldn't want to go out with him. Doris reached forward and grasping his hand pulled him inside. Clearly upset, she asked him what had happened as she indicated for him to sit down.

Seated on the wooden fireside chair holding his folded cap in his hands he looked at mother and daughter.

"Oh, my God Stanley. Whatever's happened?" asked Edith, wiping her hands on her apron. "Do you want an aspirin? It must hurt. Doris, put t'kettle on and make him some tea."

As he drank the hot sweet tea he told them how he had come by the injury. Edith shook her head at him. "Bet you won't do that again," she said. With a sigh she remembered the scrapes that her two brothers had got into as young men and was not surprised.

Stanley sat back and enjoyed their sympathy and pampering. This was a new experience for him and he accepted it with good grace.

"Ah look a right mess Doris, if tha don't want to go out wi me today it's ok. Ah don't want to show yer up."

Doris took her coat from the hook behind the door. "Don't talk soft Stanley Dale. Come on, you promised to take me out for a walk, and a few bruises shouldn't make any difference."

Her mother laughed at his expression. "If yer going to go out wi our Doris, you'd better get used to it. She's a right bossy little madam, aren't you love?" She slipped her arm around her shoulders. "Off you go you two, go for yer walk and ah'll make some tea for when you get back."

The moment they stepped out of the house they joined hands as naturally as if they were meant to be joined. Stanley looked down at her and he could hardly believe that this beautiful young girl was

284

going out with him. And then they began to talk, pouring out their lives to each other, laughing about the odd characters they knew and disclosing their hopes and fears, totally oblivious to people who passed them by. They were completely absorbed in each other.

Without any plans of where they would walk to, they arrived at Wath Wood, which was the nearest the coal blackened town could come to a beauty spot. As they reached the shelter of the trees Stanley drew her close and they kissed.From that moment he knew that there would never be anyone else for him.

Close by where they had stopped was what was known locally as the wishing well. It was little more than a pool surrounded by a low brick wall, but visitors to the wood often threw in coins and made a wish to bring them luck.

Now there was no way on earth that Stanley was about to throw hard earned money into a muddy pool whether it was lucky or not, but as Doris seated herself on a bench he took out his penknife and began carving on a tall beech tree.

Curious, Doris came to watch, but Stanley covered his work with his hand and refused to let her see. Pretending to be offended she went back to the bench and carefully rubbed the scuffs that had appeared on her new shoes.

At last he had finished and beckoned her to see his work.

"There Doris. Look. That's there forever, or until the tree blows down."

She stood close to him with her head resting on his shoulder. There, roughly carved, were their initials, surrounded by a heart. As Doris gazed at it she put her arms around him and hugged him tightly, filled with love for this tall young man, and she knew that she belonged with him.

From that first date there was seldom a day when they didn't see each other and it was soon accepted by everyone that Stanley and Doris were courting.

Doris's uncle grunted at the news and grumbled that she would end up with a houseful of children just the same as Stanley's mother had.

Doris was indignant at his remarks but mostly ignored his words, knowing him as well as she did.

Stanley on the other hand was deeply offended that William should assume he was like his father and like him would inflict repeated pregnancies on his wife, and his dislike of William grew.

Mostly, due to having little money, their outings consisted of walking, sometimes going as far as Bolton to visit his uncle and aunt where they could always be sure of a warm welcome.

It was on one of their walks around Wath that they encounted Doris's father. They had been into Sammy Bowley's shop looking at the pawned goods he had on sale and they linked arms as they left, laughing at something he had said.

Stanley saw him first. He knew Larrett Bramham by sight, as almost everyone in that small town did, mostly due to the fact that he came from a prominent and wealthy family, and also because he had gained some notoriety by parting from his wife and bringing in another woman to live in the family home.

As Stanley felt Doris grip his arm tighter he realised that she had seen him too. There was no way they could avoid each other. He glanced down at Doris.

Her lips were set in that way she had when she was upset or angry. But she held her head high and stared straight ahead.

'Surely,' thought Stanley, 'Surely, he will stop and speak to her, or at least smile and say hello.'

But Larrett gave no sign that she even existed and walked by them. As soon as her father was out of hearing, Doris said in a tight defiant little voice, "Told you, didn't I? I told you he never speaks to me. Never even notices me." Her voice broke, "But ah don't care. Me and me Mam are better off without him. He can have that woman from Scunthorpe and ah hope she makes him miserable."

But for all her brave talk Stanley could see how hurt she was. He could scarcely believe that Doris's father had totally ignored her and he put his arm around her protectively.

"Bloody hell," he exclaimed. "Ah thought my Dad was bad enough, but yours is worse! At least mine doesn't pretend he hasn't seen me."

The first time that Stanley took Doris home to meet his family she was completely overwhelmed by the number of people in that small house. His four sisters immediately took her over, admiring her clothes and dark beauty. They seated her on the sofa and sat two at each side of her, chattering non-stop until Ada called to them to let the poor girl have some breathing space. But Doris reassured her she was fine and sat with Betty, Iris, Jessie and Laura, marvelling at their long fair hair that hung in neat plaits that were almost waist length.

She was soon a regular visitor and loved being part of the large family. In contrast to her own quiet home, 93 Oak Road was always full of noise and laughter. With the working members of the family coming and going at different times it seemed that the kettle was forever on the boil, and meals were constantly being prepared or consumed. But Stanley's mother had everything under control.

Doris soon came to the conclusion that Ada was one very tough lady in spite of her delicate looks, and was usually able to rule even the adults with just a warning glance, but she could and did at times shout louder than all the rest of the family put together if they needed bringing into order.

What Stanley enjoyed most was the time spent in Doris's home. Edith often went out in the evenings leaving the young couple alone. The little cottage oozed calm and as Stanley sat on the sofa with his arm around Doris he let the peace wash over him.

Left alone, their passion and ardour could soon have turned their kisses and cuddles into deeper embraces, if it had not been for fear of Doris's grandmother or uncle popping in unannounced.

Also, Mrs Ashton had a habit of lifting the latch and walking in, calling as she did so in her strange manner of speaking that it was, "Only me" and asking for the loan of one thing or another. Stanley became quite good at imitating her and Doris laughed till tears ran down her cheeks at the outrageous things he said in poor Mrs Ashton's voice.

By this time of course, Doris was working. Within days of leaving school at Easter she began work as a housemaid at the home of a local butcher. She needed no lessons on cleaning a house, having been used to helping both her mother and grandmother since she was old enough to hold a duster, and she was a hard and efficient worker who loved to set about a room and clean it thoroughly, leaving it smelling fresh and polished.

Her employers were wealthy and Doris greatly admired their beautiful home, filled with grand furniture and valuable ornaments. One of Doris's Friday jobs was to clean the stairs. It was a wide, polished, dark oak staircase with a strip of royal blue carpet running up the centre of the treads. This was held in place by brass stair rods.

It took Doris at least an hour to clean it working on her hands and knees. Every inch had to be swept with a hand brush and dust pan, then each stair rod removed, polished and replaced.

It was when she was half way through cleaning these rods one Friday that she found the half crown. It was tucked just under the edge of the carpet, and Doris stared at it for almost a minute with rage gradually building inside her.

She knew why it was there. It had not been there the previous week, and she rightly guessed that it had been put there to test her. Firstly to see if she was cleaning thoroughly enough to find the coin and secondly to see if she was honest enough to hand it in to her employer.

With cheeks on fire Doris threw down the brush, picked up the half crown and marched, without knocking, into the parlour where Mrs Cutts sat entertaining her friends and drinking coffee from delicate china cups.

Before she had time to speak, Doris slammed the money down on the coffee table.

"There you are,"she said. "That's yours, and you can stick your bloody job if you don't trust me," and she left, slamming the door so hard that the cups rattled on the table.

The pits siren began to wail as Doris reached home, its sound carrying on the wind. For the miners it signalled the end of the shift, but for Doris it was a sign that it was dinnertime and her mother would be at home. She was not going to be pleased that Doris had walked out of her job. As she lifted the latch she took a deep breath and squared her shoulders.

Edith had just eaten her dinner and had removed her shoes and propped her feet up on the wooden stool that stood near the fender and had lit one of the few cigarettes that she allowed herself each day. She had less than thirty minutes before she had to return to work and she was relishing every moment of her relaxation.

Looking up, she smiled at her daughter until she saw the expression on her face.

"Now what?" she demanded as she put her shoes back on and nipped out the cigarette with a sigh of regret. Anger rose in her as she listened to Doris's story. She seldom lost her temper and indulged Doris in most things, but today was an exception and she banged her clenched hand on the table as she turned to face her.

"And do you mean to tell me you've walked out of a good job just for that? You stupid girl! You should have handed her the half crown and said nothing."

Doris made no reply, but the expression on her face reminded Edith so much of Arthur Bramham who was her paternal grandfather. She hesitated before continuing. "We need your wages now Doris. You know I get no allowance for you from your father now that you've left school, and you won't even get the week's money that you're owed. Not when you walked out."

Edith's temper had faded as quickly as it had risen and she was close to tears.

"Ah'm sorry Mam. Don't you worry. Ah'll get what ah'm owed, and ah'll get another job. Ah promise."

Doris buttoned her coat, pulled on her gloves and left, closing the door firmly. As she walked quickly down the hill into the centre of Wath, her mind was going over what her mother had said about her father having stopped her maintenance the very day she left school. She seethed with resentment as she thought of him living in comfort and security among his rich family while her mother worked at two jobs to make ends meet.

She decided that she would tackle Mr Cutts about the week's wages she was owed, rather than his wife back at the house that she had so recently walked out of.

As she reached the butcher's shop she could see that there was a long queue. No chance of a quiet word with him she thought, but Doris tightened her lips and fairly bristling with temper she resolved to stand her ground and demand her money.

Mr Cutts was wrapping sausages in a sheet of greaseproof paper as she entered the shop. As he caught sight of her he stopped and put his hands on his hips, his broad face breaking out into a smile.

"Hello young Doris," he said, winking at his customers. "What brings you here? Has Mrs Cutts run out of meat?"

Doris took a deep breath and drew herself up as tall as she could.

"No, Mr Cutts. I've come for my wages. I won't be working for you any longer. Mrs Cutts doesn't trust me."

His smile disappeared and he walked around the blood-stained chopping block. The customers parted like a wave until he was facing Doris directly across the narrow counter. He was a big man and towered above her, but she was not about to be intimidated and stared back at him, her cheeks bright red.

"I would like my wages for the week, and I'd like em now. I've done a full week's work."

There was murmur of agreement from the ladies in the queue.

"Quite right love. If tha's done the graft, tha's entitled to thee pay," said one very stout lady, and she leaned on the counter glaring at the butcher.

"Yes, quite right love, thee stand up for theesen. Give her money, tha tight fisted auld bugger," agreed her friend as she tucked a strand of hair inside her black felt hat.

Reaching into the till he took a handful of silver and counted it out slowly into Doris's hand.

"Ah'll speak to Mrs Cutts about this tonight young lady. If tha's walked out on t'job tha'll not get another in a hurry. There'll be no references tha knows."

Pocketing the money Doris walked out of the shop. Her legs were shaking, but her defiant parting shot was, "Ah wouldn't want a reference from your wife thank you very much."

She hadn't gone more than twenty yards when she heard her name being called.

"Doris. Doris Bramham. Wait please."

Turning around she saw a short, plump woman hurrying towards her. Doris recognised her as one of the customers in the shop. She was well dressed and as she approached Doris caught the aroma of expensive perfume. She smiled at Doris as she came to a halt in front of her.

"You are Edith Bramham's daughter?" Without waiting for confirmation she continued, "I'm Mrs Dyson. Your mother knows me. I can offer you a job my dear. It's extremely fortunate that I happened to be in the shop just now. The young lady who helps me has had to go home to look after her brothers and sisters following the death of her mother. Very sad. So I can offer the position to you. I would need you to start on Monday. There will be no need for references. You're Edith's daughter. That's good enough for me. What do you say?"

The offer was so unexpected it took Doris's breath away for a moment.

"Oh, yes, of course Mrs Dyson. Thank you. You won't regret it. Ah'm a hard worker."

Her future employer patted her hand. "I don't doubt it my dear. Your mother will tell you where I live. I will expect you at eight o'clock prompt on Monday morning."

She turned and left, giving Doris a wave as she went, her rings gleaming on her fingers.

When Doris related the story that evening to Stanley he looked at her in admiration.

"What, you went and asked old man Cutts for your wages?"

Doris nodded. 'No doubt about it,' thought Stanley, 'this shy girlfriend of mine has a backbone of pure steel.'

CHAPTER 32

By this time Stanley had been working for several years and was now an experienced farm labourer. He could turn his hand to anything on the farm and continued to learn from Mr Downing's lifetime of knowledge.

Although he loved the heavy horses that he worked with every day he was excited by the tractors and machinery that were gradually being introduced into farming, and he thought that all his birthdays had come at once when a blue Fordson Major tractor was delivered to the farm.

His first sight of it was when he returned from his day's work out in the fields. He was riding home on Punch's back, sitting side saddle, his long legs dangling loosely and his body moving back and forth rhythmically in time with the horse's slow plod.

As his eyes lit on the tractor he slid from Punch's back, his studded boots landing with a clatter on the hard packed earth. He joined Mr Downing who was gazing dolefully at the new machine.

"Ah'm not sure about this thing Stanley. Ah think ah've slipped up buying it. It could be a waste of money. Horses are doin' t'job and have been for years."

Stanley sucked in his breath. "Oh no Mr Downing. Tractors are the way to go. Ah don't think you'll regret it. Can ah av a go wi it?"

"Tha'd better do Stanley, it's beyond me."

They were joined by Eric who looked at the tractor suspiciously, and watched Stanley pick up the starting handle and insert it into position at the front of the machine. Stanley looked more confident than he felt as he turned the handle, hoping desperately that he could remember all he had learned from the demonstration he had attended down at the blacksmiths the previous week.

To his relief the engine started and he climbed up and sat on the iron seat, feeling so excited that he never noticed how cold and hard it was. Easing the tractor into gear he moved slowly forward, thrilling at the sense of power in the engine. From that moment Stanley was smitten and engines became the love of his life, second only to Doris.

That evening Edith was out and they had the cottage to themselves. Doris had laid the table carefully and cooked a meat and potato pie for Stanley. After a long, hard day out in the fields he thought it was the most delicious food he had ever tasted. With the last few drops of gravy consumed he moved to the sofa, and leaning back he sighed with contentment. Pulling Doris towards him he kissed the top of her head and whispered in her ear. "We'll do this every day when we're married."

It was the first time either of them had mentioned marriage. It was simply accepted by both of them as naturally as breathing that being married was what they both wanted. There was no question of if they would wed, it was just a matter of when, and as far as Doris was concerned it couldn't happen soon enough.

Stanley had been looking forward to introducing Doris to his sister Doll. He had told Doris in great detail about how close he was to his sister, and enthused about her sunny friendly nature, stressing how she had always understood him, and finally had described how attractive she had become as she had grown up.

He was not prepared for his girlfriend's attitude to all this information, and was puzzled and hurt when he realised that every time he mentioned her Doris became quiet and sulky, her dark eyes fairly burning with suppressed rage.

He decided to ask his mother's advice, and trying to sound casual, he described Doris's moodiness about Doll. Ada looked at him, marvelling at how dense males could be at times. She shook her head at him and gave a 'tch' sound. "Hasn't tha realised Stanley that she's probably jealous?"

"It can't be that Mam. Doll's me sister. Why would she be jealous of me sister?"

Ada returned his gaze. "Tha'd better realise lad, that Doris is not the type to share thee affections with anyone. Not even thee sister.

293

She's a deep one is that lass and tha'd do well to remember it. Nah gerr out of me way, ah've got to get this washing out."

Stanley went to work, and all day he thought about his mother's advice.By the end of the day he had come to the decision that she was right, and in future he would think about his words before he allowed them to leave his mouth as far as praise of Doll was concerned.

In the event, when the two girls finally met, Doris was completely won over by Doll's friendly personality, and as long as Stanley didn't show his affection for his sister too much, all was well.

By the time they had been courting for eighteen months both Stanley and Doris desperately wanted to get married, but as they were both under twenty one they needed their parents' consent.

Doris, at sixteen, was confident that she could persuade her mother to give permission. However, Stanley, at nineteen, was much less sure that his parents would agree. And he was right to be doubtful. When he broached the subject he chose his moment carefully and found a rare time when Ada and Harold were alone in the living room.

As he blurted out that that he wanted to get married his mother said bluntly, "No, tha bloody can't, tha's too young. Tha can wait till tha's twenty one."

Stanley's face fell, but to his surprise his father spoke up.

"Nah, hang on Ada. If he's got to get married, he'll have to and that's all there is to it."

What he was inferring was that Doris must be pregnant.

Stanley stood his ground and took a deep breath. He knew there was no question of Doris being pregnant, but he bit his lip and said nothing. If he got their permission because that was what they thought, he didn't mind. It suited his purpose to go along with the suggestion, so that's what he did, and grudgingly Ada said yes.

In the meantime Doris had approached her mother several times and was always been met with a refusal, but Doris never gave up if she wanted something, and her mother knew it only too well. After three weeks, worn down by her daughter's repeated nagging, Edith gave in.

And so a date was set for the fourteenth of January1939, probably the coldest, bleakest time of the year. But neither of them cared what time of the year it was, all they wanted was to be married and they quickly made arrangements for their wedding.

There was to be no fancy venue or expensive clothes. Doris went shopping with her mother and bought a warm new winter coat, matching shoes and gloves and a very stylish hat, while Stanley was supervised into buying a long, beige Macintosh that he was to wear over his best suit, and all topped by a new flat tweed cap. He also acquired for the first time, three sets of warm underpants and vests.

The fourteenth of January 1939 was a cold, dark day with heavy rain falling for most of the morning. Stanley was tense and nervous and anxious to be off. Dressed and ready far too early, he alternated between sitting on the kitchen stool and standing at the window, willing and praying for the rain to stop, and for his mother and father to be ready.

Just when he thought he would burst from impatience they walked into the kitchen, and he had to admit to himself that he felt proud of them.

Harold wore his best suit with his watch and chain on display on his waistcoat, and as always he looked as if he had spent the last half hour scrubbing his face. His skin was as clear and fresh as someone who spent their lives outdoors, rather than toiling every day among the coal dust.

His mother was slim and elegant in her long navy blue coat. She had trimmed her hat with new ribbon and wore soft leather gloves that hid her work worn hands.

Stanley looked at her face. She was pale and drawn. He felt overwhelmed with tenderness and the desire to protect her, but could find no words to convey that feeling.

Instead, he picked up the corsage he had had made and offered it to her. As she pinned it to her lapel she said briskly, "Come on then, what's tha waiting for? Don't want to be late does tha?"

They walked down Oak Road as far as the Oak Tree inn, and then crossed over onto Sandygate, feeling conspicuous dressed in their best clothes on what was a working day for everyone else. The narrow footpaths made it impossible to walk alongside of each other, so Stanley went first, striding out on his long legs, while his mother and father followed sedately behind.

He could hear Harold's breath, heavy in his mine worker's lungs and Ada's steel tipped heels tapping faster than his own.

To Stanley the walk seemed never ending and he burned with impatience and the fear that he might be late.

As the cottage where Edith and Doris lived came into view he could see her waiting for him outside on the pavement and his heart did a double beat.

Her face echoed his own happiness, and taking her hand he said, "This is it Doris. Today's our day."

She nodded but didn't trust herself to speak for fear of bursting into sentimental tears.

The moment was lightened by Edith, who came out wearing a large straw hat trimmed liberally with artificial flowers and fruit.

Stanley stared at it, his lips twitching, and commented, "Hey up, ah think there's a bird nesting in that lot."

Edith gave him a push. "Cheeky bugger," she said. "Thee watch it or ah'll not let yer marry my daughter."

He laughed and gave her a quick hug. "Only kidding Edi, you look grand." And he meant it. Outrageous as the hat might be, Edith carried it off with flair.

Despite Stanley's fears that they might be late, they were at the bus stop in good time and spent the next ten minutes cold and wet, huddled under two small umbrellas that threatened to blow away in the gusty wind.

By the time they were on the bus and on their way to Rotherham, Harold had become very irritable and sat alone on a seat near the front while Edith and Ada sat together and chatted throughout the whole journey.

Stanley and Doris held hands, occasionally looking at each other and smiling, happy in their own little world.

Harold turned to look at them and gave a sort of 'hmm' sound before he swivelled back to continue his silent brooding.

296

Observing his action, Edith raised her eyebrows quizzically at Ada who shrugged and said quietly, "Take no notice Edith, he's in a mood this morning."

The civil ceremony at Rotherham registry office was brief and soon over, but that made no difference to the young couple. They were now man and wife and that was all that mattered to them. If the registrar noticed that the groom's father had a different surname to his son he made no mention of it. Nor did he question why the bride's father had not signed the consent form. In fact Larrett Bramham had not been told of his daughter's forthcoming marriage and as he never acknowledged her, Edith had seen no need to inform him.

Before the midday pit siren sounded the wedding party was back in Wath and sitting down in Edith's cottage to eat the food that Doris's grandmother had prepared. She had made sandwiches and a huge apple pie liberally sprinkled with sugar, and Harold declared that it was the best he had ever tasted. He had recovered his good humour now that the wedding was over and the prospect of a session in the Royal Oak was not too far away.

Edith poured a glass of sherry for everyone, including Mrs Ashton who had somehow managed to join them, squeezing herself into the crowded room.

The couple's health was drunk and then it was over.

Harold and Ada left straight after the toast. It felt strange to Stanley, seeing his parents off. He had felt closer to them today than he had ever felt before. Ada's eyes threatened to brim over until her husband took hold of her elbow and said, "Come on Ada, let's get a move on, there's no need for waterworks. For God's sake, he's only just down t'road."

So Ada adjusted her hat and waved goodbye, pulling a face at her husband's back as she went.

Doris's grandmother told Mrs Ashton in no uncertain terms that it was time to go, and held the door open for her. Reluctantly she left and Grandma followed her, taking a slice of pie for Willie who had declined to attend the wedding celebrations, due, he said, to his 'bad stomach'.

Doris looked at Stanley on hearing that information, although she resisted saying anything. She didn't need to. Already Stanley could read what she was thinking. Doris knew her uncle and his moods only too well, and had little patience with him.

The house was silent after they had gone, apart from the chink of crockery being washed. Edith had taken charge of the job and stood at the sink, carefully washing her best china while taking puffs at her cigarette that lay in a saucer on the window sill.

Stanley took his new wife in his arms. "Hello Doris Dale," he said, holding her close. Doris was so happy she just could not stop smiling.

"I thought you two were off to Bolton?"

Edith's words echoed from the kitchen and they turned to look at her. She was speaking with the cigarette in the corner of her mouth while her hands were deep in the washing up bowl. Doris took the cigarette out of her mother's mouth and placed it on the saucer.

"I wish you wouldn't do that Mam. It looks so common," she scolded.

Edith was unrepentant and wiping her hand briefly on her apron she took another puff on the very damp cigarette.

"Aye, ah know, but it's one of me few pleasures. If you two get off now, you'll catch the next bus and be there before dark. Go on, off you go and leave me to have a bit of peace. You two enjoy yourselves. See yer later."

Within the hour the newly married couple were walking into Stanley's uncle and aunt's house in Bolton. The room was packed with relations who greeted them with a cheer. The kitchen table was laden with home baked pies and pasties and in the centre was an iced cake on a glass stand.

As usual the fire was piled high and glowing red, and as always the back door stood wide open to let out some of the overpowering heat.

Stanley knew his uncle and aunt were fond of him and had always treated him like an extra son, but was unprepared for the way John seized his hand and shook it vigorously and patted his shoulder, his eyes looking suspiciously damp.

Then he hugged Doris and said to her, "Nah then love, see tha looks after this lad, tha's got thee sen a diamond." Doris smiled and nodded, while Stanley, who was listening, thought that his uncle's words were the best compliment he had ever been paid, even if it was the ale that had loosened his tongue.

His cousin Jack had borrowed a camera and he took a snapshot of the young couple, looking very self-conscious and terribly young, followed by one of a family group just outside the back door.

Finally with only one frame left in the camera he posed Stanley and Doris, dressed in their new hats and coats, at the front of the house.

At the last moment just before the camera clicked, Doll slipped into the picture and linked her arm into Stanley's on his left side. As they stood there trying to hold their smiles while Jack fiddled with the camera, it occurred to Doris that as she was now called Doris Dale, and Doll's real name was the same. Her new husband now had a Doris Dale on each arm, and she was not at all sure that she liked that.

CHAPTER 33

They began married life sharing Edith's cottage, and also shared Doris's narrow single sized bed. In an effort to give them more sleeping room, a collection of old stools and chairs were ranged down one side of the bed and covered with Stanley's green eiderdown as padding.

For Stanley one of the advantages of living in Sandygate was his close proximity to his job. He was barely thirty yards away from Downing's farm, which meant it was very easy to get to work, but also meant that he was on call for every little emergency that arose, and he was rarely paid for the extra hours he put in.

As was usual at that time, Doris had given up her job when they married and she became a full time housewife. And she set about it very seriously. The first thing she did was to buy a notebook and she wrote down every single penny she spent.

However, even with Doris's very careful housekeeping, money was tight. Stanley had sold his Royal Enfield to his brothers, Harold and Cyril, the week before the wedding, to cover the cost of new clothes and the expenses of the registry office.

His wages were barely enough to support one, let alone a couple, and urged on by his new wife he decided it was time to ask Mr Downing for a rise.

Knowing how attached Teddy was to his money, Stanley had a sense of foreboding about asking for the rise, but there was simply no alternative.

So he waited until they had finished the milking one morning, and in the brief interval before he set out for the fields, he approached Teddy as he was leaning on the gate admiring his herd of cows that were contentedly munching on the dried pea straw in their food troughs.

He came straight out with it and put forward his request for more money in his wage packet. Teddy's expression changed and he turned and looked Stanley in the face, then looked back at his cattle. He pursed his lips and shook his head.

"Nay lad," he said slowly. "Ah think tha's gerrin' to be too big a money man for me. Tha'd better look for another job."

Stanley could not have been more shocked or hurt if he had suffered a punch in the face. But he was not about to let Teddy see that, and he turned abruptly on his heel and walked away.

For every minute of that morning as he worked, the scene replayed itself in his head. He could not believe what had just happened.

His inborn sense of fairness had taken a knock, and he seethed with the injustice that Teddy Downing had dealt him. He went over and over it again and again and wondered how on earth he could tell Doris. What would she think of him and what would she say? Only three weeks married and far from getting the rise he had hoped for, he had lost his job. He dreaded breaking the news to her. It was a long morning, but at last dinner time came around and he could put off the moment no longer.

As he walked into the cottage Doris was placing his dinner on the table. Steam was rising from the piled up plate and normally he would have sat down and demolished the food, but today he had no appetite.

Doris's cheeks were flushed from the heat of the stove and he kissed them before sitting down and giving a big sigh.

"Ah've got bad news Doris."

She looked at him as she took her place at the other side of the table, and listened as he related his conversation with Teddy Downing. As he spoke her lips tightened and her dark eyes looked black with rage. Stanley thought she was angry with him until he stopped speaking and ended with, "Ah'm sorry love, maybe ah shouldn't have asked him."

Doris took a deep breath before she began. "Why that tight fisted old bugger. All these years you've been working and slaving for him.

You've every right to ask him for a rise. He's only paying you a lad's wage but getting a man's work out of you, and all the extra hours you put in for free. Ah'll go and give that old bugger a piece of my mind," and she pushed her chair back, heading for the door.

Stanley reached it before her, and placing his back against it he took hold of her arms.

"Nah, steady on Doris. Let's think about this. No good you flying off the handle and making matters worse.

Edith, when she arrived home, took the news more calmly.

"Well Stanley, I'm not surprised. Teddy Downing hates parting with his money. He's done this sort of trick before. He'll get another young lad and work him same as he's worked you, then finish him when he wants full pay. Don't worry. You'll get another job. Just make sure you get a reference from him, and you Doris," and she pointed at her daughter, "you'd better keep quiet till he's got it, or it'll be twice as hard for him to find another job."

Stanley took heed of her words and approached Teddy the following evening when he had finished work for the day.

"Aye, ah'll give you a reference lad. Ah'll be sorry to see you go, but it's a matter of finance. Ah can't afford to pay more. Money's tight."

After making it clear that he would like the reference right away, Stanley waited on the doorstep. Inside his head he was repeating the words, 'money's tight', and he could have laughed out loud when he thought of the shiny new car, polished and gleaming in the garage at the back of the house. But, he kept his bitter thoughts under control and accepted the reference that was handed to him in a sealed envelope with every outward appearance of good grace.

The Mexborough Times was open on the table when he arrived home. Doris was leaning over it and beckoned to him as he walked in. "Come here quick Stan, look, there's a job advertised at Swinton, and a cottage goes with it. It's at Norman Flint's, have you heard of him?"

Stanley shook his head and quickly scanned through the advert. Straightening up he rebuttoned his coat and walked through the kitchen towards the door.

"Where are you going Stan? Tea's ready."

"Tea'll wait. Ah'm off to Swinton on me bike. Ta-ra. See ya when ah get back." And before Doris could say any more, he was off.

He raced along the road to Mexborough and uphill to Swinton, powering the heavy Raleigh along with his strong young legs. It was fully dark by the time he found the farm. He stopped at the gate and tried to calm his breathing. In spite of the cold icy wind he was sweating, apart his hands that were so cold he could barely unclench them from the handlebars.

Adjusting his cap, he walked up to the farm yard, propped his bike against the wall and knocked on the door.

Apart from one window the entire house was in darkness and Stanley worried that he might not have been heard, but the sound had been picked up by the dogs and loud barking made him take a couple of steps back from the door.

The voice that quietened the dogs made Stanley's nerves worse than ever and he waited in trepidation while he listened to the sound of the door being unlocked. At first he could see nothing for the light of the torch being shone in his face.

"Nah then, what does tha want at this time of night?" the voice behind the torch bellowed.

"Erm, ah've come about t'advert in t'Mexborough Times. There's a job advertised. Av ah come to t'right place?"

"Aye tha has. Tha's come at a right time ant tha? Still tha must be keen. Advert's only just gone in. Tha'd better come in and shut t'door behind thee."

Stanley followed him and the two dogs trailed behind him sniffing suspiciously at his feet. He was led into a large kitchen that was lit by a pair of oil lamps and the glow from the fire. The smell of food was strong and Stanley looked with envy at the laden table. His mealtime was long overdue. His stomach rumbled in anticipation of the food that smelt so delicious. But it soon became evident that his stomach would have no chance of anything in this house.

Not even a cup of tea was on offer, but at least his hands were beginning to warm up. He sat and waited while the farmer and his wife ploughed through the plates of ham and eggs, accompanied by the thickly buttered bread.

At last the final mouthful was swallowed and his soon-to-be new employer swung his chair round to face him. A dribble of egg yolk stuck to his chin and Stanley tried not to stare as it moved up and down as he spoke.

"Nah then young man what's your name? Ah don't suppose tha's got a reference has tha?"

As Stanley took the envelope containing the reference out of his pocket he gave a silent sigh of relief that he had asked Teddy for it.

Norman took the envelope, obviously surprised, and turned it over several times before he took a knife from the table, wiped it on the cloth and slit it open.

The kitchen was quiet as he read; just the sound of the grandfather clock ticking in the corner and the hiss of the logs on the fire broke the silence. Norman's wife sat close to the lamp darning a sock and the dogs crept close to Stanley and lay at his feet. He hardly dared to breathe for fear that Teddy had written a bad reference.

Replacing the paper back in the envelope the farmer looked up and stroked his chin wiping off the dribble of egg. He gazed at it on the end of his finger then slowly put it in his mouth as he began.

"Well," he said, "Downing seems to think well of thee, he say's tha's a good worker so ah'll tek a chance on thee. There's a cottage wi t'job and ah can pay thee," and he hesitated, and then mumbled a figure as if it pained him.

Stanley tried not to let his expression change. The wage was five shillings more than he was being paid at Downing's.

"Thanks Mr Flint, tha'll not regret it."

Little did Stanley realise that he would go over those words many times in the not too distant future and it would be himself that would have regrets.

But at that moment all he felt was relief that he had found another job so soon.

Together that evening, he and Doris made their plans and worked out the cost of moving. Stanley did toy with the idea of asking Teddy Downing for a loan of one of his horses and a cart, but Doris refused to consider it.

"We're not asking that old bugger for anything. I'd rather carry the stuff myself."

In the end it was Edith that stood the cost of a carter to move their few belongings. He gave Teddy Downing his written notice on Friday evening when he received his wages. Teddy looked at it dolefully.

"This is not very convenient," he said. "Tha's leaving me in the lurch Stanley. Ah've not much time to find a replacement."

"Aye well, ah were told to find another job so that's what ah've done," he replied, and left, feeling a little core of triumph burning inside him.

His employment with the Downings ended the following Friday evening, and the very next day Stanley and Doris moved into the promised house that went with the job at Swinton. It was actually half of a large old farmhouse with no gas, no electricity, no running water, and, of course, no bathroom or any modern conveniences of any kind.

But Doris was not the kind of girl to let that stand in her way of making a home, and she soon had their meagre household goods arranged around the empty rooms.

Without telling Doris, Stanley took his Raleigh down to Sammy Bowley's and exchanged it for a double size wooden bed, with a base of saggy chain linked meshed springs. But at least they had a full sized bed to sleep on.

A large spanner accompanied the bed. It was intended to use to tighten up the spring base, but the bed had obviously supported far too many heavy people in its time and no matter how he tried there was still a deep hollow in the centre. Fortunately the feather mattress that they had been given helped to fill the hole and they were both too young to worry about the state of the bed, they were just happy to actually be sharing one.

It didn't take long for Stanley to discover what a bad employer he now had. No matter how hard he worked it was never enough. There were none of the perks that it was customary for farm labourers to receive. No milk, eggs or potatoes that would have made the low wages go a little further. And to make matters worse, Norman made a habit of paying him his wages late on Saturday evening as if it gave him some sort of perverse pleasure to make life harder for the young couple

Of course by that time, most of the shops were closed and they were left with no food for the following day. But Stanley soon found a way to even things up by encouraging some of the hens to lay their eggs under the hedge just outside their back door.

He took a bottle to work every day and filled it with milk straight from the cows and he told Doris he had absolutely no guilty conscience about doing it. On the contrary he considered he had earned it, and was delighted to be able even up the score with his employer.

On one Saturday evening, when he was feeling particularly aggrieved about his wages, Stanley decided to provide them with a Sunday dinner. With a quick swipe he grabbed one of the cockerels that was being fattened up for the farmer's pantry. Before it had time to squawk its protest Stanley had wrung its neck. He carried it into their kitchen, still warm and flapping, and soon had it plucked and dressed it ready for a feast the following day.

As it happened, it was a day that Edith was coming to visit and she walked in to be greeted by the delicious aroma of roasting chicken.

Stanley had just finished telling her about the origins of the bird cooking in the oven when Norman Flint knocked at the door. Edith froze with fright, imagining her son-in-law being carted away to the local prison. Whiteas a sheet she clung to Doris's hands as they stood behind the door.

To Stanley's relief, his boss had merely called to give him instructions for the next day's work. Stanley hadn't realised that he was holding his breath until he let it all go at once. He nodded and gave a sort of strangled sounding, "Ok."

Before he went, Norman sniffed. "By, thee dinner smells good, ah must be paying thee too much money if tha can afford a roast dinner."

As he closed the door behind him Stanley crossed his fingers and hoped that Norman had lost count of how many cockerels he had.

Discontented though he was with his new job and employer, Stanley knew he had no alternative but to stick it out for the time

306

being and hope that things would change. And change they did, and much faster than he ever expected.

Norman's brother, Tommy, was also a farmer and actually owned a farm right next door. He had watched Stanley from the first day and wanted him working on his own farm.

He had no scruples about poaching his brother's employee and approached Stanley at the first opportunity.

"Nah then lad," he said, "ah'll not beat about t'bush. How would you like to come and work for me? Tha could stay in t'same house. Me and Norman are joint owners."

Stanley was taken aback by the suddenness of the offer but had long since learned when to speak and when not to. And right then he decided it best to keep quiet, and that probably worked to his advantage.

Sensing that Stanley was doubtful Tommy continued, "Ah'd make sure tha were paid on time, ah guess that's a bit of an issue wi our Norman. Am ah right?"

Stanley nodded but still said nothing.

"Ah might want thee to work some weekends. Ah sometimes have business on then, but tha'd get paid extra. How does that sound?"

Stanley's nod came again. "Aye, ah don't mind working extra if ah get paid."

Then Tommy dealt his ace card. "Tha knows ah run a bit of a coal business along with t'farm? Well it'd mean tha'd have to learn to drive t'lorry. How about it?"

The grin on Stanley's face said it all. One of his ambitions was to learn to drive a lorry. He held out his hand. As they shook on the deal Tommy said, "Right, that's settled. Leave Norman to me. Ah'll sort him out."

The following week, when it was time for Stanley to move over to work for Tommy at the adjoining farm, Norman suddenly decided that his young employee was the best worker he had ever had and there was a fierce argument between the two brothers. Stanley felt uncomfortable about it all and decided to keep out of the argument.He turned, walked quietly away and left them to it.

He soon settled into working for Tommy and discovered that the business that kept him occupied at the weekends was gambling, and as there was an extra half crown in his wage packet for feeding the stock and doing the milking, Stanley was all in favour of his employer's gambling streak.

The next few weeks were like Stanley and Doris's honeymoon. With a little more money, and their own home, they were at their happiest. True to his word Tommy paid his wages regularly every Friday evening, which meant Doris could do her shopping at Mexborough market on Saturday morning. Thrifty from the beginning, Doris kept an account of every penny she spent and was even able to put an odd shilling in their savings each week.

But this was 1939 and war was imminent. The mood throughout the country was solemn and disbelieving that this should all be happening again so soon after the first world war which, supposedly, had been the war to end all wars.

When war was actually declared in September of that year Doris was filled with fear that Stanley would be leaving her to go away to fight. In vain he tried to reassure her and reasoned that if he had to go there would be nothing he could do about it.

Doris's uncle, in one of his rare conversations with Stanley, urged him to stay out of the war at all costs.

"Tha's a farmer," he said. "Thee concentrate on growing stuff to feed t'country. They'll need it before long, thee mark my words."

And for once Stanley was in complete agreement with him. He had absolutely no desire to don a uniform and march away to fight, leaving his young wife alone. So it was fortunate for him that farming, like mining, was a reserved occupation.

A large proportion of the able bodied men in Wath worked down the mines and of course the coal they brought out was essential for both the homes and the factories. The exceptions were the men who had joined the territorials.

Stanley's eldest stepbrother, Bill, was one of those who had been a keen member for several years and consequently was one of the first to be called to join his regiment.

As Stanley shook his hand he thought about Herbert who had died down the pit, and reflected that he too would have been going if he had still been alive, as he had been in the same territorial regiment as Bill.

There were too many differences between Stanley and Bill for them ever to have got on well; they had never seen eye to eye.But now that he was leaving Stanley found he had more affection for his stepbrother than he had realised, and had a lump in his throat as he shook his hand and wished him a safe return.

Ada was distraught that one of her brood was going away to war and shed many a tear into her apron after he had left.

Everyone was apprehensive about the future and when a letter from the ministry arrived for Stanley, he opened it while Doris stood beside him, filled with dread.

After an anxious week he presented himself as instructed at the offices where the interview was to take place. Still dressed in his working clothes he took his place at the end of the queue and stood with his palms sweating and his teeth gritted. The lad in front of him looked barely out of short trousers and seemed to think the idea of war was exciting.

Stanley was in no mood to reason or argue with him, but he gave him a withering look and said, "Don't talk so bloody stupid. They won't be firing pop guns tha knows." Turning his back on him he clamped his mouth tight shut and waited impatiently for his interview.

When his turn eventually came it was brief. He handed over the letter from Tommy Flint confirming that he employed Stanley as a farm labourer. After a cursory scan through it, the clerk handed it back to him, along with a stamped card that declared he was exempt from conscription, but as he prepared to leave he was told curtly that he would probably be sent to Jersey to help with the potato harvest.

Doris received the news with mixed feelings, relieved that he was not going to war but upset that he would have to go away to Jersey.

"Let's count our blessings Dot," he told her, using his pet name for her. But Doris turned away, unwilling to be consoled. There was a part of Stanley that relished the idea of travelling to the island but realised it would not be a good idea to admit it to her.

Tommy took the news that he would not be eligible to be conscripted with a smile but when Stanley told him of the possibility of him having to go to the Channel Isles his face changed.

"Oh and what am ah supposed to do while tha's away on a jaunt to Jersey then? Who's going to do t'work that ah employ thee for? Who's going to help me?"

He said it with such anger that Stanley was taken aback.

"Well," he said, "ah'm sorry, but it's not my fault is it?"

"No, and it's not mine either." He paused, and Stanley watched as expressions crossed his face. But he was not prepared for Tommy's next words.

"Well, ah'll tell thee what Stan, if tha goes off to Jersey ah can't let Doris stay in t'house. Ah might need it for somebody else."

That statement was totally unexpected and Stanley was thankful that he had several hours of work in front of him before he needed to give Doris the news. He turned it over and over in his mind and by the time he had finished the milking his decision was made. They had to break free from living in a tied cottage.

Somehow they had to find a house to rent and somehow they had to find the extra money to pay the rent.

There was no question of Doris moving back in with her mother as Edith had given up the tenancy of their cottage and gone to live with her mother and brother.

"Ah'm sorry love," said Stanley as he told Doris of the latest development. She looked at him and around at the kitchen she had turned into a bright and cosy place. Her chin lifted and she rose to the challenge.

"Well, we'd better start looking for somewhere else then hadn't we?"

By teatime next day she had walked the whole of Swinton searching for houses to let. The rents were far too high on the few she found, and she returned to prepare Stanley's tea with her brain seeking alternatives.

As the days passed by they began to realise how difficult it was going to be to find a place they could afford, and Doris's mood darkened and her anger grew.

Her feelings of resentment towards her father were never far below the surface and they burst out now as she complained bitterly to Stanley and her mother.

Her grandfather had been a rich man who owned many properties. When he died he bequeathed a substantial house to Doris, but stipulated that her father could live in it in his lifetime and it was to pass to Doris on his death.

Living as they did in a small town she saw her father frequently, but never once did he acknowledge her, and sometimes Doris's sense of rejection burned so fiercely that she could barely contain it.

Today she slammed the tea pots into the washing up bowl so hard that she broke the handle from her favourite cup. Bursting into tears she turned to Stanley and cried on his shoulder.

With her words almost incoherent she raged that her grandfather had been a rich man and here she was unable to even find a house they could afford to rent, while her father lived in comfort in what she considered was her house by rights.

"I bet I never get it," she fumed as she dried her eyes.

Edith was well used to her daughter's tantrums and put her arm around her. "Doris," she said, trying to soothe her, "it's written in your grandfather's will. It's there in black and white. All legal. They can't go against it. The house will be yours one day."

Sadly, time would tell how wrong she was.

Edith pulled on her hat and coat and set off home. As she glanced back she saw that her daughter and her husband were still standing at the gate watching her go. Stanley had his arm around her shoulders, while Doris wrapped hers around his waist. With a lump in her throat she waved to them before she turned the corner, and as she waited for the bus she reflected on the last year that had been so eventful.

Many people had criticised her for giving her daughter permission to marry at such a young age, but when she saw the young couple together she knew she had made the right decision.

She thought of the other decision she had made, so many years ago, when she had refused to divorce her husband and in doing so had condemned herself to a single life. It was assumed by many that her refusal to divorce Larrett was based on spite, and if she searched her conscience there was an element of that.

She still raged inwardly when she thought of how 'that woman' had stolen her husband and her home. But apart from that there were other facts to consider.

By refusing to divorce her husband, Edith knew that any children he and his new partner had would be illegitimate, which would disbar them from inheriting any of Doris's birthright. Edith's mouth set in a determined line as she thought about the terms of Arthur Bramham's will, a copy of which lay in the bottom drawer of her dressing table. It stipulated that if there was no further issue from Larrett Bramham, then his daughter Doris would inherit the house in Moore Road.

Edith was still in a thoughtful mood as she got off the bus and almost collided with her brother William.

"Nah then Edi," he said clasping her hand, "tha's in deep thought."

Edith stared back at him. For once he had a smile on his face.

"Tha looks fed up lass. Come and have a drink wi me before tha goes home."

She linked arms with him, her normal good humour restored.

"Ok Willie, ah could just fancy a port and lemon. Won't have to be long though, ah don't like leaving Mam on her own."

"Stop worrying Edi, she's sat in front of t'fire wi a pot of tea and t'Weekly News. That'll keep her happy."

William headed for his usual corner in the Red Lion and ordered the drinks. He was in a talkative mood and Edith listened as he reminisced, sometimes about his time in France and then about their childhood.

"Does tha remember Edi, when me an ar Harry fell through t'ice on t'canal?" Without waiting for a reply he went on. "Does tha remember we stood in t'front of t'fire trying to get warm and t'steam started rising from our trousers. By hell, we got into trouble that night. Does tha remember it Edi?"

Edith laughed. "Aye ah remember it well. We had happy days then. Ah wish we could go back to em. We never knew what were in front of us did we?"

William's face had dropped into its usual solemn expression. "Tha's right there lass. We didn't have a clue what were waiting for us." And drinking up the last few drops from the half pint that he allowed himself every night he stood up.

"Is tha ready Edi? We'd better gerroff home. It's work in t'morning."

William's talkative session was over and they walked back up Sandygate in silence. As they passed Edith's old cottage she looked at the window, noting the fresh red and white gingham curtains hung at the window and the geranium on display. It had been let to two elderly ladies almost as soon as Edith had left, and she felt a pang of regret that it was no longer hers.

Crushing the thought she concentrated on her present circumstances.

It had made sense in every way for her to move in with her mother and brother. Their cottage had enough room to accommodate all three of them and meant they had only one rent to pay.

If only William wasn't so difficult. But at least it now meant there were two of them to stand up to him. He could be easy company at times, when it suited him, but the problem was it didn't seem to suit him very often. Edith gave a sigh as these thoughts tumbled through her head.

They crossed the road together and he led the way up the well-trodden path that led to the cottage. The path was simply hard packed earth and cinders that were strewn along it every day in an effort to bring about an improvement, but nothing seemed to cover the stones and bricks that lay just above the surface waiting to trip the unwary.

William turned to her. "Watch thee step Edi," and just as a warm feeling crept over her at his concern, he added, "ah dunt want to av to pick thee up."

Edith pulled a face at him behind his back and gave him a two fingered gesture but said nothing. Their mother looked up and smiled as they entered the cottage. It was good to see two of her offspring together and she thought of how, in spite of their frequent differences of opinion, they seemed to have a special bond. The gas lamp hissed and spluttered and gave off a soft light, and though the noise of it irritated her she had to admit it was a big improvement on candles and oil lamps.

The kettle rested on the bars of the fading fire that was just managing to keep the water on the boil for their evening cup of tea. Edith lifted it up and gently blew away the soot that rested on the spout before she filled the teapot.

William declined a cup, grumbling that he would be up and down all night if he had any more to drink. Lighting a candle he opened the door that led to the staircase.

"Shout me up at six Mother," he called, and closing the door behind him he made his way up the steep stairs by the light of the flickering candle.

As she poured out the final cup of tea for the day, Edith glanced at her mother and thought how tired she looked. Without asking, she unpinned her hair and began to gently brush it.

CHAPTER 34

It was September when Stanley and Doris heard about the house in Winifred Road. It was available to rent immediately, and cheap.

Stanley at first refused to even consider it, but Doris argued that they could always move again when something better turned up. So they caught the bus into Wath and walked along Doncaster Road towards Manvers Main.

Stanley hesitated at the top of Winifred Road. His heart sank. It was every bit as bad as he had expected it to be. Identical terraced houses lined the street, following the contours of the road that ended in a brick wall. Above it he could see the railway leading away from the pit and the never ending loaded trains carrying the coal.

It was not the houses, but the dirty, rundown appearance of it all that appalled him. Every brick seemed to be coated in grime; the atmosphere was full of the black dust and the stench from the coke ovens filled the air.

This was the part of Wath he hated the most, and the thought of bringing his lovely young wife here filled him with dread. Packmans Row had been bad enough, but this was much worse.

"We're not moving here Doris," he said, turning away. "It's bloody awful. Just look at it."

But Doris was not to be deterred, she reasoned that it would be better than being homeless, and had visions of being thrown out of their tied house at Swinton if Stanley was sent to work in Jersey.

"Come on Stan," she said, as she gripped his hand. "Let's at least have a look at it now we're here."

Number twenty seven was near the bottom of the street, and holding hands they set off down the fairly steep slope, passing a shop that was just slightly larger than the houses that it served.

They glanced in the window, and like all the back street shops it displayed a variety of mundane household goods, but at least this one had a background of clean white paper and an absence of dead flies.

Their progress was observed by a group of women, all of them wearing aprons and turbans. They stood with arms crossed outside one of the houses. Their conversation halted as they watched Stanley and Doris approach.

Doris lifted her head high as she gave them a slight nod, and saw the look they exchanged and knew what they were thinking.

She swore to herself that she would never be part of such a group, and would never waste time standing around on corners criticising passers-by.

As they opened the door of number twenty seven a sour smell met them. The previous tenants had obviously not been over fond of cleaning, and Doris gave a shudder as she looked at the greasy patches on the doors and the grime that ran in a band along the wall between the two rooms.

As they moved into the back room the smell became so overpowering that they covered their mouths with their hands.

The cause of the foul aroma became obvious when they realised that the stone sink in the corner was blocked and full of vomit that had grown a considerable fur coat.

"Dirty buggers," swore Stanley. "This is no good Doris, we're not stopping here." He turned to leave.

"No, wait Stan, it only needs cleaning, and Mam'll help us. It'll be ok when it's had a good scrub. There's a stove and a copper at the side of the sink."

The living room was designed to also serve as a kitchen, with everything contained in that one room. The traditional fire and oven occupied most of one wall, and to its right was a brick built copper for the laundry with a stone sink and cold water tap over it. On the opposite side of the stove was a cupboard in the recess under the stairs that served as a pantry.

Doris persisted. "It'll be ok Stan. Look, it's got all we need. Once we get it clean, it'll do, and we can afford the rent."

Stanley was won over. "Aye, well, if you're sure you can settle here, we'll take it but ah'm going to have a word with t'landlord and see if we can get some time rent free for cleaning this lot up."

But his words hid the depression that filled him as he looked out of the window at the communal yard, with the water closets and coalhouses lined up at the far side.

Doris wrapped her arms around him. "It'll be ok Stan, and at least we don't have to share a toilet. We can keep ours locked so no one else can use it."

"Aye and we bloody will an all. Ah don't want us sharing toilet seats wi some of the dirty buggers around here. Some of em look as if they haven't seen soap and water for years."

He gritted his teeth pushing his strong jaw line into a determined position. "It won't be long before we're out of this Dot. This is not what ah want for us."

Within the week Doris and her mother had scrubbed the house from top to bottom. Not an inch had escaped their disinfectant soaked brushes and cloths. The outdoor toilet had been newly whitewashed and stocked with squares of newspaper threaded on string. Doris hung them on a nail that Stanley had hammered into the wall, and then closed the door firmly and padlocked it.

Edith noted the expression on the face of a neighbour who was watching, and once back inside the house she mentioned it to her daughter. But Doris tossed her head.

"Ah don't care Mam, it's our water closet and we don't want any of that lot using it. If they don't like it they can lump it."

Stanley borrowed the coal lorry from Tommy Flint and once again they moved their few belongings.

As they turned into Winifred Road they were spotted by the children hanging about on the pavements playing, and were surrounded as soon as they stopped. Then the chorus started. "Can ah av a ride in it mister? Is tha comin' to live here? Has tha got kids?"

But Stanley was having none of it and told them, "Bugger off."

As they scattered, Doris looked at him reproachfully and he shrugged his shoulders as he said, "It's no good Doris, it's t'only sort of language they understand. Give em an inch and they'll tek a mile."

The front room of number twenty seven would have to remain empty for the foreseeable future but the living room looked cosy enough when Doris arranged their furniture and lit the fire.

"Ah'll go an tek t'lorry back Dot before them little buggers start tekin' it to pieces, ah'll be back at teatime," and giving her a quick hug he left.

Alone in the house for the first time, Doris walked through the four rooms. Only the living room at the rear and the front bedroom had any furniture. The back bedroom had nothing but a few empty boxes, while Stanley's old bike, the one he had once sold to his brother Ernest, had the front room all to itself. Ernest had long since abandoned it in the allotment shed and Stanley had reclaimed it for himself, intending to use it to get to and from work every day.

Doris knew nothing about cycles, but even to her it looked in a sorry state with twisted mudguards, no brakes, and only a stump for a pedal at one side.

Stanley had assured her he could manage on it for a few months until they could afford to replace it.

Putting her hands on the rusty handlebars Doris pushed it back and forth. She had never learnt to cycle and could not imagine how on earth Stanley was going to be able to ride this bike five miles to and from Swinton every day, and she made a silent promise that a better bike would be at the top of their list.

Gradually they settled into their new home. Once they closed the door behind them and drew the curtains they forgot that Manvers Main was just a few hundred yards away, and they tried to ignore the sound of the loaded trains rumbling by at the end of the road.

They spent their evenings reading and playing cards. Doris began work on a pegged rug, so called because it was worked using half of a clothes peg that had been sharpened to a point. Stanley laboriously cut old clothing into four inch length strips, using a pair of scissors so blunt that they that left blisters even on his tough, work worn hands, while Doris, using the half peg tool, prodded holes into a square of hessian sacking and pushed the strips of fabric into it.

At the end of every evening she laid it on the floor and admired it.

"Ah look Stanley," she said, every single time, "we've done a lot tonight." Then she rolled it up and stowed it away under the couch.

Stanley's younger brothers, Harold and Cyril, were now both miners and working at Manvers Main and of course they were frequent visitors at number twenty seven. As they walked through the door the room charged up with energy and life, and the house echoed with their laughter and jokes.

There seemed to be seldom a day without them having something hilarious to relate. Doris remarked to Stanley that she didn't know how on earth they managed to find everything so funny.

"It's the only way they can cope with it Dot," he said. "There's nought funny about working down t'pit love. Without makin' a joke of it they'd never cope."

Humour may have helped Cyril get through his days working underground, but there were two fears that he had not come to terms with. One was his fear of deep water following his experience as a child at the swimming baths, and the other was an aversion to dogs, in particular, big dogs that barked.

Unfortunately for him, one of Stanley and Doris's neighbours had a big mongrel dog. A fierce scruffy mutt that hated almost everyone, and it had taken a particular dislike to Cyril. It was kept chained up outside its owner's house and it only needed a glimpse of him to set it snarling and straining at its chain.

Cyril always gave it a wide berth and would burst through the door of number twenty seven and slam it shut behind him.

"That bloody dog," he swore on more than one occasion. "It needs putting down. Did tha see it Stan? Mek us a cup of tea Doris, me nerves are shattered."

Doris made a fuss of him, but he got little sympathy from his brothers.

As they were now earning good money they had bought a new motor cycle to go to work on, with Harold usually doing the driving and Cyril riding on the pillion seat. At Cyril's insistence they always left by the front door to avoid a further confrontation with the dreaded dog.

But there came the day when the dog almost outsmarted them. They had called on their way home from work. Cyril was in fine form and looking forward to his game of tennis, which he had recently started playing. He lingered in the doorway telling Doris all about his new hobby while Harold mounted the bike and kicked it into life. The engine spluttered and faded before settling into a steady throb. Easing it off the stand, Harold beckoned Cyril with a movement of his head.

"Come on then, is tha comin' ar kid? Me mam'll av t'dinner ready."

Hitching his dudley and snap tin to one side, Cyril swung his leg over the bike and settled on to the pillion seat. Just as he raised his hand to wave, the dog appeared at the end of the alley, trailing its broken chain behind it. Baring its teeth, a low growl came from deep in its throat. For a moment it seemed unsure whether to bark or attack, and as Harold eased the bike into motion it made up its mind and gave chase, with Cyril clinging on tight and urging his brother to get a move on. But Harold was enjoying the situation and played it as a bit of fun, only going just fast enough for the dog to snap at Cyril's legs without actually reaching them.

As they disappeared up the road with the bike wobbling and spluttering up the hill and the dog not quite managing to catch them, the watching neighbours applauded.

Harold was cursed all the way home but by the time they sat down to dinner it was a huge joke that was to be retold many times in the years to come.

The first visit they had from Doris's cousin Les almost ended in an argument. His first words were, "What the hell is Stan doing bringing thee to live in a place like this Doris?"

Unfortunately for him, Stanley, who was in the empty front room trying to repair his bike, had overheard him. Rage built inside him. Who did Les think he was coming in and criticising him? He walked into the living room his blue eyes cold with outrage and glared at Les. Realising his remarks had been overheard Les tried to make amends.

"You've got it nice and cosy in here Doris," he said, his face colouring with embarrassment.

Stanley was in no mood to be pacified and was about to say his piece when he glanced at his wife. She looked about to burst into tears. Les was like a brother to her and she could hardly bear the thought of a fall out between the two men in her life.

Putting his arm around Doris he pulled her close and faced Les.

"Ah know what a bloody slum this is, but it's all we can afford. But don't thee worry we won't be here long, will we love?" Doris shook her head and lifted it proudly.

"No, we've got plans, we won't be here long, it's just a start."

Les was mortified that his careless words had almost caused a rift between them and his face was red as he held out his hand to Stanley.

"Ah didn't mean owt wrong Stan. Ah know tha'll look after her."

The country had been at war for six weeks when Doris realised that she was pregnant. She had refused a cup of tea that her grandmother offered. Suddenly the very thought of tea turned her stomach and she said as much with a shudder.

Her grandmother gave a knowing smile and said, "Well, no need to ask what the problem is do we?"

Doris returned her gaze as she folded the washing she had just brought in. "What do you mean grandma?"

"It's obvious, ah can see it in yer face love, you're expecting."

"Well how can you be so sure?"

"Call it the wisdom of age love. Ah've seen it too many times before, and ah dare say you've been doing plenty of what causes it.A new little baby is just what we want to cheer us all up."

Doris blushed, embarrassed by her grandmother's words, but she had to admit she was seldom wrong, even if her outspoken words made her feel uncomfortable at times.

As she walked home Doris turned it over in her mind, making a tally of the dates and came to the conclusion that it would be a May baby and hugged the thought to herself even while she worried about how they would manage financially.

For once she walked down Winifred Road without even thinking about how much she hated it.As she reached the house and closed the door behind her a smile lit up her face. No matter what lay ahead nothing could take away the joy she felt, and never for one moment did she doubt that her grandmother was right.

As she stirred the fire into life and put the remains of last night's stew in the oven she looked at the clock. Only half an hour and Stanley would be home. She couldn't wait to tell him.

Coming from a large family, news of a new baby was nothing unusual for Stanley, but this was different. His own child! He was speechless for a moment, completely overawed at the thought of himself and Doris with their own child. They would be a family.

Full of love he wrapped his arms around Doris and kissed her forehead. He put his hand lightly over her mouth as she spoke her worries about not being able to afford to pay their way.

"Shush Doris, we'll manage," he said confidently." Ah'll get some extra work. Now ah can drive ah'll try and get some weekend work. Ah've heard they're short of drivers at Dysons. It's good pay there."

"But Stan," she began, "you already work at weekends."

"Aye, ah know, but ah still av Saturday evening free, ah could drive then."

He arrived home the following day, jubilant, and waltzed Doris around the room.

"Ah've gorrit Dot. They want me every Saturday night and any time that ah'm not working for Tommy. Tha should see t'car ah'll be driving, it's a big black Austin, and sometimes ah could even be driving the Daimler for weddings or funerals."

Stanley could hardly contain his excitement and was keen to spread his good news. So on Sunday, after he returned from his weekend duties at the farm, they dressed in their best clothes and set off to walk and go visiting.

Doris wore the coat she had been married in and Stanley thought she looked beautiful and told her so as he walked proudly up the dirty street with her arm through his. They stopped at the bridge over the canal and looked at the coal black water below that barely moved.

Children played on the tow path, scruffy and uncared for judging by their appearance. Stanley pulled Doris closer to him.

"Our kids are never going to play among that lot Dot. We've got to get out of this place."

She nodded, her lips in that tight determined position that he was coming to know so well.

Moving on they walked up Doncaster Road, passing the school they had both attended with just a three year gap between. Then they paused briefly at Sammy Bowley's shop. Doris commented that the goods in the window told a story of ordinary people forced to sell their most prized possessions just to survive, and wondered if living standards would ever improve for the working classes.

But Stanley was less sympathetic and said, "Well Doris, wages down t'pit have increased. They take home a lot more than ah do, but most of em spend it on beer and cigs so it's their own bloody fault."

And with that uncompromising statement hanging in the air they continued along the high street. Doris smiled as they passed the butcher's shop where she had had her confrontation with the owner just over a year ago. She reminded Stanley of the incident and he laughed as he told her she was a right little fire cracker.

The smile left her face and she became more solemn as they approached the house that would one day be hers. Heavy, cream coloured lace curtains hung at the windows and the brass door knocker gleamed.

Stanley knew what she was thinking and squeezed her hand.

"Come on Dot," he said, "don't start. It's not yours yet, but it will be one day, and at least we've got a home of our own."

An indignant, "Hmmm," was the only reply he got to that. However, Doris soon recovered her good humour as they walked smoothly in step up Sandygate towards her grandmother's cottage.But at the last minute she changed her mind and pulled him onwards up the hill.

"Let's not bother Stan. Ah don't feel like listening to Uncle Willie moaning, he's bound to be in a bad mood. He's always at his worst on Sunday nights. He hates the idea of work on Monday morning and takes it out of me Mam and Grandma. Let's go straight up to your Mam's."

93 Oak Road as usual was bright and full of the noise of a big family. Everyone seemed to be talking at once, while their father sat calmly at the table in the midst of them, enjoying his Sunday tea. The inevitable jug of celery was in front of him and Doris marvelled again at how Stanley's mother always seemed to find a supply for her husband, no matter what time of the year it was.

Harold nodded to them as they squeezed into the overcrowded room, his face as always was as clean and shining as if he had scrubbed it. His blue eyes sparkled at Doris as he indicated for her to take a seat. He had a soft spot for his new daughter-in-law and Stanley had certainly gone up in his estimation since he had married her.

It went up even more when Stanley told him about his new part time job driving hire cars on Saturday evenings.

"Hey, that's grand, tha'll be able to give me an me mate a lift home from t'Legion."

He was referring to the British Legion Club that had recently become Harold's favourite drinking place.

Stanley, still eager to gain approval from his father, nodded even while warning bells were sounding in his head.

The young couple said nothing about Doris's pregnancy. After all, they were still not sure about it and there was the uneasy knowledge that Stanley had led them to believe that Doris was already expecting when he obtained their permission to be married.

Nothing had been said about that, even though the passing months had proved that it was untrue. However, Stanley suspected that he would be in for a telling off from his mother at some time in the near future, but thankfully it didn't look as if it would be today, and they settled back to enjoy an hour in the midst of the family.

His brothers Harold and Cyril were in good form and soon had the house ringing with laughter at their stories and jokes. One of Cyril's stories involved his father, who had walked into a lamppost on the way to work the previous week; he had hit it with such force that he had knocked himself momentarily unconscious.

324

In spite of his concern about his Dad, Cyril had been bent double with laughter, and as Harold recovered consciousness he was not amused to find himself on the floor and the object of Cyril's mirth. Rubbing his head he rose and continued to work, cursing Cyril and the blackout restrictions every step of the way.

Only Cyril, as the youngest son, could have got away with relating the story to the family, but by that Sunday afternoon even Harold had to admit to seeing the funny side of his mishap.

It was dark when they left and with the blackout precautions in place it was just as well that Stanley was so familiar with the area. Even so he walked with one arm around Doris and made a great point of holding other one out in front of him.

"I'm just warding off any lampposts that might jump in front of us," he told Doris with a grin.

There was not the slightest glimmer of light anywhere. The blackout was total, but just as they reached the bottom of Oak Road the clouds slid away from the moon and the rest of the walk home was easier.

As the weeks went past the war intensified. Already thousands of people were homeless thanks to the bombing and it was clear to Stanley and Doris that there was no prospect of them being able to move out of Winifred Road. They soon realised how lucky they were to have the tenancy of the house no matter how much they hated it.

It had also become clear that Stanley was most unlikely to be sent to Jersey. The situation there was dire, and it was obvious that the tiny island, being so close to France, would be impossible to defend and would have to be abandoned to the Germans. In some ways he was disappointed not to be going but knew better than to admit as much to Doris.

The passing weeks also proved that her grandmother's intuition was correct and together they worked out that her baby would be born in May.

Stanley was working every hour he possibly could, setting out to cycle to Swinton early every morning and returning exhausted in the evening after a heavy day farming. Thankfully they had managed to buy a better bicycle but often when he was pedalling home he thought with regret of the motorbike that he used to have.

His employer, Tommy, was fonder than ever of his card games, or bit of business as he liked to refer to it. This meant that Stanley worked almost every weekend.

One of Tommy's other side-lines was his coal business and Stanley spent part of every Friday delivering coal by the sack. Doris's father was on his round and each week Stanley carried the coal they had ordered on his back and tipped it into their coal house. As Stanley collected the money he wondered if Doris's father realised that he was his son-in-law, but if he did there was never a sign of recognition.

He said nothing to Doris about it, thinking to himself that there was no point in upsetting her.

One morning when he arrived at work Tommy was waiting for him.

"Nah then," he said, "ah've got a nice job for thee, if tha's up to it."

Stanley waited with trepidation. In his experience when a boss approached you in this way it was usually to their advantage and not the employee's.

But he changed his mind at Tommy's next words. "Ah want a load of corn delivering to a farm just outside Sheffield. Can tha do it?"

Stanley's face lit up with excitement, and eager to meet the challenge he nodded. "Oh aye, ah can do it. Ah'll need a map though, and some directions, it's a bit awkward wi all signposts being taken down."

He was referring to the fact that all the signposts had been removed in case of invasion by the Germans. After all, there was no point in leaving signs up that would help the enemy to find their way around.

Tommy was prepared and pulled out a basic hand drawn map and another with written instructions on it.

"Here tha is then," he said. "Ah've filled t'lorry up wi petrol. Thee load it up wi t'corn and gerroff as soon as tha can. Don't get lost. Ah need thee back for t'afternoon milking."

By nine o'clock the lorry was loaded and ready. It was a dull overcast day and very cold. Stanley buttoned his coat up to the neck and pulled his cap firmly down as he cranked the engine. After a couple of turns it obligingly coughed a few times and burst into life. He withdrew the starting handle and stowed it behind his seat. Adjusting the choke he eased the lorry carefully out of the farmyard, and settled back to enjoy the change of routine in his working day.

The map was on the seat beside him but until he passed through Rotherham he had no need of it. Thanks to his long bike rides he was familiar with the road. It became more difficult as he approached the outskirts of Sheffield, and he had to find his way using the roughly drawn map.

He was soon well off the main road and Tommy's instructions made no sense at all. He stopped several people to ask for directions, none were any help, and seemed to have taken the government's warnings about careless talk to heart.

One man actually said to him, "Aye, ah know where it is but ah'm not telling thee. Ow do ah know if tha's a spy or not? Nay, ah'm not helping thee."

"Tha bloody idiot," retorted Stanley, "Do ah look or sound like a German? Soft bugger. Does tha think ah'v got t'German army hidden in t'sacks? Ah'm just trying to deliver a load of corn and tha's hindering t'war effort."

"Well tha's not from round here is tha?"

Stanley closed his eyes in exasperation and tried to keep his temper.

"If ah was from round here ah wouldn't need help. Thanks for nothing tha sanctimonious auld bugger," and he slipped the lorry into gear and drove off leaving the man gaping after him.

Stanley had to smile to himself as he thought of telling Doris about the encounter. He'd quite enjoyed using the word sanctimonious. He'd only heard it the week before and had been waiting for the chance to use it.

He had gone almost another five miles before he found the landmark he had been looking for and with relief recognised his position from Tommy's description.

The entrance that led down to the farm was almost hidden by overgrown trees that brushed against the sides of the lorry as he turned sharp left, and soon realised that the drive was little more than a rough track. As he drove towards the farm the lorry rocked and creaked, its old springs protesting, and Stanley held his breath as he tried to avoid the deep water-filled pot holes.

He thought of what Teddy Downing would have said about it. He would have had the track levelled in no time, believing it was time and money well spent compared to the cost of broken machinery or lamed horses due to a badly maintained road.

Not for the first time, Stanley realised that he compared all farms to Downing's and that many of them came far short of the standards that his first employer had set. He thought about the good training he had had from Teddy and he resolved never to let his own standards drop.

He had calculated that it would take an hour at the most to unload the lorry, collect payment for the corn, and be on his way back before darkness began to fall.

But the payment was where his plan fell apart. Unfortunately it was market day, and apparently the farmer had taken a load of pigs to be sold. He was informed of this by the farmer's wife after he had unloaded the corn.

"He'll be back shortly. Ah can't pay yer. Tha'll just av to wait till he gets back," she said, and she shut the door firmly in his face.

Now Stanley would be the first to admit that he had never been any good at waiting, and he stamped impatiently up and down the farmyard trying to decide on the best course of action.

There was no way he could leave the corn without payment, Tommy had been adamant about that. "That tight fisted old bugger is well known for not paying, so don't thee leave the corn without getting the money," he'd said.

Just as Stanley had decided to reload the corn back on to the lorry and take it home, the farmer turned up with a red face and a big grin. No prizes for guessing where he'd been straight after selling his pigs thought Stanley as he took a step back to avoid the beery breath that was coming out of him in great steaming clouds.

"Nah then young man, what the hell are you doing still here? Tha should have been on thee way home by nah. Tha's gonna be drivin' in t'blackout tha knows."

Stanley took another step back and tried not to show his distaste as the beery breath came closer.

"Ah've had to wait for t'money. Ah can't leave t'corn without t'payment. That's Tommy's orders."

The farmer tried to focus his eyes on Stanley and rocked so far back on his heels that he almost fell over, but he recovered, and delving deep into his trouser pocket he pulled out a roll of notes and very carefully counted out the right amount.

"There tha is son, nah tha can be on thee way before it gets dark."

Stanley checked the notes, observing to himself as he did so that the beer had not hindered the farmer's counting ability, and tucking the cash safely away under the dashboard he backed the lorry out of the farmyard.

If Stanley had considered the outward journey difficult, he was about to find the return trip far worse, and would test his sense of direction to the limit.

Darkness was falling fast and he forgot all his principles about nursing the old lorry gently over the rutted track that led back to the road.

It was obvious he would be driving in the dark in a matter of minutes and he held his foot hard on the accelerator in an effort to get to the main road as soon as possible. He ignored the creaks and groans of the protesting springs as he bounced in and out of the deep holes.

He was still on unfamiliar territory when he switched on the headlights and despaired at the small amount of light they gave off. Due to the blackout restrictions all vehicle headlights were drastically reduced and the only thing he could see was a small area of the road directly in front of him.

To add to his problems it began to rain, and as the lorry possessed only a hand operated windscreen wiper, he was forced to drive with one hand on the wheel while he moved the wiper back and forth with the other.

He lost track of time, forgot how hungry he was, and even stopped worrying about what Tommy would say to him about not arriving back in time to do the milking.

The distance that he could see in front of him was so short that he almost ran into the rear of a horse and cart, and slammed on the brakes just in time. With his heart pounding, Stanley stuck his head out of the window and received a mouthful of abuse from the man sitting on top of the cart.

"What the hell does tha think tha's doing racin' abaht in t'dark? Tha bloody idiot."

Considering that he was probably travelling at less than five miles per hour Stanley was momentarily incensed at the accusation of him racing about in the dark, but was so relieved to see a fellow traveller that he thought it better not to antagonise him further.

"Sorry mate," he shouted, "ah can't see a thing wi these lights. Where is tha goin'?"

When the reply came Stanley could happily have got out of his lorry and hugged both the man and his horse. He was going all the way to the crossroads where he joined the main road and he knew that he could find his way easily from there.

So he bit back his impatience and resigned himself to following the horse and cart for the next few miles and blessed the fact that at least the horse knew his way home in the dark.

When he saw Tommy waiting for him at the farm gate he feared the worst and expected a severe telling off, but to his surprise he was greeted like a long lost son. Pulling open the lorry door almost before it had come to a standstill Tommy grinned up at him.

"By heck Stan, tha had me worried. My missis thought tha'd run off wi t'lorry an t'cash. But ah told her that weren't likely, not when tha'd got tha lovely Doris waiting at home for thee."

He saw the expression on his face and hastily added, "She were only joking Stan, How the hell did tha to find thee way back in t'blackout?"

As Stanley jumped down from the cab, his legs, stiff with cold, almost buckled underneath him. He handed Tommy the cash and explained how he had been kept waiting.

"Aye tha did right to wait or ah'd never have got it. It's typical of him. Tha's done well Stan and ah'll see thee right in thee wage packet."

Stanley nodded his thanks as he wheeled his bike out of the barn. He felt frozen through but hoped the bike ride home would get his circulation going.

"Aye tha'd better get off home Stan, your Doris'll be wondering where tha's got to. Tha knows, if tha'd stayed in t'farmhouse here, instead of moving to Winifred Road tha wouldn't have had a long bike ride in front of thee. That was a big mistake Stan. Tha'd have been a lot better off staying here."

Stanley looked at him. He was speechless at the audacity of Tommy. How dare he say that? It was him that had said Doris would have to move out of the house if he was sent to Jersey to help with the potato harvest. But he gritted his teeth and just said goodnight.

Tommy watched as his young worker disappeared into the darkness, then, thankful that his young employee had returned safely, he returned to the warmth of the kitchen.

As he made himself comfortable in his armchair, he remarked to his wife that Stan Dale was a funny lad at times, and had seemed to go quiet on him for no reason, and he wondered if he had said something to offend him.

Stanley, in the meantime, made the journey home in record time in spite of riding in almost complete darkness. His anger at Tommy's thoughtless words made him push the pedals round faster, and by the time he reached the top of Winifred Road he had warmed up. He could feel the sweat gathering under his collar, but his hands on the handlebars remained cold as ice.

He freewheeled down to number twenty seven, feeling unbelievably relieved to be home. Just as he stopped the door opened, and in the dim light he could just make out the outline of Doris's head. As she realised he was standing there holding his bike up with one hand she opened the door fully and practically threw herself at him with a cry of relief.

"Hey steady up Dot, steady up. Watch me bike love," protested Stanley as he struggled to keep his balance. "Come on, let me get inside, me hands are bloody frozen. And to demonstrate how cold they were he slipped his free hand down the neck of her dress as he followed her inside, causing Doris to shriek with shock.

He didn't think he had ever been so glad to be sitting in front of a blazing fire as he was that night. His dinner had long since dried into a congealed mess and Doris fretted about it, but had nothing else to give him. She need not have worried; Stanley was now so hungry he declared he would have eaten it even if it had changed into cardboard.

Between mouthfuls he told her all about his day, then sat back with a mug of tea. As he drank, he looked around his home. Doris had made it cosy. Every part of the stove and every inch of furniture was polished and smelling sweet. He drew her on to his knee and kissed her. He had never felt such love and knew he would work himself into the ground to provide for her and their unborn child.

With farming being one of the lowest paid jobs, Stanley was thankful for the frequent weekends when Tommy was away on business and he was called upon to work overtime. The extra half crown in his wages made all the difference.

However, what really helped the finances, were the few hours driving for Dysons on Saturday evenings. On the weekends when he was on feeding and milking duties at the Swinton farm, he had barely enough time to get washed and changed and bolt some food down before he left to cycle into Wath and begin his evening of taxi driving.

But to Stanley it was such a pleasure to sit behind the wheel of the stately Daimler that it didn't feel like work at all. He kept a polishing cloth under the seat and every spare moment he had during the evening was spent adding to the shine on that magnificent vehicle.

But, there came an evening in December when he thought he had lost his prized driving job.

His father, Harold, had soon cottoned on to the fact that Stanley was often driving the taxi to and from the British Legion, and that just happened to be Harold's favourite drinking venue.

For two weeks running he had managed to persuade his son to collect himself and his drinking partners from the club late at night, after they had spent the last few hours consuming pint after pint of Barnsley's best brew.

It was a mystery to Stanley how these hard drinking miners could still be standing, considering the amount they had poured into their stomachs, and he calculated that what they spent in one evening would have kept himself and Doris for a week, and yet they expected him to risk his job giving them free taxi rides.

He knew he should refuse to take them. He knew it very well. But somehow, there still remained that little boy deep inside him that sought hisfather's approval and attention. And so he agreed.

It was the second Saturday evening in December and the weather was bad, with lashing rain that only just resisted turning into sleet, and strong winds gusting in every direction.

It was late and Stanley was tired. He thought longingly of home and a warm room, closely followed by a warm bed shared with Doris. He had taken a party of pre-Christmas revellers home and received a generous tip, and he hoped that was his last job of the evening. He returned to the club just to make sure that everyone had gone home, and his heart sank when he entered the darkened hall and realised that his father was standing there waiting for him, accompanied by three of his drinking buddies.

"Ah, there tha is Stanley," he said, and turning, he beckoned to his mates. "Come on," he called, his voice echoing around the empty club. "Ar Stan'll run us home, won't tha Stan?"

All of them looked the worse for what they had drunk and all were oblivious to the dismay on Stanley's face. The last thing he wanted was this drunken quartet in the immaculate Daimler. But what could he do? For years afterwards, whenever he thought of that evening, he swore he should have made them walk home. But he didn't.

Reluctantly he led the way outside and opened the nearside rear door. Impatiently he ushered his father and his best mate Arthur Nutwell towards the back seat. Harold was none too steady on his feet and had a fit of drunken giggles as Stanley tried to push him into the car.

The remaining two were now heading around the back of the vehicle, singing a duet as they went. Stanley could see exactly what was going to happen, but his shouted warning went unheeded, and they continued.

As he watched, one of them opened the offside rear door, but failed to keep hold of it, leaving it at the mercy of the strong wind that took hold of it, and sent it crashing backwards with frightening force, smashing the hinges and the glass with a sickening sound that made Stanley cringe.

The sound even sobered Harold, and he took a sharp intake of breath before he said, "Oh bloody hell Stanley, that's bad luck. What tha going to do? Can tha repair it?"

Stanley examined the damage as best he could by the light of his torch and felt the rage building inside him. Years of anger, rejection and bitterness came boiling up and erupted, and he shouted it all out at his father, telling him exactly what he thought of him, while the four men gaped at him with slack mouths.

As he paused for breath and felt around the damaged door, Arthur said in a voice only slightly slurred, "It were only an accident Stan. Tha can't talk to thee father like that."

The comment only enraged Stanley more. "Father? Father? Tha calls him a father. He's niver been a father to me. And nah, ah've got to tek this car back and explain it all to Dyson. Ah'll get the sack for this. Get in the bloody car you two; and thee, Father." And here he paused and pointed his finger at Harold. "Don't thee ever expect me to do this again. In fact, don't ever expect anything from me ever again. Ah don't owe thee owt. Not even respect."

Not another word was spoken by any of the men. Stanley stopped the car half way up Oak Road and held open the door while they all got out. In silence they watched Stanley drive away, and then made their separate ways home, all much more sober than when they had left the club.

After he had parked the Daimler in its usual place Stanley cycled slowly home. He felt exhausted by the long day of work and the disastrous events of the evening. The emotional outburst at his father had left him feeling drained.

He decided he would have to go and see Mr Dyson first thing the next morning and take the blame himself. There was no other way. It

334

was all his own fault. He should never have agreed to give them a lift home.

He would offer to work for free until the damage was paid for. Maybe that way he would keep his job.

Just as he expected there was a row when Doris heard about it. She sat very still and tight lipped as he told her all about it.

"Ah knew this would happen," she said. "Tha should have had more sense than to agree to take the drunken idiots home. Tha'll get t'sack and tha deserves it. And ah don't suppose thee father'll be offering to stump up any money to compensate thee, will he?"

Stanley shook his head and replied, "Shut up Doris, just shut up. Ah've had enough."

Doris was not used to being told to shut up, and in a temper she banged the supper pots into the sink and broke two plates.

Stanley took a deep breath. "Look Doris," he said, trying to speak calmly, "nothing anyone says will make me feel worse. Ah were stupid, but it won't happen again, and us rowing won't alter it." He put his hands over his face in despair. At that moment he felt completely worn out and sick of the daily grind, and Doris's attitude was the last straw.

But her temper dissolved as quickly as it had risen when she realised how upset he was, and she put her arms around him.

"Aw, ah'm sorry love. Ah should be sticking up for thee, and ah am. It's thee Dad ah'm angry at really." She slipped on to his knee. "Bloody terrible fathers we've both got."

Stanley pulled her closer. "Well to be fair Doris, mine is mostly ok wi all of em except me. It's just me he seems to be at odds with. Come on love, tha'd better gerroff me knee, ah've got pins and needles in me leg. Let's go to bed. Ah'm shattered. Leave the pots till morning."

But in spite of his exhaustion it was hard to sleep. The interview he was to have with Mr Dyson the next day preyed on his mind. The sagging bed was more uncomfortable than ever and he lay awake hour after hour listening to Doris's regular breathing.

It was a relief when he looked at the clock and found it was 5.30 and time to get up. He dressed as quickly as he could, groping around on the ice cold floor in the dark to find his socks.

Downstairs it was a little warmer and he lit a candle to save on the gas light, and then put the kettle on to boil. He hated the dark mornings and thought of the miners who often never saw daylight all week at this time of the year. As always the thought made him thankful he wasn't one of them.

But the coming interview with Mr Dyson was uppermost in his mind and he couldn't wait to get it over with.

The milking and feeding at Swinton were done in record time that morning, and it was only just breaking daylight when he cycled into Wath. He stood at the door of Dyson's house and swallowed hard before he knocked. He had been rehearsing his speech all the way from Swinton and the words were there on the tip of his tongue.

Fortunately Mr Dyson was also an early riser and it was him that answered the door. In as normal a voice as he could manage Stanley said, "Good morning. Erm, ah'm sorry but I had a bit of an accident last night."

Mr Dyson's cheery expression faded as he followed Stanley to the Daimler, and listened to the explanation as to how the wind had whipped the door out of his hands. His face took on a pained look as he ran his hands over the damage.

He was silent and Stanley stammered out that he would work for free until it was paid for. Nothing could describe the relief he felt when his employer put his hands in his pockets and sighed as he said, "Well ah appreciate that offer Stan, but it won't be necessary. Ah'll tell the insurance company that a customer was responsible and then they will cover the cost of the repair."

But as Stanley thanked him and turned to go he added with a slight menace in his voice, "Tha'd better be more careful in future. Ah'm disappointed in thee. These cars are valuable tha knows. They're not bloody old farm carts." Those words echoed in Stanley's head for a long time.

He knew better than to expect an apology from his father, but thought he might have shown some sign of concern or guilt at the trouble he had landed his son in.

But of course no word came from him, and Stanley stayed away from Oak Road and said he had no desire to ever see Harold again.

In the end it was due to Ada that things were smoothed over. She put on her best hat and coat and walked down to Winifred Road and apologised on behalf of her husband.

CHAPTER 35

There were one or two neighbours in Winifred Road who welcomed Stanley and Doris and became friends. Next door on their right hand side was Mrs Lloyd, who took Doris under her wing and assumed the role of protector. She proudly showed her young neighbour into her home that shone from its daily polishing.

"Nah Doris, what does tha think of that love?" and she tucked her considerable body to one side of the fireplace in order to display the magnificent brass fender, which twinkled and reflected the flames from the blazing fire. At either end of the fender were two leather padded seats and Doris gazed in admiration as Mrs Lloyd bent over and triumphantly lifted the top of the seat nearest to her, revealing a storage space. She smiled as Doris exaggerated her surprise.

"Nah, ain't that grand Doris?" she said. "This belonged to gentry tha knows. Forty years ah've had it, and ah've alus looked after it. It'll be ar Charlie's when ah'm gone, but ah doubt that slut he's married'll even be bothered to clean it."

Doris nodded and backed out of the house, making her excuses as she left.

Much as she liked her neighbour she had no intention of being drawn into discussions about her daughter-in-law.

Mrs Sharp who owned the shop at the top of the street had also taken a liking to Doris, and rarely did she go into the shop without being told that Mrs Sharp hated, "Bloody Wath." And she invariably added, "When t'war is over Doris, me and my Arthur'll be off. They'll not see us for dust. We've gorr our eye on a bungalow at t'seaside. Oh, ah can't wait. It's only thinking of it that keeps me going.Ah hate bloody Wath and ah hate this bloody street."

Doris was in complete agreement and dreamed every day of moving elsewhere.

Her only other friend in the street was Mrs Hewlett who lived just opposite number twenty seven. In spite of bringing up a large family her home was immaculate, and her family free from the impetigo that seemed to plague almost every other child in the street. It was a matter of great pride to Mrs Hewlett that none of her children were painted with the purple medication that was applied liberally by the school nurse to the sufferers of the dreaded impetigo. Noting Doris's pregnancy, she said quietly, "Nah then love, if tha needs any help tha knows where ah am."

But there were other neighbours who both Stanley and Doris avoided whenever they could.

Doris, especially if she was alone, would discreetly cross the street to avoid almost any member of the family who lived in the end house at the very bottom of Winifred Road. The house was so full of children, ranging from babies to teenagers, that Doris never was able to work out exactly how many there were. What they all had in common was blonde, curly hair and they would have been strikingly attractive if it had not been for the dirt encrusted on their scalps and a variety of scabs decorating their faces. The look was invariably completed by two streaks of green snot progressing from nose to mouth, and Doris could not help a shudder going through her every time she saw them.

Their mother, Martha Jackson, was a thin frail looking woman, worn down by years of child bearing. Whenever she passed Doris she would take out the cigarette that hung from the corner of her mouth and spit a large ball of phlegm out onto the pavement, then give a toothless grin as she replaced the drooping Woodbine.

Her husband, Jack Jackson, completed this charming family. Thick set and of medium height with a massive head covered in curly blonde hair, he reminded Doris of a Herefordshire bull.

"All he wants," she said to Stanley, "is a big ring through his nose."

He nodded in agreement. "Aye, tha's right. But keep clear of him. He's a wrongun. Nobody likes him. Not even his work mates. He's trouble waiting to happen. Keep out of t'way of all t'bloody family."

Stanley must have had a premonition as he spoke those words. It was soon afterwards that the trouble arose.

Doris frequently went to visit her mother and grandmother after her housework was done, and less than a week after that conversation she was returning home when she heard footsteps behind her. They seemed to be walking at exactly the same pace and she glanced quickly behind.

It was four in the afternoon and being mid-December it was almost dark, but she instantly recognised Jack Jackson. Although he was in his pit clothes and helmet, and would have been identical to any of the other men on their way home, there was no mistaking him with his chunky thickset build.

Dreading coming into contact with him Doris began to walk faster, her heels tapping quickly along the pavement, but she soon realised that his footsteps, loud in his steel tipped boots, were coming closer.

She consoled herself that she was now almost home, and reached in her bag for the large key. Gripping it tight she prepared to slip it into the lock and be inside before he caught up with her.

Breathless, she reached number twenty seven and fumbled until the key slipped into the lock. But it refused to turn. Desperately she tried to twist it, first one way and then the other. 'Please,' she thought, 'not now, don't choose this moment to stick.'

And suddenly he was there, leaning over her shoulder, breathing his beer filled breath all over her, and Doris snapped. Her quick temper came to her rescue and she turned to face him.

"Keep away from me, tha filthy pig. Gerroff home to thee pigsty where tha belongs," she said, and she backed away from him as far as she could, until she was pressed up against the door.

He grinned back at her and licked around his mouth with a long tongue that looked bright pink against his coal-blackened face. He smacked his lips as he looked at her. He was so close his face was almost touching hers, and Doris could see every hair on his eyelashes and the black crustations around his nostrils and she turned her head away to avoid breathing in his foul breath.

"Well, ain't tha a right little spitfire? Shall ah come in an show thee what a real man's like instead of that long streak of piss tha's married to?"

Before the scene could progress any further the head of a sweeping brush hit him in the face, and with relief Doris realised that Mrs Lloyd was standing at her front door which was directly next to her own.

"Thee leave t'lass alone Jack Jackson. Bugger off home. Tha's a big bully. Ah'll av t'bobby on thee. It's about time tha did another stretch down t'line."

And as he began to back away, spouting a mouthful of foul language to save face, she continued, "If tha's feeling randy tek thee missis upstairs and see if tha can gerr another snotty nosed kid to add to t'litter tha's already got. Go on. Clear off," and she waved the brush after him.

Doris stared in surprise at her neighbour. She was used to seeing her quiet and motherly, and now here she was, facing up to the most feared man in the street, and he had obviously found her formidable seeing as he had done as she said.

Mrs Lloyd appeared to have taken it all in her stride and patted Doris's hand.

"Come on love, tha's as white as a sheet. Come and av a cup of tea wi me."

But Doris shook her head as she thanked her.

"No, no, ah'll go and av a lay down, then ah've got to get Stan's tea ready."

"Well. Ok me love, but knock on t'wall if tha needs owt."

When Stanley returned home an hour later he found Doris white faced and tearful, partly with shock and partly with anger. He listened to what had happened with mounting indignation.

Now Stanley, brought up within a large family in a tough mining community, could hold his own with most, and spoke his mind fearlessly, but he was no fighting man and avoided coming to blows if at all possible. However, this was not to be tolerated, and without stopping to think he pushed his chair to one side, picked up the round stick that was used to push the washing down into the copper and left the house leaving the door wide open behind him.

He strode across the yard towards Jackson's house, gripping the smooth white stick tightly, his rage boiling up inside him. As he rounded the corner that led into the small back yard, the dog that they kept tied under the window lunged towards him growling. Kept short of food it looked a sorry sight, with clumps of hair missing and its ribs clearly visible through its matted fur.

At any other time Stanley would probably have felt sorry for the animal and admired its spirit in attempting to act as a guard dog when it was in such an emaciated condition. But today was not that time, and he raised the stick threateningly, and glared until the dog backed down and crawled under the rusty tin sheet that served as a shelter.

After he had rapped loudly on the door he stepped back a pace, and waited. The door was opened almost immediately by one of the younger members of the Jackson clan. As he peered out into the darkness, Stanley said curtly, "Get thee Dad."

From within the house he could hear an assortment of raised voices and the door was closed with a slam, only to be wrenched open again by Jackson himself.

While he was standing on the top of the stone steps that led into the house, he towered above Stanley, who kept his distance, and watched his every move as best he could in the dim light that shone from within. Jackson was outlined by the faint gaslight, and Stanley gripped the stick in readiness for him to make a move.

Jackson had now realised who it was that was standing in his yard, and he laughed, "What does tha want then Daley?"

Trying to keep his voice steady, Stanley said, "Tha knows bloody well what ah'm here for. Thee stay away from my wife."

Jackson laughed again. "An who's gonna mek me? Not thee, tha long streak o piss." He lashed out at Stanley with his foot.

But Stanley saw it coming and struck his ankle with the stick. Overbalanced, Jackson fell down the three steps and landed on his hands and knees.

Without a second thought Stanley kicked him in the ribs, and then retreated backwards, saying as he went, "Me. Ah'm going to make thee. Ah've told thee. Stay away from my wife. Tha'll get worse next time."

Shaking, Stanley went home and locked the door behind him, knowing he had made a dangerous enemy. He may have won the first round, but he knew there were bound to be repercussions. Jackson had a fearsome reputation, and the chances that he would be waiting for him down a dark alley one night were high.

And so, every day, until Jackson was jailed two months later for theft, Stanley carried a brass knuckle duster in his right hand pocket and avoided any places where he could be cornered.

CHAPTER 36

Christmas 1939 came and went with little joy. So many people had family members or friends who were now far from home, and there seemed no cause to celebrate. And then of course there was the bombing. Although Wath itself was not a target, nearby Sheffield with its steelworks suffered raid after raid.

Home life had changed beyond all recognition. Every available woman of working age with no commitments was expected to work in something connected with the war effort. Rationing of food was in force and long queues at shops were a miserable and normal part of daily life.

The shop shelves were empty of luxury goods and only the very rich seemed able to live in any degree of comfort. Doris's grandmother said almost every day, "It'll get worse, much worse, before this lot's over."

With Stanley's stepbrother Bill away fighting there was another empty place at the table at 93 Oak Road. Financially, due to miner's wages having risen, the whole Corker family were better off than they had ever been, but Ada would have swapped it all to have had things back as they were before the war.

Slowly the winter passed. Doris's days were spent cooking and cleaning her home, constantly trying to prevent the grime outside from creeping into her spotless house. And like all the other millions of other housewives she spent hours queuing for their weekly rations of essential food, going from one shop to another, waiting her turn at each one while the shopkeeper laboriously cut out the little square coupons from the ration books, and handed over the amount of food they were allowed.

She managed to visit her grandmother most days and listened to her grumbles about her son's bad temper and her worries about Edith, who had recently become over-friendly with a single man who had a bad reputation. Doris challenged her mother about it at the first opportunity.

Edith denied it, but within a month she had packed her case and moved in with him.

Unfortunately, the family's fears were proved correct when Edith returned home a week later with a bruised face and a black eye.

Her brother Willie, for all his faults, sprang to his sister's defence, and wasted no time in going round to see the man who had inflicted the injuries.

He was back an hour later with Edith's belongings stuffed hastily inside her navy blue suitcase.

Typically for him, he shouted and pointed his finger at her. "Thee keep away from him in future. Ah won't be going to thee rescue again."

Edith shook her head, and as she wiped away her tears she noticed that Willie's knuckles on his right hand were bleeding.

In March, Stanley and Doris had a visit from Les, who brought the news that he had received his call up papers. As a pit top worker he was not exempt from conscription. He was not happy about it.

Les said he had no objection to serving his country as a soldier; it was love that was making him reluctant. He had recently met and fallen in love with an attractive, dark haired girl called Kate, who was four years older than him and the single mother of a young daughter. Les dreaded the thought of leaving her and told Stanley and Doris that they planned to marry on his first leave after his basic training.

His parents had reservations about the marriage but Les was determined to go ahead with or without their approval.

Doris sat and cried after he had left. Les was more like a brother to her than a cousin and she was inconsolable. But, no matter how many tears were shed, the wheels of war turned, and Les was soon waving goodbye to Wath and his lovely Kate. Life was changing for everyone.

In the early hours of Whit Sunday Doris went into labour, and Stanley rode his bike as fast as he could to inform the midwife. She took his news calmly and slowly finished her breakfast before she wheeled her bicycle out of the shed, and carefully positioned her black bag in the basket at the front.

Stanley was beside himself with impatience, but she would not be hurried.

"Calm down son," she said as she picked a piece of burnt toast out of her back tooth and shuffled it around with her tongue. "It's her first, it'll be hours yet."

Knowing how much they needed her Stanley resisted the urge to swear at her, and he rode away in front, hoping she would increase her speed to keep up with him.

He arrived home to find Doris being looked after by their next door neighbour, Mrs Lloyd. The midwife puffed and panted her way up the stairs, took one quick look at the distressed mother to be, and told Stanley to go and get the doctor.

From the bed Doris called out that they couldn't afford the doctor, but Stanley was already on his way.

Whatever magic the doctor used, Doris was soon holding her baby in her arms and Stanley was being congratulated on having a fine, healthy daughter.

Stanley, who had been hoping for a son, now found he was absolutely delighted to have a daughter and thanked the doctor three times before asking him how much he owed him.

"Well, my usual charge is ten shillings but it will be five this time. You can call round at the surgery next week and pay the money to my wife. She looks after that side of things," he said, and adjusting his trilby he nodded his goodbye and left.

Thankful that they had another week to pay the bill, Stanley bounded up the stairs to see Doris and get to know his new daughter.

Always beautiful, Doris now looked a perfect picture, with her dark hair shining and a pink blush on her cheeks. Stanley felt as if he could burst with happiness as he watched her cradling their baby in her arms.

Among their visitors the next day was Les, accompanied by his new wife. They had married two days earlier at the registry office. Les looked like a stranger in his army uniform until his broad smile lit up his face. Feeling self-conscious he gave Doris a quick hug, then bent over the cot to admire the newest member of the family.

Dipping into his pocket he produced a half crown and placed it in the cot.

"There tha is Eileen," he said. "Ah've given thee me last half crown," and he pulled his pocket inside out to prove it.

It was to be a phrase he would repeat to her often, in the far distant future.

Many years later he would say, whenever he saw her, "Does tha know, when tha were a babby, ah give thee me last half crown."

Within three days he was leaving Wath again, and setting out to join his regiment. Leaving his new wife and family behind was so hard, but it would have been almost impossible to bear if they had known then that it would be more than five years before they saw each other again.

Stanley and Doris had accepted that they would never be able to leave Winifred Road with the housing situation as it was, and in spite of their youthful impatience they realised how lucky they were to be together in their own home.

Stanley continued to drive for Dyson's whenever he had any free time from his farming work. There was little time or money to socialise, but every Sunday evening was set aside to play cards with Doris's best friend Maisie and her fiancé Roy.

With their daughter tucked up fast asleep in bed, the pack of cards came out and they gambled for match sticks, laughing and joking the night away.

They saw Stanley's sister Doll most months but the atmosphere between her and Doris was uncomfortable at times.

Stanley had quickly come to the conclusion that his wife was jealous of his affection for his sister and tried to avoid showing how fond he was of her.

Doll was delighted with her new baby niece and seldom arrived without a gift for her and appeared not to notice the black looks that Doris gave her.

If Stanley had been older he would have realised that trouble was brewing between his wife and his sister, but he failed to sense it, and when it erupted he was at a loss as to how to deal with it.

A rare outing had been arranged for a weekend late in the year. Baby Eileen had been deposited with her grandmother Edith to sleep over for the first time.

Stanley and Doris, together with Harold, Cyril, their girlfriends and Doll, caught the bus into Barnsley. They were all in high spirits and for a couple of hours they toured the local public houses. Then, with more pints of beer inside them than they were used to, it was time to catch the last bus home.

The three brothers, encouraged by the alcohol, were in a teasing mood, and the fashionable red pixie hood that Doll was wearing presented an opportunity that was irresistible to Harold. Grabbing the pom pom on the end of it he pulled it sharply downwards.

Doll pushed him away and readjusted the hood and rearranged her fringe, but Harold promptly pulled the hood down again. This went on several times and banter broke out until Doll burst into tears.

Stanley intervened, and for the first time in their lives a scuffle broke out between him and Harold. With the drink talking to them, fists were raised, and in an attempt to stop them Doris pushed her way in front of her husband and received a punch that was intended for him.

Appalled at what had happened they were all suddenly very sober and travelled home in silence.

The next morning Doris had developed a black eye and also a raging temper. She blamed Doll for the whole incident, and nothing Stanley said could change her mind and she issued an ultimatum.

With her most determined look on her face she stated firmly that Doll had to be pushed out of their lives, and if he had anything more to do with her she would take the baby and leave him.

Incensed by what he considered her unfairness, he refused to do as she demanded and they argued fiercely, but Doris was accustomed to

348

having her own way, and would go to any lengths to achieve it.In the end, saddened and upset, Stanley backed down and for many years had no contact with his favourite sister.

Edith was a willing babysitter and by the time Eileen was two years old she was spending every weekend at Sandygate with her grandmother, great grandmother and her great uncle.

The war ground slowly onwards, full of hardship and shortages of daily commodities. Every day brought more news of tragedies and loss of lives, but Stanley and Doris with their youthful, natural optimism never lost sight of their dreams, or their determination to leave Wath.

Eileen, born in 1940 and introduced to life in the midst of a world at war, thought it perfectly normal to have to queue for hours at almost empty shops, always hoping that the owner would have some goods hidden away under the counter.

It was normal and usual to see people dressed in black and in mourning for loved ones lost in battle or bombing raids. Like all the other working class children she had never known any different and so she accepted it all.

She pretended to be enthusiastic about the cloth bodied doll with the ugly pot head that appeared on her fourth Christmas, and cared little when it broke two days later. What she really wanted was a teddy bear like the one she had seen pictures of in a story book.

She listened to descriptions of a mythical fruit called a banana that was delicious and would be available again, 'when the war was over', and in the meantime munched on a slice of turnip as a treat. And she was quite used to having a miniscule amount of egg or meat on her plate and no butter to speak of but cried bitterly when her mother spread lard on her toast instead of dripping.

But at last it was over. The day dawned when Germany was finally defeated. Overjoyed, Doris hugged her daughter and told her that the war was ended.

"Will we be able to buy toys now?" asked Eileen, "And bananas?"

When told, "Not just yet," she couldn't understand why they were not available immediately. After all, the war was over. That was what everyone had been waiting for, wasn't it?

It was indeed what everyone had been waiting for but it soon became clear that nothing was going to change very quickly.

VE night was a national celebration. A party to surpass all parties, but it was bittersweet for so many. The war had been won at a price too high for families who had had to bear the loss of nearest and dearest.

The survivors gradually began to be discharged from the forces and arrived home dressed in ill-fitting demob suits provided by the government, carrying cardboard suitcases filled with what few personal belongings they had managed to preserve.

It became commonplace to see the small houses decked out with bunting, and often painted sheets hung from bedroom windows proclaiming 'Welcome home Bill/Jack/Tommy', or whatever was the name of the person expected.

Stanley's stepbrother Bill was one of the lucky ones. He arrived home unharmed and was soon back at his old job down the mine, working on the coal face alongside his father and brothers.

Doris's cousin Les also came through the war unscathed and at last he was able to return to Wath, and found his beloved Kate waiting for him. After all the long years separated they were, of course, overjoyed to see each other. Eventually they were given the tenancy of a brand new council house at New Hill and settled down to enjoy a long happy life together.

CHAPTER 37

Eileen began school in 1945 at the Queen Victoria on Doncaster Road where her parents had received their education. The rocking horse still stood in the hall in pristine condition due the fact that it was still untouched and had never been played on.

The nursery classroom was still heated by the coke burning stove at the front of the classroom, surrounded by a large fireguard that was invaluable for drying wet trousers and knickers of youngsters who had not made it to the toilet in time.

The only obvious change was the two huge underground air raid shelters that had been installed in the playground. The entrances to them were gaping arched doorways approached down ridged concrete paths. The actual doors had been removed at the end of the war and they now resembled dark, man-made caves.

Pupils were strictly forbidden to enter them and only the bravest and toughest disobeyed that order. The ruling was totally unnecessary as far as five-year-old Eileen was concerned. Nothing in the world would have persuaded her to descend into those shelters. They were the centre of many of her nightmares.

The toilets were alongside the air raid shelters and they were cold smelly places in poor state of repair. Few of them had seats and most of them were regularly blocked and full of foul water and unmentionables.

Eileen avoided using them and consequently her knickers were frequently among the many others drying on the fire guard.

At the end of Winifred Road, between the last house and the railway line, there was a narrow strip of coal blackened ground that was designated as an allotment. When it became vacant, Stanley and

Doris grabbed the opportunity to rent it and began their first poultry keeping enterprise.

The land had been neglected and was overgrown with dust covered grass and perennial weeds that had flourished in spite of the impoverished soil.

From the scrap heap on Tommy's farm Stanley rescued several old corrugated sheets, some metal and some asbestos, and from them built a crude shed and the base of a fence. The wire netting was harder to source, but eventually with the help of brothers Harold and Cyril they acquired some from the pit yard. It was crumpled and rusty but Stanley painstakingly straightened it all out and they were able to finish the enclosure.

It was a great day when Stanley arrived home with the new livestock in a large cardboard box. He had rode with it balanced on the handlebars of his bike all the way from Swinton, but it was worth it to see the look on Doris's face as she peeped through the holes in the lid. Carrying the box gently she set it down in the new chicken run. Slowly she unfastened the string and lifted the lid.

Inside, still crouched low, were six young pullets. Half the neighbours were out by now, watching with bated breath as if they had never seen poultry before.

As Stanley opened the gate and slipped inside to join Doris he looked across at the end house, and noticed Jack Jackson standing on the step of his back door leaning against the jamb, a cigarette in his hand and a sneer on his face, watching the proceedings.

A shiver went through Stanley and he said quietly to one of the neighbours, "When did that thieving bugger get out of jail then?"

Doris had missed what he said, but Mrs Lloyd, standing holding the gate had heard. "Last night Stan," she said, "Pity they didn't throw the bloody key away, Wath's been a better place wi out im in it. Tha's gonna av ta keep a close eye on them chickens lad. Cos he'll av em; as soon as he as the chance."

Never were six chickens better looked after. Several times every day Doris was there, checking on them and filling their water trough and taking them titbits to supplement their regular feed. Eileen trailed after her, watching her mother, but was totally unimpressed by the new livestock and quite failed to see what the attraction was.

What did impress her was the trick that Cyril demonstrated. Taking a half full bucket of water he swung it around in a circle above his head without spilling a drop. She had long hero worshipped her uncle Cyril but now she declared she would marry him when she grew up.

The chickens thrived under Doris's care, and the day the first egg arrived she carried it reverently back to the house and placed it on a saucer in the centre of the table, and admired it all afternoon.

When Stanley arrived home from work it was boiled and waiting for him to enjoy with a plate of fresh bread and butter. Doris had already got her calculations made as to how much money they could make selling the surplus eggs as soon as the hens were in full production.

But alas, they never had the chance to lay any more. Less than two days later Doris discovered that the lock had been broken and all six hens were gone, and their first poultry keeping venture was finished.

Of course Jack Jackson was the chief suspect, and they reported the theft to the police. The constable listened to them and sympathised, but shook his head and said sorry, but there was nothing they could do without proof.

But barely a week had gone by before they had cause to consult the police again. The dog that Jackson kept chained up just outside his back door managed to slip out of its collar and bit Eileen's leg while she played in the communal yard.

Looking at her daughter's leg, Doris's rage erupted and she had a monumental row with Mrs Jackson, who at first tried to shout over Doris but soon backed away at the look of sheer fury in her dark eyes.

From there Doris went straight to the police station, and sitting her daughter on the counter, showed them the bite marks.

Fortunately the walk to the station had allowed Doris's temper to cool a little, and she gave a calm but firm account of what had happened and demanded that something be done.

The police sergeant gave a sigh and a sort of "Hmm" sound, when he heard Jackson's name and assured her that he would attend to it.

Jackson was duly up in court charged with keeping a dangerous animal and fined and the dog disappeared.

Stanley and Doris felt that justice had been done but the tension between the two households increased and made living in Winifred Road more uncomfortable than ever.

Inside Stanley, the spirit of adventure burned strong, and if he had been born at a later time or into different circumstances, he would have travelled far and explored different places. But these were hard times, and like most people he had to work long and hard every day just to earn enough to survive.

However, that did not prevent him from exploring the surrounding countryside whenever he had a spare hour. He took to his bike riding again. He fitted a little wooden seat to the cross bar of his bike and took his daughter with him, pedalling his way out of the Dearne Valley and to the outlying villages, pointing out places of interest to her as they cycled along.

On one outing Stanley headed for Wentworth and after a long uphill ride they reached Hoober Stand, which was, and still is, a famous folly built in the sixteenth century by the Marquis of Rockingham.

As Stanley came to a halt he lifted his daughter down from her seat on the crossbar and together they gazed and marvelled at the triangular shaped monument that stood on the highest point in the countryside.

"One day," said Stanley, "we might be able to climb to the top and look all around and see for miles." He read out the history on the plaque that said it had been built by the Marquis.

Then to himself, he added, "That's a laugh. Fat lot of building he'd have done. Sent some poor folk up to do it more like. Ah wonder how many of the poor souls were killed or injured just on the whim of some chinless bloody gentry."

It was while Stanley was out on one of his bike rides that he came across an area where coal was being outcropped. Even though it was late Saturday afternoon work was in full production. Huge machines were gouging out the soil and extracting coal that lay close to the surface.

As he watched, a lorry pulled up very close beside him. It was too close for comfort and Stanley snatched his bike and his daughter to one side.

"Nah then Stan. Ah've not seen thee for a long time."

Stanley looked at the driver for a moment before he recognised him as Walt Smith who used to be in the same class at school. Reaching through the cab window they shook hands.

"What's tha doing round ere then Stan, is tha sightseeing?"

"Aye an a right sight it is an all. It looks worse than Manvers. Talk about destroying t'countryside."

Walt ignored Stan's comment and continued, "What's tha doin' these days then? Tha's not still farmin' is tha?"

When he received a nod in reply Walt tossed his head in derision. "That's a mug's game Stan. No money in farmin'. Tha wants to see about gerrin' a job ere. Tha'd get twice as much. Tha can drive can't tha? Ah'd put a word in for thee. That's foreman over there. Him wi t'big cap. Ah've got to go nah. Go on, ask him. Tell im ah know thee. He's a big mate of mine. Tha'll be ok, go on."

Stanley thought for only a moment. With twice the wages they could build up some savings. Lifting his daughter from the bike he took her up the slight slope among the dust covered trees, and setting her down instructed her to sit there and not move until he came back. He leaned his bike against a tree and straightening his cap he strode across to speak to the foreman.

By the time he returned he was finding it hard not to grin. He'd got it. He'd got the job. He was to start in a week's time, and just as Walt had said, his wages would be over twice what he earned at Tommy Flint's.

The way back home was mostly downhill, and he sang as he cruised along, his head full of hope that the extra money would help them to get out of their present situation.

He handed Tommy his notice the next day and by the following Monday was employed by Mowlem's as a lorry driver. Over the next six months he gradually adjusted to his new line of work, and although he missed the farming life he enjoyed the new experiences and the modern machinery.

His mechanical talents developed, and the extra wages finally put them in a position where they could save for their future.

But then the word came that the coal seam they were working was running out, and Stanley found he was unemployed for the first time in his life.

The employment authorities decreed that Stanley, as a fit, able bodied man, could not receive any kind of benefit, but his wife and child could have a meal ticket that entitled them to one cooked meal per day.

Doris, with her child, was to report to a sort of canteen that had been opened in a church hall just across the road from the Queen Victoria School.

Eileen thought it a great experience, and loved the warm cheerful hall full of people sitting at the long trestle tables and thought the food was wonderful.

She was unwise enough to say as much to her mother and received a scowl and some sharp words. Doris felt humiliated and practically dragged her daughter out of the canteen and refused to ever go back.

She had a blazing row with Stanley that night and swore she would rather starve than eat at the canteen again.

Their savings were quickly dwindling away and in desperation Stanley decided he would have to do what he had always said he wouldn't do.

He would go down the pit to work. And he went to see his father to ask if he could use his influence to get him a place down the mine.

But to his surprise Harold was dead set against it. "Tha's not cut out to be a miner Stan, tha knows tha's not."

When Stanley insisted it was the only way for them to manage, Harold arranged for him and Doris to make a trip down the mine on a Sunday morning. Doris was shaking as she stepped into the cage to descend down the pit shaft and Stanley was not much better, although he tried to be blasé in front of his father.

To try and lighten the atmosphere Harold looked up at his tall son and said, "Well tha's too tall to be a miner for a start."

Stanley managed a smile but was thankful that the darkness hid his real expression of horror as the cage dropped like a stone and no one was more relieved when the expedition was over. He freely admitted that his father was right, and his respect grew for the men who spent all their working lives underground.

He swallowed his pride and went to ask Teddy Downing for work. There was no full time work available but he was offered a few hours every weekend, tending a herd of bullocks that were kept on a separate farm at the other side of Wath, not far from Manvers Main.

The rate of pay was low even by farm workers' standards, but Stanley was in no position to be choosy and he accepted. He had reached the point where he was glad of anything that brought in money.

Dyson's agreed to give him work driving whenever they had a funeral or a wedding in addition to his Saturday evening work, and by being even more frugal than ever they just about managed to pay their rent and eat.

As Christmas 1946 approached, Stanley decided to try his hand at toy making to earn some much needed cash. Rationing for many items was still in place, and goods like toys were in short supply. So, temporarily, he turned the empty front room into a workshop and made dolls' pushchairs.

Stanley was no carpenter, and the pushchairs he produced were rough constructions, but the generation of children he was supplying had been starved of toys and were happy to accept almost anything. And so he found buyers for whatever he produced and was able to add a little more to the housekeeping.

That Christmas was a disastrous one for the Dale family. It started out full of happy anticipation. They had been given a couple of armchairs and a folding bed settee and as soon as the toy making venture was over Doris was at last able to furnish the front room. Stanley had brought home the top of a pine tree and they had decorated it with homemade trinkets and paper chains.

But by Boxing Day Doris was sick of it. She said it made dust and dropped its needles. She was already in a bad mood due to a parcel arriving from Doll containing a miniature baking set for Eileen. She was not prepared to make friends with her sister-in-law, and she put the parcel in the dustbin. She had quarrelled with Stanley about it and in a fit of temper she took hold of the Christmas tree, complete with decorations, and pushed the whole lot on to the fire and up the chimney.

Of course the fire took rapid hold of the dry oil-filled pine needles and the flames threatened to set the chimney alight. It was consumed in minutes but sparks continued to shoot out of the top of the chimney for some time. Eileen curled up in a chair and sobbed, partly from fright and partly from the loss of their first Christmas tree and she wished she was with her grandmother in Sandygate.

Early in the new year of 1947 another use was found for the front room. Now that it was considered furnished they sublet it to a young newly married couple. They were to have the room as a bedsit, with shared use of the kitchen facilities and they also shared the outside toilet.

But Doris was not able to come to terms with sharing and claimed the young woman did not come up to her standards of housekeeping. Within a week it was over. Doris had turfed them out at a minute's notice and justified her action by bristling with indignation at having had to share the sink and cooking facilities.

The snow began at the end of January and 1947 turned out to be the coldest on record. Having just come through a devastating war, the nation as a whole was ill-equipped to cope with the bad weather. Many people were in poor health following years of rationing and badly clothed due to the shortages. Houses were cold and in many cases in a bad state of repair following the bombing and lack of materials to carry out even basic maintenance. The outdoor toilets were often frozen solid, adding to the misery.

Unemployed men were set to clearing the footpaths and for months pyramids of dirty snow lined the edges of the roads.

For a short time with each fresh fall of snow Wath was transformed into a white fairyland. It didn't last long of course. It was soon discoloured by the black film of coal dust that settled everywhere.

For the children it was heaven. Winifred Road, being on a hill, was the perfect place for sledging. The snow was soon hard packed and the whole street was taken over by dozens of children speeding down it on an assortment of homemade sleds.

The canal was frozen over and for weeks it was a playground for the hardy who could stand the cold and a skating rink for the few who possessed skates.

But at last it was over, temperatures began to rise and a late spring arrived and with it came hope. And for Stanley and Doris, there came a renewed determination to leave Wath.

Farm jobs were becoming more available and with them usually went a cottage. Stanley had reluctantly come to the conclusion that a job with a tied house was their only way out and he began scouring the pages of the 'Farmer and Stock Breeder' for jobs.

He posted letter after letter of applications. Some were answered, some were not, and some offered positions that were so poorly paid that they would have had difficulty feeding themselves on the amount of money on offer.

But eventually two letters gave him hope and interviews were offered. The one they favoured most was at Hooten Pagnell, a village that Stanley had visited on his bike rides.

They scraped together the bus fare and arrived in the village as the church clock began to strike. Stanley had described the village to Doris and it was just as attractive as he had said it was. Already she could imagine them living here in one of the lovely stone built cottages.

The cottage that went with the job had been described as being on the outskirts of the village, but it turned out to be all of two miles out of it and reluctantly they agreed that it just was not suitable.

Back at home Stanley looked at the second letter. A Mr Smith had suggested that he come to interview him and if he thought that Stanley was right for the job he would take him to see the farm and also the cottage that went with it.

Stanley wrote back and a date for the interview was arranged. Doris went into a frenzy of spring cleaning; dusting and scrubbing the house that was already spotless.

The big day arrived. Eileen was dressed in her best clothes and sent out to play with strict instructions not to stray too far from home and at all costs not to get dirty!

Mr Smith's arrival, in his black, shiny Humber, was witnessed by most of the neighbours, and by the time Stanley opened the door and invited his visitor into the house a gossip committee was already gathering in the alleyway.

It was clear Mr Smith was satisfied that he was right for the position and he offered it to him almost before he had finished reading his references. He was prepared to take them immediately to see the farm and the cottage, but they would have to catch the bus back.

Stanley was to be the cow man, in charge of the milking morning and night, and would also tend the herd of bullocks. In between that he would work as a general farm hand. They would have the cottage rent free, two jugs of milk per day, as many potatoes and turnips as they needed, and four pounds ten shilling a week plus overtime when available.

Trying not to sound too eager Stanley agreed and Eileen was called inside.

Doris made a face at the state of her hands but Mr Smith laughed.

"Don't worry," he said, "I've got four youngsters myself. They attract dirt like a magnet attracts iron filings."

The curious neighbours that had gathered outside attempted to wave them off, but Doris gave them a withering look and then totally ignored them. Stanley didn't even need to look at her to know that she was muttering, "Nosy buggers," under her breath.

Eileen was always a quiet, shy child but was now struck completely speechless by the splendid interior of the luxurious car they were in. She gripped her mother's hand tightly as they sat close together on the soft leather seats, and although not a word passed her lips she just could not stop smiling.

Stanley sat at the front talking to his new employer and learned that he actually ran two farms, one at Adwick le Street and one at Hooten Pagnell where he and his family lived.

They were soon pulling up outside the large pebble-dashed farmhouse where they were handed over to the foreman, Mr Bert Dunning, who gave them a friendly welcome.

Stanley was immediately impressed by the neat appearance of the farmyard. The house was in the lower yard and surrounded by a long stretch of brick built cart sheds with granaries above them. Every door and window was freshly painted a dull orangey red colour, and not a single weed grew in the courtyard.

The foreman showed them around the farm and described again what his work would entail. He made a point of explaining that Mr Smith's mother, sister and her husband lived in the farmhouse, and as staunch chapel goers they would only tolerate the bare essential work being done on Sundays.

He also hinted that it would be highly desirable for their daughter to attend the Sunday School and the morning service at the chapel just up the road.

Stanley and Doris nodded their agreement to all this while waiting impatiently to be shown the cottage where they were to live.

But Bert Dunning was about to come to that detail, and walked with them out of the farmyard and along the road as far as the corner.

"There you are," he said pointing to a cottage at the end of a row. "I can't show you inside. It's still occupied at the moment, but you can see what it's like from the outside."

They exchanged glances. They liked what they saw. The outside was painted a dirty shade of yellow with green, flaking paint on the front door, but they had fallen for its old fashioned charm.

Outside, the garden stretched at least fifty yards, and that so delighted them that they barely noticed that the outside tap was the only water supply.

They agreed on it immediately and shook hands with Bert Dunning who was destined to become a good friend.

He directed them to the bus stop after arranging a date for them to move in.

When Doris asked anxiously about the present tenants, Bert smiled.

"Don't you worry, the house will be vacant on the date I have given you."

As they waved him goodbye and walked for the first time up the village street, their heads were spinning with plans and the thought of their new life away from Wath.

The date for them to move was just two weeks from that day. A van was booked for the removal and they took great pleasure in handing in their notice to the landlord of 27 Winifred Road.

Edith's face fell at the news of their move. Not only was she losing the regular visits from her daughter, she was also losing her granddaughter's company every weekend. Eileen had been staying with her each week from Friday till Monday ever since she could walk.

Her brother Willie was gloomier than ever, he was used to taking his great niece out walking on Sunday mornings and did not like his routine being upset, and he stomped up the stairs to his room when he heard the news, muttering about the young being bloody selfish.

Three days before the moving date Stanley heard about a border collie going free to a good home, and he cycled to Barnsley to claim her.

He returned with Meg, a beautiful black and white bitch with long silky fur and a face that expressed her every emotion.

He had carried her under his arm on the downhill parts and she had run alongside him the rest of the way. She was absolutely exhausted and after drinking a bowl of water, she flopped down under the table and fell asleep. Eileen crawled alongside and lay on the floor with her until bedtime. Meg was to become her constant companion.

Moving day arrived at last. The van was packed with all their possessions. Doris sat in the passenger seat in the cab while Stanley, with his daughter and dog, sat in the back among their assorted household goods.

As the van pulled slowly up the hill and out on to Doncaster Road, Stanley took one last look at the street that he had hated from the first day he had laid eyes on it.

When they first moved there they had regarded it as temporary, and never imagined that it would be seven years before they were able to leave it.

He swallowed the lump in his throat and clenched his teeth to prevent his face from betraying how emotional he felt.

He'd done it. He'd got his family out of Winifred Road.

Today their new life would begin.

Yon Lad Out There

Leaving Wath upon Dearne in 1947 marked the beginning of a new era for Stanley and Doris.

It was to be a time of great change that saw them settled in their tied cottage in Adwick le Street and a time when they were blessed with the birth of a second daughter.

As the years passed their ambition to have their own farm grew but it was a seemingly impossible dream when they had no money or assets.

What they did have was the optimism of youth, determination and an absolute refusal to be beaten.

Together they set out on the long path to achieve their ambition.